Agri-Food and Rural Development

Contemporary Food Studies: Economy, Culture and Politics

Series Editors: David Goodman and Michael K. Goodman

ISSN: 2058-1807

This interdisciplinary series represents a significant step towards unifying the study, teaching, and research of food studies across the social sciences. The series features authoritative appraisals of core themes, debates and emerging research, written by leading scholars in the field. Each title offers a jargon-free introduction to upper-level undergraduate and postgraduate students in the social sciences and humanities.

Kate Cairns and Josée Johnston, *Food and Femininity*
Peter Jackson, *Anxious Appetites: Food and Consumer Culture*
Philip H. Howard, *Concentration and Power in the Food System: Who Controls What We Eat?*
Terry Marsden, *Agri-Food and Rural Development: Sustainable Place-Making*
Emma-Jayne Abbot, *The Agency of Eating: Mediation, Food and the Body*
Further titles forthcoming

Agri-Food and Rural Development

Sustainable Place-Making

Terry Marsden

Bloomsbury Academic
An imprint of Bloomsbury Publishing Plc

BLOOMSBURY

LONDON · OXFORD · NEW YORK · NEW DELHI · SYDNEY

Bloomsbury Academic
An imprint of Bloomsbury Publishing Plc

50 Bedford Square	1385 Broadway
London	New York
WC1B 3DP	NY 10018
UK	USA

www.bloomsbury.com

BLOOMSBURY and the Diana logo are trademarks of
Bloomsbury Publishing Plc

First published 2017

British Library Cataloguing-in-Publication Data
A catalogue record for this book is available from the British Library.

ISBN: HB: 978-0-8578-5545-9
      PB: 978-0-8578-5740-8
    ePDF: 978-0-8578-5679-1
   eBook: 978-0-8578-5745-3

Library of Congress Cataloging-in-Publication Data
Names: Marsden, Terry, author.
Title: Agri-food and rural development : sustainable place-making / Terry Marsden.
Description: London ; New York, NY : Bloomsbury Academic, 2017. |
Series: Contemporary food studies: economy, culture and politics,
ISSN 2058-1807 | Includes bibliographical references and index.
Identifiers: LCCN 2016057193 (print) | LCCN 2017022313 (ebook) |
ISBN 9780857857453 (ePub) | ISBN 9780857856791 (ePDF) |
ISBN 9780857857408 (pbk.) | ISBN 9780857855459 (hardback)
Subjects: LCSH: Rural development–Great Britain. |
Sustainable agriculture–Great Britain.
Classification: LCC HN400.C6 (ebook) |
LCC HN400.C6 M37 2017 (print) | DDC 307.1/4120941–dc23
LC record available at https://lccn.loc gov/2016057193

Cover design: Eleanor Rose
Cover image © antb/Shutterstock

Series: Contemporary Food Studies: Economy, Culture and Politics, ISSN: 2058-1807

Typeset by Deanta Global Publishing Services, Chennai, India

To find out more about our authors and books visit www.bloomsbury.com. Here you will find extracts,
author interviews, details of forthcoming events and the option to sign up for our newsletters.

To Kathleen Marsden and all of those who served
in the Women's Land Army

Contents

List of figures

Acknowledgements

Many colleagues and friends have helped me formulate and shape the arguments in this book. However, I am particularly indebted to Ina Horlings, Jessica Paddock and Yoko Kanemasu who acted as extremely valuable and productive researchers on the succession of projects which led to many of the empirical arguments and analysis in Chapters 4 and 5 of the book. These projects were funded by the EU and the ESRC (UK), and I am also grateful for this support. I am also grateful for the assistance and long-term commitment of many of our respondents in Devon and Shetland to the research. I would also like to sincerely thank Karolina Rucinska (for her help with the text and bibliography), Justyna Prosser and Ana Moragues-Faus for their discussions on some aspects of my arguments here.

My family, as always, have given me a lot of support directly and indirectly (Mary Anne, Joseph and Tilly, Hannah and Tom, and my late mother, Kathleen). My invaluable and long-standing discussions with rural friends in my own rural 'hinterland' in Staffordshire should also be mentioned, as they have provided unending commentary on the current state of rural affairs. Steven Goundrey, our research institute manager, has also been very supportive, both in helping at times with the text and in keeping my diary in shape in ways that have meant that I could successfully bring this book to a conclusion. I must also thank the series editors, David and Mike Goodman, for their patience, and also for their supportive feedback on reading drafts of the book, together with three anonymous reviews. All of these comments were both invaluable and supportive.

Terry Marsden
Sustainable Places Research Institute, Cardiff University.

Preface

Replacing the bio-economy – the necessary renaissance of agri-food and rural development

There are few occasions in the passage of generations when we begin to feel and sense a moment of real significant change and transition. This book provides one thesis for how to conceptually and empirically engage with such a contested transition; caused as it is by a range of factors internal and external to its condition. It is now clear to most of us that the planet upon which we feed and sustain ourselves will not be able to grant us, or our future generations, the unlimited natural resources we have for so long expected of it. As multiplex energy, food and overall resource demands increase for an ever-expanding population that has been increasingly disenfranchised from its own natural habitat, we are witnessing, step by step, the need for fundamental change in the governance and management of resources that this requires.

We will, however difficult this might be for some, need to shift to a 'post-carbon economy'. This is, as this book demonstrates, easier said than done of course, as it is fraught with severe contestations and contradictions. Nevertheless, we also know that the early decades of the twenty-first century will be crucial in setting up this platform for the transition. And a central part of this involves creating a new governance infrastructure for a more sustainable agri-food and rural development system. Rural areas and their various governance frameworks around the world are having to redefine their roles and positions in their respective national and multilevel governance structures, as they become increasingly significant for managing and supplying a growing urban and cosmopolitan society with the necessary sustainable resources and services they require and demand. We are and will continue to witness then a contested transition to a completely new set of functionalities between the rural and the urban, the rural and the nation, and the rural and the world. It will be one which will require a host of new, revised and less carbon-based sustainable rural development models and practices. And one in which agri-food production and consumption systems and practices will become re-calibrated.

So far, however, at least until the combined crises which exploded during 2007–8, there has been an overall tendency to disguise and deny the significance of this realm for too long, as we have been busy continuing to plunder the earth's biospheric resources. A sort of 'business as usual model'. It is now recognized by many that the current period (2015–30) will be a critical one for the necessary policy and resource governance changes needed. The question becomes, how and in what direction will these changes come about? What will be the re-assembled power networks and frameworks which will achieve this? These questions and their varied answers will, I argue, become major drivers for rural and agri-food development over the coming decades.

Probably not since the dawn of industrialization and urbanization in the early nineteenth century have we witnessed such a profound process of transitional change in the use, management and spatial arrangements of natural resources. Then it led, amidst a triumvirate of local and regional land enclosures, 'free-trade' polemics and regulations, and intensive urbanization of the labouring classes, to the development of a vibrant and critical social science which tracked and critically examined the nature of this urbanized capitalist-led process of modernization. Central then, as now, was the balance between the towns, the expanding cities and their countryside. How would the rapidly urbanized populations feed and sustain themselves? How would the surrounding countryside provide and procure the goods and services needed? What would be the outcomes of the social protests associated with these transformations?

It sounds familiar? Today, with the majority of people living in cities and increasingly detached from the countryside, this also begins to provide a profound platform for a revised critical and, I would suggest, normative debate on how to recast these sets of relationships given the end of carbonized industrialism and modernization.

The main aim then here in this book is to provide one basis, a conceptual platform, upon which this necessary transition might begin to be debated, re-drawn, examined and progressed; and to pose critical questions of its changing and contested governance and articulation. It does not suggest there is only one answer. It does not suggest it may work. What it attempts to do, however, is to suggest that the necessary transitions will need to be nourished with new conceptual insights and theoretical paradigms that have been so far, at best, rather timidly dealt with by academic scholars, and, usually, continually denied and attacked by the current neo-liberal governance orthodoxy operating in most advanced societies.

This is an orthodoxy, as we shall see, which has progressively perceived and enacted a governmentality which has rendered rural areas as marginal to the global competitiveness agenda on the one hand, and the increasingly powerful and concentrated nature of cities and corporations on the other. It is a governmentality which continues to render the primary production and processing of natural goods and services as marginal and of 'low value' compared to the concentrated 'value-added' service and 'tertiary sectors', like food retailing, banking and energy distribution. It is a governmentality which continues to ignore and exclude the true and full ecological and environmental costs associated with its necessary value creation and valorization processes.

Now is the time, I argue, to openly return to the biosphere; and to do so by developing a new, engaging and more empowering approach to the bio-economy and the sustained role of agri-food and rural areas within it. It is this sphere and its sustainable management that will save and enhance future generations; yet it is this sphere, and the people who work in it, and are intimately close to it, who are often subject to the most extreme forms of societal and ecological exploitation, vulnerability and exclusion. Scholars in the agri-food and rural development field have been asking such questions for a long time, but it is now clear to the thesis I map out here that we cannot any longer just rest upon the critical analysis of the extant problematic alone. We have to find and propose new ways to design the bio-economy – or as I prefer the eco-economy – in ways which valorize rather than devalorize its basic and vulnerable agri-food and rural resource. Rurality, I argue, thus becomes central to the post-carbon economy and needs refreshed governance frameworks which both recognize and promote this.

In all of the contested debates currently about climate change, resource depletion and its environmental justice impacts, it is somewhat surprising that a key axis of 'sustainable adaptation' sits on our, largely unrecognized, doorstep. That is the doorstep of what we do, both as consumers and producers every hour of every day, of managing and changing our relation with food and its rural provenance. It is this contested reconnection that this thesis also introduces and explores. It doesn't provide even half the answers, but it opens the door.

In this preface to the narrative, I want to propose four postulates for debate which the succeeding chapters attempt to address. These are:

(i) We need to provide more design as well as critical examination of the ways out of the current lock-in neo-liberalist governance frameworks;

(ii) One way to do this is to shift the balance of design to develop sustainable place-based approaches in rural areas.

(iii) We need to connect the case of agri-food and rural development to the wider and more volatile macro-bio and political economy;

(iv) We need to develop a more engaging and empowering 'post-normal science' for more place-based reflexive governance frameworks.

Here I argue that agri-food and rural areas are now bound up in the centre of both contingent and 'contested sustainabilities'. In order to elucidate their emerging framings, it is timely to critically and openly address their underlying and competing conceptualizations and theories. In short, *Constructing the Countryside* (Marsden et al., 1993) is still very much under contested and critical construction.

These are challenging times to be talking like this. But that's exactly why we need to propose these ideas. There will be a need to relocate rural development at the heart of the post-carbon economy and polity. Let's see if we cannot speed it up and challenge the orthodoxy of the present.

Finally, here in preface there needs to be a comment on my use of 'governance' throughout this work. Over the past two decades it has been common to introduce this expanding concept as one which embraces not just formal governmental and institutional arrangements but also the wide variety of networks and associational activities which surround it. To this perspective I fully agree. However, in my usage of the concept in what follows, I also would like to make the two following additions with regard to its usage and development here.

First, I use the concept throughout to connote the ways in which those networks and associations are actively and dynamically assembled in ways which create effective combinations of state, policy, technology, science, corporate, market and civil interests into coherent and often concrete mobilizations and framings, which can then gain and hold onto, and indeed contest, relational power. The networks and associations, thereon, are far from devoid of power, action and intention. They are far from 'empty vessels'. They hold and fix nature, over time and space, both human and physical. In a world which is increasingly recognizing the 'scarcity' of its natural resources, the character of the intentional governance of those resources becomes all the more critical.

This inherent intentionality is the second important point regarding my usage and application of governance. That is, that more and more of these agents and networks of governance, be they state-, market- or civil-society-led, are indeed focusing now upon the bio- and the eco-politics of 'natural powers'. This 'natural' intentionality of governance becomes the life-blood of linking human and natural 'agency' with unfolding and contingent 'structures'. In this sense, and indeed unlike the great twentieth-century modernization phase (see Chapter 1), we can no longer contain, exclude or render as marginal bio-power or its consequences. So the point is that governance of nature is not just about more, or the proliferations thereof, of networks and fluid associations and coalitions for their own sake, however important and relevant these indeed are. It is also crucially about how these multiplex and combinational governance interests – not least in their modus of science and its framing of rationality – intentionally mobilize, institutionalize and then render marginal their opposed and alternative framings. This is inherently a dialectical process of active and contested sustainabilities. This is the new 'natural powers' dialectic. Sustainability, and more specifically sustainable place-making, I argue now provides the new and relatively unmapped political and conceptual terrain upon which this contestation and dialectic is taking place. And, indeed, I argue that rural areas, and their customs and practices, will play an increasingly central and pivotal role in shaping this contested terrain. In this sense 'contested sustainabilities' represent a generational 'battlefield of knowledge', which in the context of the planet's exhausting resource base is, I am afraid, at the moment, something of a 'zero-sum game'. But – and an important 'but' – is that it doesn't have to be that way.

Chapter 1

Governing for agri-food security and rural sustainability: Antecedents and transitions

Introduction

One of the great historical ironies of the recent British history of governance of agri-food and rural development has been the strong tendency to have significant neo-liberal bouts in which the significance of agri-food and rural development for domestic well-being and sustainability is downplayed. This most drastically took place after the enclosures and subjugation of the peasant classes. With the repeal of the Corn Laws by 1846, whereby domestic agricultural markets were opened up to world trade, the British imperial regime placed precedence on the export of manufactured goods and commercial services in return for expanding imperial preferences for the importation of both domestic and exotic colonial foods and beverages.

By the beginning of the twentieth century, the UK, despite its global hegemony, was heavily dependent upon imported food, with a great variety of tropical products imported as well as three-quarters of the country's staple consumption of wheat and cheese, and half of its meat products. From 1860 to the start of the Second World War in 1939, rural UK faced a long agricultural recession, largely as a neo-liberalized domestic cost for its urban-based and landowning and merchant-class wealth accumulation, developed by imperial export of its industrial manufacturing and commercial goods and services.

I make these historical points as they become increasingly relevant today, when again, as we shall see, in the early decades of the twenty-first century, the peculiarly British tendency to create long-running and self-inflicted domestic vulnerabilities in its rural hinterlands has in many cases reappeared. As an introduction then to this book, it is thus relevant to paint something of an overview of some of these significant historical antecedents and transitions for two main reasons. Historical accounts are useful in that they give at least some clues as to the present situation and governance conditions we witness with regard to agri-food and rural development. Also, and this is especially the case with regard to the distinctive evolution of governance of agri-food and the position of rural areas, there have been successive waves of highly intentional macro-political actions and ideologies which have held profound consequences for the abilities of rural areas and their natures to sustain themselves. In particular, and in different guises, these have swayed from waves of productionism and modernization on the one hand to protectionism and romanticism on the other.

In many cases we should perhaps find it quite remarkable that the British countryside has indeed sustained itself to the extent it has. Our present generation is left with a countryside which has surely 'been through the mill', as successive waves of changing and contested governance have shaped the physical and social landscape. The long-running, 'taken for granted' (modernist) ideology born in the 'free-trade' and imperial mid-nineteenth century was of course also partly responsible for the emergence of an increasingly (romanticist) vibrant rural and amenity environmentalist lobby which played a key role in the twentieth century for at least protecting large segments of the British countryside. The oppositional status to neo-liberalism survives and, indeed, becomes even more vehement today, and sets a stage for the playing out of many of the contemporary dimensions of 'contested sustainabilities' that. I will focus on this in the book. First, however, let us identify in more depth some of these important agri-food antecedents and transition points.

Imperial 'outsourcing' of productionism

By developing manufacturing and allowing domestic agriculture to shrink through a policy of free trade, the nineteenth- and early-twentieth-century UK became by far the largest importer (and processor and re-exporter) of food and raw materials. For many later industrializing countries, the UK was their prime export market: for example, for Russian and American wheat, Argentinian meat and Danish butter and cheese. The British market was vital for many colonial products – for example, Australian butter, wool, wine, beef, dried and canned fruits, sugar and lamb; New Zealand butter, cheese, lamb and mutton; Rhodesian tobacco; West Indian and Mauritian sugar; Ghanaian cocoa; and Malayan rubber. By the early 1890s, Canada was becoming a significant exporter, joining the United States and Russia, and the newly opened Suez Canal was facilitating imports also from India and Australasia.

With such an extensive food-producing empire, the UK's domestic food security depended critically upon its then-undisputed mastery of the seas and its steam ships, combined with its continuing manufacturing strength, all of which could arguably be harmed by any counter policy of domestic agricultural self-sufficiency in peacetime. The explicit neglect of UK's domestic agriculture and rurality (save for its private estates and grouse moors), and indeed the relative impoverishment of much of its rural population, was compensated by the exported and imperial gains of facilitating the exploitation of the natural resources of the empire, through the very encouragement of emigration from the UK and the supply of capital on favourable terms. This was a profound and quite lasting natural and spatial, and indeed, ecological 'fix'. The policy of imperial preferences, through which imported food and raw materials received concessions on some customs duties, further encouraged the expansion of primary production in the empire for the British market. For example, in Australia, whole tracts of land were newly settled for fruit growing and grape growing. Back home, rural infrastructures were collapsing on the back of lower-cost imports and a failure of the British state to recognize the significance of the domestic rural local economy.

By the time of the First World War, and especially by the onset of the Great Depression of the late 1920s and 1930s, it was becoming clear that this loss of UK's rural capacity was indeed a strategic issue. The UK entered the First World War with food shortages and shortages of labour (Lloyd George, 1933); and the Acland Committee (1913: 27), just before entering the most costly of all wars, lamented the state of rural affairs thus:

The matter is very urgent; the remaining portion of rural England, here as in other countries subject to constant encroachment by the towns, is a precious possession which must be rightly used, not for the benefit of individuals only, but with a constant eye to the best National and Imperial interests. Why as a Nation are we so sluggish in this matter? Do we realise how essential a rural population is and that Germany has 13 persons employed in agriculture to every 100 acres of cultivated areas, and France 10, while in the UK there are slightly under 5. ... It is obvious that it is not a question of climate and soil which makes this enormous difference. It is that, with our common tradition of *laissez-faire*, we have allowed the State to look on and make no really effective effort to increase the rural population. We must get a public opinion which warmly approves every rural village where a healthy, independent and prosperous set of families is being added to the countryside.

It was of course more likely to be in the new settler countries of Britain's far-flung empire where such vibrant networks of family farms and villages were being established.

The emergence of post-war UK productionism and modernization

The imperial position of the UK, and along with it its dominant free-trade policy, emerged as significantly weaker both after the First World War and the Great Depression. Trade protectionism was growing around the world by the 1930s. More politicians, facing declines in manufacturing, came to support more protective tariffs. Between the 1930s and the years of post-Second World War reconstruction, most Western nations introduced measures to counteract the instability and volatility of their domestic agricultural markets, and to attempt to lift their rural areas out of the impoverished conditions of the interwar years. This was part and parcel of a more general (Keynesian) shift in the management of national policies in response to the Great Depression, the war years, and their recognition – countering explicitly classical and long-running liberal orthodoxies of public finances – that the state was critical in developing a modern agri-food and rural sector.

But here again we see the irony and paradox of the distinctive British rural and agrarian condition. For at just the point that the UK state belatedly turned to its rural heartlands for strategic national productivist needs, we find that the rural heartlands, due to their secular decline, were bereft of the capacity to immediately deliver. The long-running experience of the imperial food order had by the 1940s rendered the UK rural space incapable of meeting these new modernizing and productivist demands. The lengthy agricultural depression had led to thousands of acres of arable land lying unkempt and put under grass; and thousands of farm workers unemployed or suffering from low wages (Hall, 1941). The National Farm Survey of 1941 revealed a devastating picture of the extent of social and economic unsustainability in the countryside and the economic and social weaknesses and vulnerabilities of farm families. The UK debt crisis, food rationing and the horror of the German U-boat campaign experience, all indicated the need for a national productivist agricultural policy built upon more stability in supply and national self-sufficiency.

The UK then entered, from the early 1940s up until the 1980s, a period of unprecedented, and in many ways, remarkable modernization and state-supported growth in its agricultural and rural base. Ironically, again we can see this as a tacit realization of the 'success' of its earlier phases of neo-liberalizing imperialism. For despite the impoverished state of its domestic rural parts and much of its national food system, it had indirectly created and outsourced a settler-intensive 'Fordist' model of food supply in its former colonies, upon which it now needed access as a declining imperial power. The warning signs of this food security crisis came well earlier, during the costly and imperial First World War. Given the parlous state of the British rural land base, as Acland had reported, food security became an immediate concern. And it ushered in (imported) Fordist mechanization, which was later to become the harbinger of post-war and state-supported agrarian productivism. David Lloyd George (1933: 774) echoes the urgency of these conditions in the midst of the First World War thus:

> Here we were up against a two-fold difficulty. On the one hand, we had not got tractors. On the other, the farmers were not at all eager to use them. Steam ploughing they were in some districts more familiar with, but of the 500 sets which existed in the country, nearly half were idle as their engine drivers had left for the army or the munitions factories, and many of the sets were out of repair. ... At this stage Mr Henry Ford came to our aid. ... He offered to present his 'Fordson' tractor to the British Government as a model, together with all the drawings, patterns, jigs etc., needed for its production, free of cost. ... Motor and steam power represented only one aspect of the very great resort which we made to mechanical aids in our campaign. The Ministry of Munitions was called on to furnish every kind of improved agricultural implement which could save labour and assist mass production from the soil.

Here we see the big transformation emerging, with the UK increasingly reaping the disbenefits for neglecting its domestic agricultures and rural areas at the altar of its past imperial zest, at the same time in significant times of national crisis having to rely upon the newly found Fordist vibrancy of its colonial partners. Everything that happened during the onset and ending of the Second World War exacerbated this new industrial dependency. Slowly, at first, the UK rural space was emerging from a system dominated by the 'manurial utility' (Lloyd George, 1933) of horsepower, hoe and then steam, to one built upon imported mechanical and chemical technologies from its colonist progeny. The system of American 'Lease-Lend' served to further mechanize the deeper parts of the British countryside which was still largely dependent on horsepower after the war.

The period 1945–84 thus emerges as a remarkable period of state-induced agricultural productivism and agri-industrialization. This was borne out of both the wartime and imperial crisis, and a renewed intensity and political consensus for securing more and more of the domestic population's food needs from its own shores. These basic tenets of the productivist period were maintained largely intact until the end of the 1970s, dominating the White Paper *Farming and the Nation* in 1979 and the earlier *Food from Our Own Resources* in 1975. Both espoused a strong function for the UK rural space to contribute fully to reducing national balance of payments deficits, and to give as much land as possible to domestic production, duly aided and abetted by a strong R&D science base and price guarantees.

What was so unique in food and rural governance terms about this period was the synergies that were created between different arms of national policy, such that aspects of science policy, treasury and fiscal support, planning and land use, as well as wider welfare policies all contributed to raising both the national security and sustainability of rural and agri-food infrastructures. This was based less, of course, on horse and steam power and more, increasingly, upon imported and domestic carbon in the form of coal, oil and gas. Artificial fertilization was greatly enhanced which contributed to rapid increases in yields per hectare. The governance system also put in protectionist measures to assist hill farmers and the more isolated rural communities (such as in Wales, Scotland and much of Northern England). For example, the Hill Farming Act (1946) paid hill livestock subsidies, which were eventually encapsulated into the European Community's Less Favoured Areas Directive.

Security of land rights, through an extension of farm tenancy legislation, gave impetus for family continuity for farm tenants; and security of agricultural land use was dovetailed with the 1947 Town and Country Planning Act which secured a priority for agricultural land use in rural areas (protection) as well as restricting residential developments (urban containment). This had the social consequence of creating a sharper distinction between town and country, warding off spasmodic 'ribbon development', and maintaining a cheap supply of rural labour for the farm population (see Hall et al., 1972; Newby, 1977). Financial security of farm businesses and the provision of relatively cheap supplies of food for consumers was created by a system of guaranteed prices and deficiency payments, which were also absorbed into the EU CAP payments systems post 1974. Farmer's unions, especially the National Farmers Union (NFU) came to play a strong corporatist role within successive Labour and Tory governments, influencing directly the annual review of farm prices and incomes, and in return implementing the productivist policies on behalf of the government to their distributed and diverse membership (Self and Storing, 1962).

This highly synergistic policy regime brought about significant structural change both to land holding and agricultural management. Without directly taking over or nationalizing land rights per se (as in the Soviet bloc at the time), there was a growth in owner occupation of farmland by farm families (75 per cent of land) by the 1980s, and a further diminution of landed estates. This was also associated with an increase in the average size of holdings since the 1950s, and a rise in large mixed tenure holdings. These trends continued throughout the 1970s and 1980s.

For quite a considerable period (1947–80) – indeed a period we might look back on as a period of 'high farming' – agri-food governance in the UK as well as much of the EU progressed as a productivist regime which seemed to successfully combine the effective public management of both food security and sustainability. Food consumers were now able to access an increasing variety of nutritious foods, with the days of rationing long gone; farmers and landholders were far more secure in their businesses and could plan on family succession of their farms for future generations. A complex and supportive scientific and advisory apparatus had been established to continue to mechanize and chemicalize the industry; and the farming lobbies were disproportionately and, some argued, exceptionally empowered in their role as national government guardians charged with keeping national balance of payments deficits and inflation rates under some type of control. Moreover, the state-supported system had stimulated nationalized, and increasingly internationalized agri-business in the upstream and downstream sectors. This was, for a time, an industrial as well as an agricultural and food nation success story (see Wormell, 1978).

The onset of contradictions and the rise of post-productivism

Such a seemingly resilient national and EU productivist regime however came under continuous pressure, as in the 1970s international oil price hikes destabilized the Western economies. The food sector increasingly became an arena of uncertainty and struggle between nation states in the North and the South and in the East and the West, despite the EU's best efforts to manage trading arrangements. Trade wars re-emerged, and the tensions between national, economic and political (protectionist) strategies, on the one hand, and multinational (globalizing) corporations, on the other, was increasing the instability of food commodity prices (Goodman and Redclift, 1991).

Neo-liberalized globalization of trade was re-emerging and highly and heavily supported agricultural policies now emanating out of Europe came under heavy critique by a new breed of 'new right' politicians who were to eventually be led by Margaret Thatcher and Ronald Reagan. As with the 1930s, the 1970s presaged geo-political change, but this time in the opposite political direction. Welfarism, Keynesianism and, as part and parcel of this, highly state-supported agricultures and food policies were increasingly seen as too costly and inefficient. While the EU's agricultural support ballooned to over 80 per cent of its total expenditure, farm incomes were now falling due to cheaper food imports and high input costs. The growing cost-price squeeze placed on farmers, under conditions of guaranteed prices, only encouraged them to produce more and more, thereby swelling the already overflowing EU intervention stores, and increasing overall support costs.

These economic fractures emerged just as the political power and security embodied in the post-war corporatist partnership between national EU governments and farmers unions also began to wane. These two processes were closely related. Internal conflicts between different commodity producers ('corn' vs. 'horn'), and scales of producers became more frequent, and the EU commission, as well as much of Whitehall, became a place for what seemed to be, in the public's eye, the inordinate wrangling over farmers 'featherbedded' prices and incomes. A signature moment in this crisis – a crisis of transition to a more post-productivist regime – came when the EU suddenly imposed milk quotas on dairy farmers so as to curb overproduction in 1984. The Thatcher-inspired abolition of the Milk Marketing Board occurred in the same year. What was dawning – faced with embarrassingly overflowing food stocks, on the one hand, and a re-invigorated neo-liberalist politics which wished to cut farm subsidies in line with what it was achieving in other branches of the recession-hit economies, on the other hand – was a new post-productivist policy landscape, whereby overproduction and excessive subsidies were to be severely curtailed and redirected.

Of course, the financial and political crisis which ensued, especially during the 1980s, with the UK reforming 'new right' government, was also reinforced by the recognition of a growing environmental crisis associated with the very externalities the increasingly intensive productivist agri-food regime had produced. While the productivist regime had largely 'solved' the problems of national food security, the profound and multifarious ecological problems of sustainability were now clearly emerging (see Lowe, Marsden and Whatmore, 1990; Goodman and Redclift, 1991). It seemed during the 1980s that the age of productivism was clearly doomed, prostrated as it was across a reforming and deregulating neo-right politics on the one hand, and a broadening (and largely anti-farming, left of centre) environmental movement on the other.

National government departments and EU directorates spent much of the 1980s and 1990s attempting to assuage these new pressures, largely with a set of compromised and post-productivist measures (such as 'set aside', extending conservation areas, payments for agri-environment schemes), which attempted to contain carbon- and intensive-based agricultures, without necessarily changing their modus operandi. Meanwhile the strength of a multifarious environmental lobby grew, and as it grew it also became anti-farming.

The extent of the deregulatory drive by successive Thatcher governments and successive neo-liberal governments since was also impacting upon the reconstitution of the food consumer interest. Central to this political drive was the unleashing of wider consumer rights, whether it was associated with housing, education, health or, indeed, food. It was no coincidence, therefore, that we saw, especially during the last two decades of the twentieth century, the rise of the private corporate retailers as 'the new masters of the food system' (Flynn and Marsden, 1992). The incidence of BSE, among a range of other public food scares (e.g. Salmonella), was yet another severe and long-lasting blow to the intensive production and processing sector; but it was a crisis from which much of the corporate, but not the independent butchery and grocery sector, would come out largely unscathed.

Private-interest governance and post-productionism in the 1990s and 2000s

By 1993 (p. 14) Wyn Grant, studying agri-food politics in the EU and the UK, was able to argue:

> Britain displays many of the characteristics of the company state. In a company state the most important form of business-state contract is the direct one between company and government. Government prioritises such forms of contract over associative intermediation.

The rise of the corporate grocery retailers was closely tied to the growth in consumer choice and the equal growth in imports (especially of fresh fruits and vegetables from around the world). Above all, we should see the period of post-productivism (1984–2008) as very much an unfinished and ongoing compromise which significantly empowered European consumers, some environmental pressure groups and, above all, the corporate retailers (see Spaargaren et al., 2012). This was intended as a *private-interest-governance* regime bestowed, especially upon the retailers, by the reforming and deregulating 'new right' and the then Blair governments in order for them to provide a vast array of food choices while also keeping food inflation under control. In this sense they had adeptly replaced farmers and landowners as the key government delivery agents for ensuring food security and food sustainability. In particular, then, it reduced the hitherto political power of both domestic and European producers (and indeed many of their rural areas), in favour of corporate interests, all in the name of widening consumerism and consumer sovereignty. In this sense it was a particular compromise with the growth of consumer-based neo-liberalism, which in the context of Europe and agri-food, encouraged the rapid and profound growth of retailer-led supply chain regulation – indeed in itself, a new form of private retailer-led supply chain regulation and corporatism (see Busch and Bain, 2004; Marsden et al., 2010).

It is important to recognize that, again as in the Imperial past, by partly exporting its production and environmental externalities on production platforms in developing countries, post-productivism managed to politically stabilize the wider neo-liberal project by calibrating both food security and food sustainability largely by privately regulated means. Household food costs could be kept under control while facing the consumer with an increasing array of food choices. To be a citizen meant being an effective consumer. In turn, consumer politics began to play a powerful role in sustaining the new right and neo-liberalism more generally. Food supply and security were thus a fuel for continued neo-liberalization. Meanwhile, a myriad of EU environmental regulations could fend off, or at least ring fence, the destructive ecological effects of domestic intensive farming systems as long as imports from outside the EU could be expanded with relatively low transport costs and private sector quality standards of regulation. By 2006, 72 per cent of all UK grocery sales took place in the corporate supermarkets, an increase from 67 per cent in 2000, with sales increasing by 26 per cent over the same period. For a time then up to the Food, Financial, Fiscal and Fuel (FFFF) crisis of 2007–8, this corporatist model seemed to deliver rewards for government, retailers and consumers/householders, while the farming interests continued to lose political power. Tight supply chain regulation drove down prices, further influencing government in progressing a largely laissez-faire approach to food policy.

Over this period too, it can also be seen that the British countryside became a more differentiated and a consumption countryside (see Murdoch et al., 2003), whereby both agricultural employment and net farm incomes continued to decline. The intensive livestock farming community continued to be beset with problems of animal diseases, most notably foot-and-mouth disease in the early 2000s, followed by the controversial bovine TB linked to the swelling badger population (see Woods, 2008; Enticott, 2014). DEFRA was left to pick up the pieces from these mismanagements, as well as to administer the deepening labyrinthine allocation of CAP support systems on which farmers increasingly relied. While the waves of growing ex-urban populations were, from the late 1950s, colonizing much of the British countryside, upholding much of the romantic and rural 'idyll' cultural features of the countryside, the dwindling number of neighbouring farmers were struggling to uphold the vestiges of the earlier productivist and modernizing paradigm many of them had been reared on.

The post-productivist phase of the 1980s and 1990s in the UK especially, but more generally in Western Europe, created a revised public and private hybrid governance model in which both the public and private sectors strived to codify, regulate and rationalize the safety and quality of foods. They did so while attempting to maintain the growth and legitimacy of the technologically driven intensive food production and processing systems, especially now outside of Europe as well as within. These systems are though highly vulnerable to ecological and food quality crises, as the long-running controversies about the role of Genetic Modification (GM) and a range of pesticides have demonstrated. The EU and UK approach was to create independent scientific-based institutions like the European Food Standards Agency (EFSA), and the Food Standards Agency (FSA) in the UK to manage food risks and increasing public concerns about the adulteration of their foods. The retailer-led hybrid model of governance – which combined sets of basic public standards below the more privately competitive quality standards set by the retailers – was thus still highly vulnerable to abuse and public concern. This has been demonstrated by the horsemeat scandal of 2013, among others.

Rural development, relocalization and the rise of alternative food networks (AFNs)

It is also important to recognize that at the time the dominant and mass hybrid system emerged in the 1980s and 1990s, and Europeanization of much of the UK food, agricultural and rural policy was providing many distributed and fragmented local rural development interests with the means to develop alternative local food networks, often based upon a more diversified local agricultural base. In the extensive upland areas of Wales, Scotland and England, in particular, a rejuvenated movement was beginning to take place whereby groups of farmers, regional and local development agencies, and some local landowners, and community leaders collaborated to create new forms of local value added through combinations of local food and tourist/amenities. This was very much a 'bottom-up' process, but was given significant added impetus by a range of EU rural development funding mechanisms, most significantly associated with regional structural funding, protected names of geographical origin designations, and the rural specific programme of LEADER. This significantly stimulated the birth of what some European scholars, and eventually the Organisation for Economic Co-operation and Development (OECD), entitled the 'new rural development paradigm'. We shall focus on this later in the book, but here it is important to outline its origins, not least because, by the turn of the century, there was indeed an explosion of diversified rural development initiatives in the UK and in mainland Europe, and this was being seen by many as a real alternative to the dominant conventional agri-food paradigm.

'Rural development' in the UK context had historically been very much the 'Cinderella' policy field, being conveniently located outwith the more dominant agricultural and the environmental policy fields. However, since the time of the Acland Committee (1913), and Lloyd George as we saw above, there has been a continuous strand of political concern for the plight and welfare of the (non-agricultural) rural economy. The Development Commission was set up as early as 1909, with a strong rural economy focus. This evolved in the 1920s into the Rural Development Commission which merged with the Council for Industries in Rural Areas in the 1980s, and then the Countryside Commission in the 1990s. In rural Wales there was a long history of rural economic and social development with the setting up of the Development Board for Rural Areas (DBRW) in the early 1960s, in Mid Wales. However, it was Europeanization and the availability of substantial grant funding for local rural projects which became particularly relevant during the 1990s and early 2000s leading to the proliferation of integrated rural development projects across rural UK.

As with significant areas of agri-environmental policy, many local rural development advocates began to bypass Westminster and turn to Brussels for policy intermediation, funding possibilities and networking. They largely had a warmer reception than in Whitehall. The Delors EU policy statement (EC, 1988) entitled *The Future of Rural Society* lay the framework for later EU rural development programmes upon which much of the early rural development initiatives began their lives. This was welcomed by the British rural development fraternity, especially in the upland regions that had long been marginalized (as 'peripheral') by the productivist regime. Under the Eurosceptic Thatcher administration (who not least seemed to be in perpetual conflict with the Delorsian philosophy of EU regional integration, balance and diversity) it held little sway in Whitehall. How could you have a 'future for rural society' when 'there was no such thing as society'? The telling hearsay and negotiating talk around reducing UK's EU financial contributions at the time in Whitehall was the Faustian quid pro quo: 'Let the French keep their supported agricultures, we will keep and support our financial services.'

Now, almost as in the 1900s, it had to be left to the eventual devolved regions of Wales and Scotland, and some notable Lords (like Donald Curry, Henry Plumb and Christopher Haskins) to articulate the plight of local rural economy needs. The Curry Commission of 2002 on the *Future of Farming and Food*, as well as a series of White Papers and devolved strategy papers, began to give more weight to, on the one hand, the value of short food supply chains and re-localized foods and, on the other, the role of these food supply chains and re-localized foods in generating local economic development (see Marsden and Sonnino, 2008; Morgan et al., 2008). The early Blair governments, as Ward (2008) argues, by setting up a new rural White Paper process, did begin to espouse a more integrated, holistic and territorial approach to rural development and this coincided with the reformed CAP policies bringing in the 'second pillar' rural development policy. Although the foot-and-mouth crisis in 2001–2, and what can only be regarded as (but highly charged) political side issues like the ban on fox hunting, tended to crowd-out and dilute the overall territorial agenda, especially in England.

More promisingly, however, and as a run up to the financial and fiscal crisis (2007–8), as we shall see in the next chapter, what we witnessed by the early 2000s was a gradual and perhaps somewhat tacit confluence of interests and emergent coalitions between (i) local and regional territorial rural development interests (which were given a fillip by the devolution process in Scotland and Wales, and European funding programmes); (ii) a growth in consumer and some producer movements to demand shorter and locally grown foods (Goodman, DuPuis and Goodman, 2012); and (iii) the arrival of sustainability debates and their connections with the agri-food and rural spheres. In this sense, while there were significant disappointments among commentators about the early Blair reform agenda, through devolution, and in upgrading the status of sustainability and climate change debates, it began to lead to a far more integrated and holistic thinking across the policy community. Indeed, even in agricultural circles this was beginning to be recognized. This was, in many respects, influenced greatly by Europe and the growth of EU Environmental Action Programmes, and rural and regional support programmes which empowered many local and regional actors and networks (see Milone and Ventura, 2010; O'Connor, 2006).

Conclusion: A postscript and the rise of food quality

In 2003, Henk Renting, Jo Banks and I published one of the first empirically based and comparative papers on the extent and growth of alternative food networks across seven EU states, including the UK (Renting, Marsden and Banks, 2003). This occurred in the midst of a revival of interest and activity around countering the conventional and industrially organized agri-food supply chains, and the growth in Europe of newly emerging food networks that have since become known under the headings 'alternative food networks' (AFNs) and 'short food supply chains' (SFSCs). The paper was part of a wider scholarly endeavour which we initiated regarding the understanding and explicit normative development of a sustainable rural development countermovement which was attempting to progress a wholesale paradigmatic shift in thinking and in practice with regard to re-integrating agriculture – more specifically 'farming' – into the wider need to create sustainable rural development (see Marsden, 2003; van der Ploeg and Marsden, 2008; Lamine, et al., 2012; Horlings and Marsden, 2014). This involved putting more intellectual and empirical impetus into the OECD's call at the time for a 'new rural paradigm' (OECD, 2006) which espoused a far more diversified and multifunctional rural economic base linked to meeting growing urban consumer as well as production demands. The tendency prior to this endeavour, both in policy and scholarly circles, had been very much to separate agriculture from wider aspects of rural development. In the UK, especially, this has long had the effect of marginalizing non-agricultural aspects of rural development. Even though, as the Foot-and-Mouth Disease (FMD) crisis had so markedly shown, the farming economy was highly integrated into the amenity and tourism functions of the consumption countryside for its economic well-being.

These issues have been far from eclipsed in 2017, not least with the increasing recognition of a continuing ecological crisis, climate change, food and health concerns, and the contested processes involved in developing a 'post-carbon' economy (see OECD and EU recent papers, OECD, 2013; EC, 2015). The 2003 paper that I co-authored with Renting and Banks helped stimulate an explosion of empirical work both in Europe and then in North America on AFNs as an antidote to the conventional system, and there was considerable debate about AFNs' relevance and long-term viability. Some of our North American colleagues were, to say the least, sceptical about our paradigmatic ambitions (see Goodman, 2004 and van der Ploeg and Renting, 2004 for a reply), but nevertheless also had to admit that even in their more neo-liberalized realm the explosion of AFNs was a growing reality (see Goodman, DuPuis and Goodman, 2012; Morgan et al., 2008).

In the paper, and especially in the conclusion, we emphasized that while we saw the growth of AFNs as a significant and growing phenomenon in rural Europe, and thus a major touchstone in the wider and deeper development of the rural development paradigm, we were cautious to point out the significant countervailing tendencies of appropriation, co-option, dilution and market closure around their continuing and, indeed, long-term development. In a word, mainstreaming of these alternatives has not occurred since, despite their growth and significant embeddedness in many European regions. This does not, however, call into question the continued need and relevance of the sustainable rural development paradigm; but it does give us an opportunity to assess, now with significant hindsight, how its significant contested status has fared since the early 2000s. Here then I want to outline some of the barriers that have constrained and contained the sustainable rural development paradigm and the role of AFNs as part of it with regard specifically to the EU. What I argue and develop in succeeding chapters, is that this has been caught up in wider shifts in the political economy, of which food, indeed, plays a growing and significant part.

Reasons for the 'glass ceiling'

1. Neo-liberalized consumerism and the growth of AFNs

It is important to recognize, as we have argued here, that the late twentieth century and early 2000s represented, not least in Europe, a period 'of plenty' with regard to agri-food. Continued growth in household incomes combined with the progressive declines in household expenditures for food and energy were still coupled with an explosive growth in consumerism, fed by a growth in imports from the Global South and the East (not least in both temperate and exotic fruits and vegetables). This continued 'spatial fix' and growth in household disposable incomes allowed, especially among the middle classes, for an explosion of consumption of novel foods and take-away and out-of-home eating practices (see Spaargaren et al., 2012). At the same time more food producers, faced with the long-running cost-price squeeze associated with the still highly regulated conventional markets, saw increasing advantages and opportunities in meeting these new and novel demands. This provided a rich empirical opportunity, especially for the more postmodern of scholars, to study the proliferation of farmers markets, box schemes, community-supported agricultures and the like.

Hence, we had a collision here between neo-liberalized hyper-consumerism and the growth of AFN niches at this particular time period of the early 2000s. This has also put pressure and constraints on the development of AFNs and SFSCs, especially those with a stronger commercial orientation, that have seen themselves caught in a need for scale enlargement and cost-price reduction, and created vulnerability for conventionalization and appropriation by mainstream intermediate supply chain actors. AFNs and SFSCs in their development over the last decade, at least in the European context, have been weakening, further strengthening and consolidating collective forms of action that potentially might have counteracted the individualized focus of neo-liberal consumerism.

2. The financial and fiscal crisis of the national state and contested sustainabilities

As we will explore in more detail in the next chapter, the 2007–8 price hikes in fuel and food were combined with the deepening crisis of neo-liberalism which resulted in the financial and fiscal crisis of the national state, (not least the UK) and indeed as we have seen also of the European state. In addition, the collapse of the post-Cold War settlement and the global volatility of markets only fuelled new rounds of financialization (and of course associated 'land grabbing') which in turn has made this volatility even more stark as we write now in 2017. As Jason Moore (2015) has documented, the onset of this period was also more profound as it witnessed a crisis in globalized and neo-liberalized capitalist world ecology, which among other things, meant that the convenient spatial fixes upon which the UK and wider European food economy had come to rely could no longer be so effectively sustained. In short, to use the transition management lexicon, the dominant agri-food system or regime *and* its myriad forms of AFN niches which we empirically display in our 2003 paper come under the severe effects of new and recombinant 'landscape change' factors, including growing and volatile financialization of food systems, climate change effects, food shortages and resource limits, sovereign debt and political volatilities.

3. The reactions of the state: more of the same

The reactions of national and supra-states to this now long-running financial and fiscal crisis has in many ways further entrenched a neo-liberalized, as opposed to welfarist, model for dealing with it. This has occurred in a context where: (i) the long-running 'Engels law' of continuing declines in proportional household costs for food and energy has now been reversed in most EU nation states; (ii) due to rising household costs and cuts in welfare budgets there has been an explosion in widening social and spatial inequalities with regard to access to healthy foods; and (iii) the national state has allowed the continued oligopolization and hence surplus value-creation of much of the retailers' corporate-controlled food system in ways which have, at the same time, increased the cost-price squeeze for producers and provided poorer quality and 'discounted' options for those consumers especially on low incomes. It is no wonder then that a recent growth in academic work has now moved to incorporate questions of food, poverty, insecurity, sovereignty and the 'right to food' (De Schutter, 2014), alongside its more established AFN and food quality concerns.

4. Reasons to be cheerful? From AFNs to transformative change

These shifts, caused by the continuing financial and fiscal crisis of the national state, and particularly by the specific (and highly regulatory) neo-liberalized reactions of nation states and their privatized dealings with corporate food firms, thus set a renewed and challenging context for progressing the sustainable rural–urban paradigm. They also imply limitations for the type of policy responses that nation states and the EU developed in response to emerging AFNs and SFSCs, potentially embodying a fundamental challenge to neo-liberalized, dominant development models. While in recent years within the EU we have seen a recognition of the magnitude and role of emerging AFNs/SFSC (e.g. Kneafsey et al., 2013), in policy debates and processes these have systematically been framed in ways that deny and contradict their potential transformative capacity: they are considered a 'niche market', that are only relevant in as far as they result in extra income for mainstream professional farmers, and which can only be subject of policy from the perspective of the 'responsive state' (see also Marsden and Sonnino, 2008).

But as we shall see in succeeding chapters to this book, all is by no means lost. The crisis is engendering its own social and political oppositional status; there is an explosion of connections between collective farming – food-health-biodiversity-energy – and community concerns which can and are challenging the neo-liberal orthodoxy around agri-food in different urban and rural spaces. It does imply that relevant and potentially transformative responses often do not come from the side of the 'usual players'. One such development is the rise of the City and the city-regions as food policy actors, perhaps most symbolically expressed by the signing of the Milan Urban Food Policy Pact by over 115 city governments from around the world in which local governments claim their role in governing their local food systems, including the development of SFSCs in collaboration with their communities (Forster et al., 2015; see also Moragues-Faus and Morgan, 2015). Also, as indicated elsewhere before, this is not so much the realm of state-based governance but rather civil society-initiated governance mechanisms – all with a focus on enhancing local territory – and community-based food sovereignty and democracy, where in the context of the multidimensional crisis of the neo-liberal agri-food model relevant dynamics and promising innovations occur (Renting, Schermer and Rossi, 2012).

This means that the agri-food scholarly and policy arena is now a far larger, more community-engaged vector for wider social movements (see Constance, Renard and Rivera-Ferre, 2014) on both sides of the Atlantic. In this sense agri-food studies, and the contested progress of the sustainable rural (and urban) development paradigm can no longer be restricted to the in-depth elaboration and dissemination of agri-food or AFN 'niches'. Rather it requires the adoption and ambition to create real transformative change – 'places of possibility' – by harnessing the social and natural politics of both rural producers and city consumers who will demand more sustainable and circular linkages between urban and rural functionalities which will reduce the natural and human wastage in current conventional systems of food provision.

In progressing these ambitions we may have to look beyond the nation and supra-state for guidance and support (to the local, regional, civic and translocal assemblages), but as scholars we will also need to become more normatively and politically engaged with these existing conventional institutional structures in critically articulating more variant post-neo-liberalized and more sustainable food systems. More diverse and a denser web of SFSCs and the wider rural–urban development paradigm can play a major role in fostering more effective urban–rural and producer–consumer coalitions, building upon our earlier work. In moving our agenda forward we should, thus, not abandon the central role of innovative and multi-governance as a key arena for comparative empirical analysis.

Chapter 2

Contested sustainabilities in agri-food and rural development: Exploring sustainable pathways of green growth and the bio-economy in the UK

Introduction: Shifts in the governmentality of rural areas and agri-food

This chapter explores the changing and more fluid regulation and governance of rural areas and agri-food in the UK during and after the combined food, financial, fiscal and fuel crisis (FFFFc) which emerged during 2007–8 across much of the world. There is no doubt that this was, and indeed still is, a crisis of neo-liberalism as many commentators have argued. However, in much of this book I wish to link this directly to the growing environmental and ecological crises, and indeed its political and scientific reactions, of which this is a significant part (see Moore, 2010; Marsden and Morley, 2014).

Building on earlier studies of British rural development which traced and positioned the evolution of rural governance from post-war corporatist productivism to the emerging 1980s–2000s neo-liberal forms of consumption countryside, this chapter postulates that the British countryside is at the centre of a now more unstable, possibly more uncontrollable and contested, period of bio-resource governance: *one of contested sustainabilities*. This is not leading, importantly, to the complete abandonment or the maintenance of significant remnants of either corporatist or private-interest forms of neo-liberal governmentality in the rural sphere; but it is creating new spaces and places of possibility and agency for new forms of empowered and more sustainable forms of resource governance to take hold.

Our previous studies of rural development both in a wider European and UK sense are in need of refreshment given the shifts and crises the world has experienced, especially since 2008. In earlier monographs, some of my colleagues and I had aimed to chart the development and macroeconomic positionality of the rural and agricultural sphere as being associated with two main trends. First, since the 1980s we charted the development of the more diverse consumption countryside (see Marsden et al., 1993; Murdoch and Marsden, 1995; Murdoch et al., 2003). This demonstrated the growth in a more diverse 'post-productivist' countryside which was now far more reliant upon the vagaries and distinctive features of its regional and global economic conditions than upon the previous post-war national governance priorities of agricultural productivism and food security. As agriculture was economically and politically receding into the background, the use and sociopolitical drivers for much of the countryside seemed to be coming from the metropolitan demands for housing, amenity and environmental protection. This has since been seen as EU-wide trend, especially around its major conurbations, like Amsterdam and Helsinki (Andersson et al., 2008, 2016).

A second feature, identified in the volume *The Condition of Rural Sustainability* (Marsden, 2003) and developed as part of a sustainable rural development paradigm (see van der Ploeg and Marsden, 2008; Marsden, 2010), was the contested, but nevertheless significant, development of alternative, broadening, deepening and re-grounding strategies adopted in many rural areas, which amounted to the re-birth of more endogenous and diversified land-based eco-economies. This signalled what we called the start of the 'rural development paradigm' at the time. These were emerging as local responses to both the growth in the consumption demands of the countryside and, more long term, to the new realization of the need to create more sustainable forms of development within the rural realm. This approach was codified and connected further by the OECD's pronouncement of a 'new rural paradigm' (see Chapter 4) which was relinked to its urban counterparts in providing a diversified range of functions for urban as well as rural society.

It is important to now recognize that both of these treatises on the new positionality of the rurality in Europe were presaged upon a relatively 'golden period' of neo-liberalizing European consumerism and post-productionism (see Marsden, 2013). For instance, neither the impending food/energy security crisis of 2007–8 nor the related financial and fiscal crisis was predicted. However, both of these related events have and are having profound conditioning affects upon the structure, role and future policy direction of the European countryside. I thus call this new more unstable period one of 'contested sustainabilities'. While the countryside had been a major site for contestation before the crisis occurred, I now want to argue that both the need to demonstrate and to promote the sustainable condition has become more critical for a wider range of actors and institutions associated with rural areas. Also, at the same time, there are now more divisions and contestations in the views, articulations, intentions and visions as to actually how this sustainability condition should be taken forward.

Indeed, what we are now witnessing, given the scale and depth of both the (carbonized) resource and wider (climate) environmental crisis, is a growing necessity to relocate rural areas as key zones of, and in, the post-carbon transition, during a period of rapid and 'locked-in' con-urbanization and population growth in many parts of the world.

As such Europe (and indeed the UK specifically) can no longer look in upon itself for the solutions to these problems. Prior to 2007–8 Europe and its member states were still highly internally focused upon enlargement of its single European market and the project of harmonizing many of its social and environmental policies and frameworks. At the same time, its economy benefitted in capturing increasing volumes of 'cheap' food imports from outside its borders. We have now entered a period when the ecological and economic crises have become not only inextricably intertwined, but also more globalized. As such there are no more quick spatial or national fixes whereby ecological costs can be exported or distanced, as indeed they had been during the 'golden period'. Hence, from a European perspective then, the global ecological and economic externalities have come home to roost, and as such we are likely to witness a redefinition of the countryside as a contested way of trying to cope and resolve some of these new global challenges.

Since the 2007–8 crisis at least three major trends have been superimposed upon the rural realm making its governance and development far more contingent and contested. These concern (i) the somewhat dominant reaction to the new crisis of sustainability and food/energy security being to promote a new politics and science of 'sustainable intensification', a reincarnated form of neo-productivism; (ii) to creating new privatized and positional rounds of consumption countryside investments as forms of safe haven investments by the rich and the financial sector; and (iii) using rural space and its links with sustainability initiatives in urban contexts and innovative platforms for alternative sustainable development in the areas of food, cooperative housing, community gardens, and sustainable transport and business developments. While all three trends vary in their degree of intensity and spatial variability, and of course map onto, as we shall see later, preexisting socio-economic and political conditions, they also represent a new period of redefinition of rurality with regard to its human-natural conditions. In short, they represent a refocusing upon the unique socio-natural features of the countryside –what I term the bio-eco-economy.

This incorporates the multiple ways in which rural and urban people and their institutions manage and manipulate the biosphere which sustains their existence and creates economic value out of its non-renewable and renewable resources. In this sense, under the relatively new crisis conditions the race is on, both by external agents and endogenous rural peoples, to redefine their natural bases and assets in ways which re-create livelihoods for an increasingly cosmopolitan world. This is a world which cannot now sustain itself on carbon-based consumerism. We are thus witnessing a period of contested sustainabilities, whereby the rural and its resources become a key arena for playing out of different economic strategies over natural resource use and value.

Taking a Foucouldian (2007) perspective we can argue that we are now witnessing a redefinition of the coordinates of rural and agri-food *biopower* whereby contested framings of the bio-economy and the eco-economy vie for position in and through rural spaces. Indeed rural spaces and their effective governmentality become, I argue, a key macroeconomic and political site for the playing out of bio-politics more generally, and their property and knowledge rights in particular. Perhaps not surprisingly this leads to a generalized macroeconomic and political perception that rural areas and their economies are increasingly sidelined to mainstream economic development and financialization (see Chapter 6). And indeed conventional Gross Domestic Product (GDP) statistics and data continue, falsely, to portray this image of rural areas as receding economic backwaters. But this is, I argue in this book, increasingly a misnomer once one considers the transition to the post-carbon economy and the need to cultivate the bio-sphere. Current standard metrics about agriculture tend then to reinforce its economically marginal status, just at the time that we need to revalorize its multifunctional capabilities.

In some significant cases this misconception is, as I argue below, leading to the promotion of more centralized, monopolistic or, at least, oligopolistic rights over land and intellectual property rights (see 'land grabbing' and rural cash purchases, and seed patents as exemplars). But this is also a more decentred battleground where new place-based knowledges and practices, often organized translocally across the countryside and cities can now literally 'gain ground'.

Contested sustainabilities become dominant also because of the mere universalism of sustainability framings (weak and strong, narrow and deep), whereby significant polities, private and civic interests all espouse some variant of a sustainable futurity. Indeed since the crisis emerged in 2007–8, there has been an urgency on the parts of both dominant 'regimes' and significant 'niches' to claim 'sustainable' solutions, especially implicating different types of rurality. 'Sustainable intensification' – getting more for less – has indeed become a dominant neo-productivist framing which encapsulates neo-liberalist notions of the bio-economy (see Goven and Pavone, 2014). Notions of the place-based eco-economy emerge also espousing radical implications of science, local knowledge and more reflexive post-neo-liberalized governance (see Marsden and Franklin, 2013).

We can thus witness then in the UK the maintenance of an outmoded official statistical reality or construction which renders rural areas and their agrarian economies as declining and marginal, and tends to mask, on the one hand, the social and political realities of monopolistic biopower and class positional buying power and, on the other, the uneven emergence of more decentred eco-economic strategies. In this sense traditional types of governmentality over the very definition of the rural and agricultural are increasingly distorting the realities and re-location of ruralities as part of the post-carbon transition. This distortion also comes into play with regard to the EU Common Agricultural Policy of continuing to be seen to subsidize farming, when in fact this is indirectly a major subsidy for the downstream corporate processing and retailing sectors providing highly subsidized cheap farm-gate inputs which are then used to promote downstream 'value-added' products.

So this book is in many ways a significant rejoinder to earlier works on the variable and contested conditions of rural sustainability started over two decades ago. More significantly, however, it provides a new treatise upon how the re-location and redefinition of the countryside in the twenty-first century will emerge out of deep-seated contestations of what is regarded as sustainable in the medium to long term. It is not just that the terminology and condition of sustainability is contested, it is how such contestations emerge and are then configured in rural and urban spaces in ways which give opportunities or obstacles for new forms of real sustainable rural development to take hold. I shall address what constitutes real forms of sustainable rural development in conclusion to the book. What is becoming increasingly clear is the need to reintegrate economic as well as social assessments of rural and regional change with their bio-eco-economic bases. This is, at heart, therefore a rejuvenated humanist 'more-than-human' endeavour in that it problematizes the reintegration of the ecological into the economic and the social. It asks:

1 How will rural areas and their peoples contribute to a more post-carbon economy?

2 What will shape and who will control the combination of technologies, policies and science applications for this to occur?

3 Can rural areas and their peoples begin to revalorize both their labour and ecological practices through these developments? Or will it be 'business as usual' with regard to the devalorization of rural resources as in the last modernization period?

4 Are we witnessing the dawn of a new period of real ecological modernization in the emergence of the bio-eco-economy with respect to rural areas?

5 How do we reconceptualize and politicize space and place in ways which promote and stimulate the reconstruction of 'real' forms and processes of rural sustainability? What sort of governance and market mechanisms will this require?

New productivism and the bio-economy

It is somewhat remarkable how little debate there is, especially on the political left in the UK, on the types of economic and social growth the countryside so desperately needs. Despite a pressing need, the depth and significance of the combined FFFFc has ironically seemed to stifle the debates about new forms of sustainable 'green growth'. Yet, the impacts of the combined resource and fiscal crisis require a radical overhaul of our assumptions concerning the relationships between green markets, the state and civil society.[1] As the food banks and rates of food and fuel poverty across the UK grow, real sustainable thinking also still seems to be marginalized. This is a particular problem for the Labour Party in their quest to represent themselves, at recent elections, as potentially responsible fiscal and macroeconomic governors (e.g. 2010, 2015). This tends to wrongly reinforce the restricted zero-sum assumptions about 'jobs versus environment'. Meanwhile, the Conservative Right still sees growth through a lens of a more deregulated, and continuing carbonized, growth model which embeds 'frack, slash and build' as the harbingers for the next round of speculative economic growth.[2] This chapter begins to create a new compass with which to open the space for these debates with regard to the challenges and opportunities around rural land resources and their contribution to a more sustainable and national 'green growth'.

It is in this context that we need to critically explore the potential opportunities of the (post-carbon) revolution occurring in the scientific and policy advancement of the bio-economy: the creation of new bio-based resources as a basis for sustainable economic and social development, and the production of plant- and animal-based renewable products, goods and services. In Europe the bio-economy already has a turnover of 2 trillion euros, employing 22 million, or 9 per cent of total EU employment. It includes the interconnected sectors of agriculture, forestry, fisheries, food production, as well as parts of chemical, bio-technological and renewable energy industries. It encompasses sustainable production and renewable biological resources and their conversion, as well as the integration of waste streams and bio-based products (like bio-plastics and building materials), biofuels and bio-energy (OECD, 2011; EU, 2012).[3] The EU is expecting that each euro being invested in bio-economy R&D will generate 10 euro of value added. It is clear from a host of authoritative policy documents from the EU, North America and now Asia, that this involves the potential for significant levels of employment and economic development in areas like bio-refining; in reducing municipal and food wastes by combining heat and power generation; and within the food and forest sectors, by using different plant and fibre materials for a wider vector of bio-based markets in food, energy, waste and material chains.[4]

Whatever the longevity of a declining carbon-based energy and food system, it is increasingly clear that large petro-chemical companies (e.g. BP/Shell/Exxon) and many regional authorities are, in parallel, developing positive and green growth strategies around progressing their bio-economies (such as the Alberta and British Columbia strategies, 2012).[5] In addition, in Europe, countries like Finland and Sweden are investing heavily in converting their food and fibre sectors into centres of international innovation in biofuels and biomass products and services. Germany is busy converting its ageing chemical industries in North Rhine-Westphalia and in Baden-Württemberg into 'bio-regions and valleys', developing bio-refinery facilities for the nexus of new demands around heating, energy, transport and waste recycling. In the food sector, second- and third-generation genetic engineering is moving into the realms of more health-related and functional food designs as well as continuing to create plants which are capable of coping with droughts and a gamut of pests and diseases which are on the increase as a result of climate change.[6]

The UK so far has been less explicit and strategic about the potentials of the bio-economy. There is no overriding strategy despite evidence that the green economy is already worth more than £120 billion, employing nearly a million people, with over 25,000 jobs being created in 2012. In addition, the UK is committed to obtaining at least 15 per cent of all its energy from renewable sources (including half through bio-energy) by 2020. Despite the fact that the green sector employs more than the automobile, aerospace and telecom sectors, it receives far less political or policy attention.[7]

While renewable energy and reducing wastes and carbon are a major driver it is also recognized now that the UK needs to exploit the huge advances in bio-sciences, agricultural science, technologies and their links to agricultural and forest practices. Rising global demand for food, feed, fibre and fuel is linked to the development of more sustainable farming practices both in advanced and, especially, developing countries. This growing demand is emerging across sectors in food and non-food markets. The OECD estimates that the bio-economy could contribute over \$1 trillion of gross value added in OECD countries by 2030, of which 36 per cent could come from what is traditionally known as primary agricultural production.[8]

These bio-based developments are linking science and R&D strategies largely, but not exclusively, with corporate food, fibre-based and fuel firms, and significant public and private investments. The bio-economy, for instance, is a major feature of the enhanced EU (Horizon, 2015–20) science budget which assumes clear and exponential growth in jobs and gross value added from every euro invested in its R&D programme.[9]

The UK recent government statements suggest plans to embrace new bio-economy technologies (HM Government, 2015). Such ongoing developments present real opportunities and challenges for the UK economy and polity, and especially for its rural regions. So far the UK, despite some rather restricted and narrow approaches to this agenda (see, for instance, the discussion on UK strategy for agricultural technologies, July 2013), is failing to comprehensively grasp and deal with these challenges and debates, or indeed rationally discuss in strategic policy terms what sort of approach to adopt to stimulate and harness this new agenda. The arrival and development of the internationalized bio-economy, I wish to argue, reinforces and brings into sharp relief the public policy need for a more effective debate about how the UK can create a sustainable and green economic strategy. However, it needs to be recognized that there are significant political and ideological barriers here. As the recent British business minister stated (DEFRA, 2015):

> Food and farming are cornerstones of our communities, providing one in eight jobs and generating billions for our growing economy. We are working with industry to develop a long-term plan to ensure a bright future for food and farming that supports a One Nation economy.
>
> We are hugely ambitious for the industry's future – we want to champion technology, build skills and bring a new generation into food and farming by trebling apprenticeships. British food already enjoys a world-beating reputation for quality, traceability and fantastic taste, but there is more we can do to boost our global brand. We're asking those at the heart of UK food and farming to lead the way to ensure the industry can thrive.

Again, improving rural productivity is more generally seen as a major vehicle for ensuring wider economic prosperity as this recent policy statement indicates (HM Government, 2015: 2):

> Productivity, or the amount of output produced per unit of input (often per worker or hour worked), is the single most important determinant of living standards. Achieving growth in productivity is critical for achieving sustained economic growth. The UK economy is expected to be the fastest growing of the G7 in both 2014 and 2015, according to the OECD. However, UK productivity is estimated to be currently 17% below the G7 average. Narrowing the UK's productivity gap with other countries is a key economic priority for the government.
>
> On average, productivity (measured in terms of GVA per workforce job) is lower in rural areas than it is in urban areas. In 2013, productivity in predominantly rural areas was around 17% below the level of productivity for predominantly urban areas, including London. When London is excluded the difference in productivity in 2013 was around 7%. There is significant scope to harness recent economic trends to strengthen productivity levels in rural areas.

In tackling these issues, the established political right do not accept the need for new and more integrated and balanced economic and regional planning or policies upon which much of the innovative potential of the bio-economy elsewhere now relies. Rather they favour new forms of de-regulation and 'cutting red tape' as the primary means of increasing standard notions of 'productivity'. At the same time many environmental interests are now so fractured and fragmented around different aspects of bio-economic, energy and food and residential developments that their overall impact usually starts and ends in a (Not In My Backyard) 'NIMBY' condition of veto. Both trends also create the conditions for a lack of public engagement, knowledge, deliberation and social learning which is needed as part and parcel of making such bio-economic transitions possible. This is leading to further local and national vetoes on potential developments (e.g. wind farms, mega-farms, biomass and bio-refining plants, tidal energy, etc.) which are needed to create more food and energy security and resilience for future generations in the UK. There is then something of a policy void in the UK regarding how to deal with the onset of the bio-economy, with environmental interests tending to wish to restrict developments at any cost, and governments largely leaving the onus on private and mainly corporate developers. In this policy context effective deliberation on real 'green growth' for rural areas is seriously lacking and, one might argue, missing many opportunities.

We can explore these (less than optimal) sets of conditions with a focus on their implications for agri-food and rural land issues in the UK. This shows how aspects of the bio-economy, especially through a renewed emphasis upon agricultural production, and what is generically labelled as 'sustainable intensification', are creating new opportunities and challenges for the rural domain. This suggests, in conclusion, the need to broaden a more engaged concept of the bio-economy/eco-economy which allows more diversity of real sustainable development possibilities to be considered.

Rural land: A new bio-economic frontier?

A major implication of the contested move towards a post-carbon economy, and the bio-economy more specifically, is a redefinition and new premium being placed upon the use and potential multifunctionality of rural land and property rights (as well as water and aquatic resources).[10] As soon as it becomes unprofitable or unacceptable to mine for geologically deep, non-renewable resources (such as coal, oil and gas), the emerging post-carbon world has to face a renewed challenge of obtaining the bulk of its energy as well as its food needs from the land surface. This was the case in pre-industrial times when horse 'power' meant that draught animals had to be fed and catered for from the same land resource (as in early settler agricultures in North America and Australasia). The difference today, some two centuries later is that (i) populations are of a significantly greater scale and urban complexity; and (ii) we have found during the carbon period all sorts of new demands and amenity functions for the exclusive use of land, such that it is now no longer an extendable but very limited resource; coming with high social and economic costs. Hence the onset of the bio-economy, continued urbanization and growing land-based demands for food, fibre and energy are creating and are set to continue creating more intensity of land use. This is being expressed in the speculative 'land grabbing' experienced in Africa, but as we shall see here it is also occurring closer to home.

In the UK, particularly after the food and fuel price hikes of 2007–8, and the ensuing financial and fiscal crisis, we have seen a renewed political and economic need to intensify the demand and use of rural land. This is reflected in the persistently high price values accorded to it, and, as in the economic crisis of the 1970s, the attractive option of rural land as an investor's 'safe haven' for individual and institutional surpluses and bonuses. The British countryside, as the financial crisis has unfolded, has become a major location for surplus investment and cash which has ratcheted up the positional good and market value of land and rural housing, far beyond the reach of the majority of Britain's urban and especially rural populations. This has further rendered much of the British countryside as a positional and exclusive space – a 'consumption countryside' where the economy is dominated by ex-urban lifestyle spending. Ironically then, the onset of the FFFFc since 2007–8, has tended to re-enforce the exclusive positionality of the British countryside, making it more of a cash-rich consumption and amenity space.

One measure of this is the number of rural homes bought as 'cash purchases' without mortgage or loans. This was significantly higher in sparse rural areas (26.9 per cent) compared to urban areas (19.1 per cent) in 2007. This differential increased by 4 per cent as the recession in 2008 ensued, despite an overall nationally slower housing market.[11] Similarly, agricultural land prices rose as the recession hit in 2008, the first time for a decade, rising by 28 per cent, and fuelled not least by city bonuses. In 2013 prices were forecast to continue to rise both for agricultural and forestry land at 5 per cent per year.

Unlike the 1970s and 1980s inflationary rounds, when we lived through a period of food surpluses and generally decreasing food and energy expenditure in households (see Murdoch and Marsden, 1995), we now witness the need to again see the rural land base as an intensive production *and* consumption space.

Since the food crisis hit in 2007–8 we have also witnessed the not-unrelated emergence of a new scientific-bio-economic paradigm around the concept of 'sustainable intensification'. That assumes farming the land base in such a way as to further intensify production and productivity, while also attempting to reduce environmental and ecological costs and externalities. 'Having more for less' goes the mantra. This bio-economic paradigm is now at the centre of the UK government's agri-food and green growth agenda. In England and Wales this is reopening the door for the development of 'mega-farms' (especially in the dairy, pig and poultry sectors), with a less dramatic intensification process in the conventional agricultural sector. The latter is taking many forms, including the reduction in the actual number of family run farms; the amalgamation of holdings with some 'farmers' only keeping their registered status for tax purposes; and the growth of contract farming of amalgamated parcels of land. In Wales over 250 dairy holdings were lost between 2009 and 2012, yet average head size increased from 76 to 84. The overall number of dairy farms fell by more than a half between 2006 and 2016 (from 3,054 to 1,336). By 2016 England and Wales were losing six farms per week, with a reduction from 15,000 to 9,500 between 2005 and 2016. Herd sizes increased as farm businesses declined. All the signs are that there will be further reductions in dairy farms, which, along with UK horticulture, will be increasingly practised as a mono-intensified system rather than as part and parcel of the more variegated mixed farming systems. Meanwhile, and despite much talk of 'sustainable intensification' and 'taking back control' from Brussels (post Brexit), the UK as a whole is increasingly reliant upon food imports and is facing significant declines in its food self-sufficiency, with some analysts suggesting this is now as low as 54 per cent.

These conditions allow both agri-business interests and the cash-rich ex-urban incomers to create a new Faustian bargain, whereby whole (and newly redundant) farmsteads can become converted for private residence, while the surrounding farmland is further intensified for production purposes. This dislocation of farmsteads and farmland is further polarizing the rural communities across England and Wales; allowing a particularly more intensified model of the productivist bio-economy to develop on the one hand, while furthering the more exclusive ex-urban gentrification of the rural housing and estates on the other. Low-cost homes for locals and especially the young become further restricted.

Against the backcloth of both sustainable intensification and the increasingly exclusive ex-urban colonization of much of the inner countryside, it is important to recognize the more fledgling development of the growth of urban-based food movements and AFNs over the past decade. Indeed, partly as a consumer response to the intensification processes, and the growing disenchantment of sizeable proportions of the British urban population about the provenance and adulteration of their foods, there has been a growth in alternative- and community-based food growing and consumption (farmers markets, food hubs, community land trusts, etc.).[12] While these so far have been mainly urban-based and have largely been ignored by rural residents and farmers, they are posed to play a more significant role not least in demanding land and property rights in rural areas, as demand for short-supply chains proliferate, but the supply of productive land to meet these demands remains restricted. For instance, the Community Land Advisory Service is a collaborative brokering service aiming to increase community access to land across the UK; and it liaises with community groups, local authorities, private landowners and other institutional landowners about providing more land for community-based food and energy initiatives. In the United States and Canada, these 'back to the land' movements are proliferating through such mechanisms as Community Supported Agriculture (CSA) schemes and city-based food councils.

We can witness, then, three highly varied but nonetheless significant trends, all leading to the current and future intensity of demands being placed upon rural land and its existing property rights in the UK: (i) An expansion and deepening of ex-urban cash-rich investment opportunities; (ii) Ongoing 'sustainable' intensification of agri-food; and (iii) The proliferation of alternative, more eco-economic community-led food and energy developments. As land, food and energy resources get tighter and urban and suburban populations grow, so will these multiple demands upon the UK rural land base. We need a national-level policy debate about how to capture and, indeed, spread the sustainable value and opportunities these trends provide; yet this is not seen as much of a political priority by the political Right or Left.

Towards a sustainable bio-economic strategy for the UK

Unlike during the Blair and Brown governments of the early 2000s, when a succession of crises, such as the foot-and-mouth disease, lingering concerns over bovine spongiform encephalopathy (BSE) known as mad cow disease, and the food and energy price increases in 2007–8, led to a raft of policy strategy documents in the form of Rural White Papers and food strategy documents, we now more recently see a paucity of strategic public policy concern in the agri-food policy and rural nexus. This is perhaps surprising given that both former Liberal and Conservative governments have more traditionally given what might be regarded as exceptional attention to the British rural realm given their own electoral geographies. A new rural and wider spatial strategy for the UK is long overdue, as is the need for a redefining debate about food policy and the role of rural land in it. As well as a series of public–private initiatives (e.g. 'responsibility deals' on obesity, etc.), one significant development is the published *UK Strategy for Agricultural Technologies* (July 2013), which explicitly espouses a bio-economic paradigm of science- and technology-led 'sustainable intensification'.[13] A leadership council made up of mainly corporate food industry representatives and science research funding bodies has been formed to oversee and review this strategy before its implementation. It is argued that the strategy 'is not about championing any particular type of farming or food, we want consumer choice to be the driver of investment through the supply chain. It is about ensuring the UK has a vibrant sector developing a wide range of new innovations across the supply chain whether using organic, conventional or GM techniques' (HM Government, 2013: 16).

However, there is no further mention of the alternative or agro-ecological sector, or the significance of the urban-based consumer movements, and the definitions of success are narrowly focused on the increased productivity through applying more rapid take-up of technologies in food supply chains. The strategy gives a strong green light for more intensification of production while, at the same time, relating this to the need to fit this intensification within some parameters and metrics of sustainability. This is the challenge it sets for the industry and science sector, with more public–private investments being encouraged to achieve this.

While wide-ranging groups like the Association of Agricultural Engineers,[14] and many within the agro-ecological movement, may criticize this strategy as adopting a far too narrow definition of innovation, technology and bio-economic-led sustainable innovation (for instance, there is no mention of investment in agro-ecological or organic research and development infrastructure), there can be no doubt that the strategy does express a renewed national attempt to reposition the UK as a leader in agri-tech innovation and development. And, indeed, by default, it upgrades the political and economic status of the land-based sector and its somewhat fragmented skills base. In this sense it calls out for a range of sister strategy statements on rural development and integrated agri-food policy so as to address *all* of the key dynamics and challenges identified above. The question is, Is the very idea of renewed national food and rural planning too ideologically indigestible for the Conservative government? It clearly should not be for an aspirant centre-green-left government, as the *National Plan for the UK: From Austerity to the Age of the New Green Deal* published by the Green New Deal group suggests.[15]

Conclusions: Towards a broadened sustainable bio-eco-economy

In earlier papers (see Kitchen and Marsden, 2009; Marsden, 2010; Horlings and Marsden, 2014) we have made the distinction between the bio-economy and the eco-economy in relation to current agri-food and rural developments.[16] As we shall explore in succeeding chapters, it is important to see the latter as a radical variant of the former in that it starts with the premise of generating social and economic goals for our agri-food system based upon wider definitions of agri-ecological productivity, social justice and food sovereignty. The onset of 'the bio-economy' does not necessarily have to suggest one dominant technologically driven and framed paradigm around sustainable intensification; but could presage more of a plurality and diversity of approaches based upon a range of ecologically and socially grounded agri-food initiatives and movements.

This is the major theme of the book: how could the onset of the bio-economy be captured and nurtured in ways which would lead to real sustainable and eco-economic development for the UK and the wider European countryside? The question is posed in the countervailing and contested context as we have outlined here of considerable asymmetric drivers currently occurring: growing social exclusion, reduced state support for rural programmes, further agricultural and bio-economic intensification, reduced farm-based and wider SME business infrastructures, and deeper control over rural property rights by cash-rich and mobile social groups.

In this regard it will be important – given the public and private demands ensuing on rural land – to envision a more pluralistic and diverse approach in shaping bio-eco-economy developments, on the one hand, and more sustainable land-based management, on the other. In conclusion, we can identify some key research and policy desiderata which need attention in informing these strategic debates.

- Consider how to open up and manage rural land and aquatic resources as part of the wider and growing demand of eco-system goods and services. This will entail developing both national and regional eco-system assessment of rural resources, which encompasses a wider definition of both production and consumption of these resources and links these to urban as well as rural needs.[17]

- Create socially based objectives which harness the new bio-economy design technologies in ways which create social, ecological and economic diversity and a more distributed system of rural provision. Critical here is catering for low-income and working-poor households, and the young and the elderly who still reside in rural regions. Can they benefit from more distributive and localized forms of energy and food/fibre production in terms of employment and consumption?

- Create more flexible rural landholding arrangements for urban-based consumption actors and players: develop gateways for the use of rural resources for alternative urban-based food and energy groups. Here, there is a growing need for more land 'sharing' and community land initiatives which engage both urban and rural groups.

- Envision a far wider R&D and extension farm- and forest-based system which encourages diversities in the bio- and eco-economies: a plurality of approaches for diverse and place-based bio-economy. This needs to encourage more mixed and bio-diverse farming practices through demonstration farms and facilities.

- Invest in the 'missing middle' of food supply chains, not just food but the nexus of fibre, timber, energy and waste. Create more infrastructure and spaces for short-supply chains, including community food hubs, local markets and food processing plants.

- Increase multilevel state procurement of all of the above such as it overcomes trade rules and competition policy on the basis of place-based economic development and more health-related food production and consumption. This is particularly necessary concerning the stimulation of the regional horticultural systems of provision, linking sustainable production with institutional procurement of healthier food options.

- Promote and evaluate the balance between 'mega-farms', multifunctional farms and the stimulation of mini/ecological farms. This needs to consider the farm structures question in the UK context and how a more effective balance between intensive and potentially exporting sectors (like dairy and lamb) can be developed while enhancing 'economies of scope', rather than just scale on smaller and more multifunctional holdings.

- Foster and reinforce emerging webs of social capital and skills in land-based practices. This holds important implications for educational provision, from primary to higher education, and in the development of entrepreneurial and land-practice-based skill development.

- Create social conditions which promote economic resilience and dynamism, rather than vulnerability and exclusion. This could build upon local- and community-based 'sustainable place-making' initiatives, whereby community groups begin to envision and redefine their communities according to their particular sustainable assets and opportunities. Across the UK and much of Europe, these types of alliances are forming with differing degrees of arms-length support from local councils and municipalities.

- Create urban–rural green infrastructures which recognize the urban demands on rural land. This recognizes the need for a more integrated planning process which creates opportunities for 'green corridors' between urban and rural areas (for instance, through the canal and rivers networks). This could create more healthy lifestyles and jobs.

Towards a new rural paradigm: From crisis to capacity-building

Current policies and politics need to urgently turn their attention to, and foster a more expansive and inclusive, 'new rural paradigm' of 'green growth' around the rural bio-economy. But this currently tends to be largely and actively marginalized by, as we shall see, a prevailing EU- and British-governance framing which favours a restricted and neo-productivist approach to the bio-economy, together with a broader neo-liberalizing approach to resolving the current macroeconomic crisis by reductions in state interventions (austerity, not least in the rural and environmental domain). The central question and conceptual challenge then is: what would an alternative to this look like and on what principles should it be based, given the new arena of economic vulnerability post-carbonism and, in the UK especially, increasing counter-urbanization which is set to be demanding more rather than less from rural land-based resources?

There are ways of shaping this agenda which could create a triple dividend of healthier urban consumers, more diverse and productive value-added rural production of goods and services, and an enhanced eco-ecological rural infrastructure upon which to create the adaptive capacity for real sustainable rural development. These are the challenges for the macroeconomic policy agenda and, more broadly, for locating the UK and especially its rural regions at the vanguard necessary for the sustainable development transition.

The rest of this book, then, critically considers the current and combined crisis conditions with regard to contested sustainabilities on agri-food and rural development. First, the crisis itself has introduced, and is reinforcing, bi-polarities of paradigms which are attempting to arrest and 'solve' the crisis in their own ways using different and contested 'sustainability' framings. These are in themselves creating asymmetrical social, economic and ecological outcomes. Second, it goes on to propose a more nuanced and deeper critical and normative framework for sustainable place-making – around an enhanced conceptualization of the eco-economy – a major conceptual and practical approach for delivering this in the medium term.

It argues that unless these timely intellectual and praxis challenges are indeed grasped urgently, it will be more and more difficult to arrive at a resilient and sustainable condition for rural (and indeed urban) development. Indeed, more generally, unless the true and fundamental significance of rural-based resources is recognized in terms of new rounds of real ecological modernization, it is unlikely that the planet can sustain itself. In this sense the overarching notion of the bio-economy as we explore in the next chapter (Chapter 3), needs critical treatment as to its dominant framings. This occurs when, and especially since 2007–8, scientific policy and market and corporate interests are competing to frame the concept in ways which deliver their particular brand of 'sustainability'. In the subsequent chapters (Chapters 3, 4 and 5), we empirically examine how these dominant framings need challenging in ways which could potentially enhance the real sustainable role of the rural domain. This is outlined using empirical evidence from the UK and Europe in Chapters 4 and 5. In order to progress this 'new rural paradigm', we need to reconceptualize the governance of rural nature, of scientific policy and practice in ways which prioritize sustainable place-making and rural development as part of a wider and engaging sustainability science, (Chapter 6) such that it can begin to deliver at least some of the agenda outlined here.

Notes

1. See, for instance, the latest National Plan for the UK. *From Austerity to the Age of the New Deal*. Green New Deal Group, September, 2013. And for a broader macro-perspective, see Hall, Massey and Rustin (2013) After neo-liberalism: analysing the present. Soundings Manifesto Online.
2. See Ross (2013).
3. OECD (2009).
4. Hoff (2011).
5. Alberta Bio-economy Strategy, 2013, and British Columbia BC-Bio-economy, 2013.
6. Second- and third-generation GM is the generic term given to the new raft of bio-technologies, many yet to be commercialized, associated with quality traits, such as flavour-enhancing feed crops tailored to consumer nutritional needs and improved nutrition of crops like vegetables and rice (e.g. rice with additional vitamin A and iron). First-generation GM was mainly concerned with rearranging input traits associated with herbicide, insect, disease and water resistance.

    BP, Shell and Exxon, among others, are entering the bio-energy fields to an estimated sale of $400 million per year. Conference on 'Growing the Bio-economy' October 2012, Banff, Alberta, Canada.
7. See Green New Deal Group (2013).
8. A UK strategy for Agricultural Technologies. HM Government, July 2013.
9. EU (2012).
10. I concentrate here specifically upon the terrestrial land base. But it is important to recognize that important bio-economic developments around protein and energy innovation also relate to the aquatic environment, not least the use of algae and sea grass as rich bio-economic resources. See: Houses of Parliament, Parliamentary Office of Science and Technology Post Note. Biofuels from Algae, no.384, July 2011.
11. See Commission for Rural Communities (2010) State of the Countryside Report; and given historical depth in the volume: Constructing the Countryside. Murdoch et al. (2003).
12. It is difficult to put a figure on how large the alternative- and community-based food sector is in the UK in relation to the conventional food system given the lack of systematic data. But see: Marsden and Sonnino (2012); and Marsden and Morley (2014).
13. HM Government (July 2013).
14. http://www.aea.uk.com/
15. New Deal Group (2013).
16. Marsden (2012).
17. See National eco-system assessment: follow on study. DEFRA/UNDP. Cambridge, UK.

Chapter 3

Socializing and spatializing the bio-economy: Reconstructing natural powers

Introduction: From post-productivism to the bio-economy

As we discussed in Chapter 1, since the end of the twentieth century, and especially since the food and fuel price hikes of 2007–8, we have witnessed a reorientation of agri-food in both advanced and developing countries. This is now necessitating the reconceptualization of agri-food, and especially land- and water-based food production, not only in terms of agri-food's functional significance (ecological, metabolic, economic, social) but also in terms of how it provides a new or, at least, revised basis for real transitions towards a post-carbon-based set of conditions. I want to argue in this chapter that under the current circumstances we need to reconceptualize agri-food in terms of a wider bio-economic and eco-economic framing. This sees it as, once again, a natural and distinctive basis for the wider bio-economy, an economy which will increasingly have to provide the means of satisfying the bulk of society's food, energy and fibre needs.

In this sense we are now at a juncture whereby the dominant policy frameworks of 'post-productionism', as we see still prevalent in some quarters, are giving way to neo-productivist concerns, not only around framings of 'sustainable intensification' but also with regard to wider technological, political and economic developments and recognitions of the need to extract more function and material out of plant, animal and biospheric materials. Indeed, as 'peakism' of fossil fuels and its related minerals continues to become a reality, however much this may be denied, growing 'prospective knowledges' as well as the all-too-present realities of climate change and resource shortfalls is stimulating both the rapid development of the bio-economy, on the one hand,

and, at its centre, the redefinition of agriculture and agri-food, on the other. This chapter explores some of the cardinal dimensions of this contested redefinition, and some of the ways in which it can be conceptualized.

Some might see this as a further stage in a more chaotic capitalist development, whereby resource constraints are leading to more desperate means to intensively appropriate, substitute and expropriate land-based agricultures (Goodman, Sorj and Wilkinson, 1987; Pechlaner, 2012) through the development of new bio-technological techniques. These change reproductive life courses in favour of new functional and economic necessities (such as the first generation of GM crops (1996–2006), which were largely aimed to act as a palliative to the industrial ecological vulnerabilities that are endemic in the conventional- and commodity-based food system). As we shall see below, however, this is only part of a wider and more complex story, whereby questions of sustainability, sovereignty, security and governance now surround and interact with a highly contingent and contested bio-economical terrain. Agriculture and land- and water-based production and consumption systems now sit within this multidimensional context, in ways which render many of our earlier conceptualizations as only partial explainers of this growing complexity and contingency. It now embraces interrelated questions of sustainability, sovereignty, security and governance.

Sustainability: Weak and strong conceptions of sustainability now underlie much of the scientific research agendas and corporate strategies in the food and energy sectors; and these conceptions are being variably supported by national and regional government R&D policies which, as we shall see, are promoting the bio-economy to varying degrees as a major investing 'green growth' strategy.

Sovereignty: The post-1980 neo-liberal conceptions of widening consumer sovereignty and growing absolute consumption are reaching severe limits both materially and economically. Both producer and consumer sovereignty are being increasingly curtailed, leading to more inequality in access to quality food and relatively cheap forms of food and energy. This is creating social and political unrest and revitalizing alternative social movements which are attempting to reshape the bio-economical pathways in new more sustainable and just directions. This is occurring at multiple spatial scales and social contexts.

Security: Food and fuel security concerns are now developing a new geo-politics and security mercantilism in the increasingly interconnected food, fuel and forestry sectors (see McMichael, 2013), as well as spawning local and community post-neo-liberal developments. National and regional governments are increasingly seeing the development of their bio-economies as a national security issue (see McKibben, 2015), as well as, domestically, as a social legitimatory issue which can no longer be taken for granted. Access and ownership over land and water resources, often too economistically framed as 'eco-system goods and services', become a new focus of attention in 'solving' the security issues.

Governance: The tensions between neo-liberalizing governance and more reflexive (post) neo-liberal approaches are becoming greater within and between the multilevel states. The failure of market-based mechanisms, such as carbon trading, and the inertia of many agricultural and commodity programmes means that much of government policy is antithetical to the sustainable development of the bio-economy. Yet it is important to recognize that this requires positive and facilitative governance.

What we see now emerging, therefore, in albeit, uneven and contested ways, is the redefinition of agri-food as part and parcel of a wider and multifunctional bio-economy. This clearly implies in itself an inherently multifunctional question with regard to the historically dominant land- and resource-user agriculture. This question is: How is it to share its functions as a food, fibre, fuel and wider energy and amenity producer given both the recognized global limits of its land- and water-based resource and the increasing and polyvalent growth in the demand for a wider range of potentially renewable products and services? How will it adapt to being part of a wider interconnected matrix and nexus?

This will involve and activate our four interconnected arenas, as well as one fraught with dangers and vulnerabilities for the sustainability of configured human, animal and plant life. Its development will inevitably change 'natures matrix' (Perfecto, Vandermeer and Wright, 2009) over both time and space. And, to varying degrees, this will involve an understanding of how combinations of public, private and, importantly, civic, sections of society gain some level of control and access which can shape these bio-economical developments. In this sense, we are at a critical juncture of new social and public design. It is no longer a matter of ecologically modernizing in ways which create more secure natures, although this is an important part. Nature is not as uncontrollable as many scholars would have us believe. What we witness is the opportunities to be far more participatory in shaping sustainable natures through managing (rather than denying) the bio-economy, on the one hand, and, probably more immediately and materially, being able and enabled to do this, not least through the active lens of a more sustainable paradigm for agriculture and food, on the other.

We are thus at a juncture, therefore, where the reconceptualization of agriculture and agri-food shows great conceptual and material potentiality. In order to grasp this, however, demands that we critically begin to position it within a more complex, contested and contingent bio-economical context, not least by examining some of the scientific, technological and political drivers for its early development.

Unpacking the sustainable bio-economy paradigm: Explorations of green growth in rural and regional development

In order for the globe to cope with population growth, rapid depletion of resources (especially energy, food and minerals), environmental pressures and climate change, there is increasing recognition that it will be necessary to radically transform approaches to the production, consumption, processing, storage, recycling and disposal of biological resources (see OECD, 2009, 2011; EC, 2012). One major cross-sectoral means of achieving this is to develop the 'bio-economy'. This is defined by the OECD (2009: 9) as

> that part of economic activities which captures the latent value in biological processes and renewable bio-resources to produce improved health and sustainable growth and development. A second concept mentioned here, the bio-based economy, deals more narrowly with industrial applications: it is an economy that uses renewable bio-resources and eco-industrial clusters to produce sustainable bio-products, jobs and income.

The development of a 'post-carbon' bio-economy – one which uses biological resources from the land and the sea, as well as waste, as inputs to food and feed, industrial and energy production, and delivers a wider vector of environmental goods and services in a more sustainable way – represents a paradigm shift in developmental thinking and application (see Langeveld, Dixon and Jaworski, 2010). It also becomes a major driver for future agri-food and fibre system dynamics, management and sustainability (Thompson and Schoones, 2009; McMichael, 2009). The OECD has estimated that by 2030, the use of biotechnologies will contribute up to 35 per cent of the output of chemicals and other industrial products (like bio-plastics), up to 80 per cent of pharmaceutical and diagnostic production, and some 50 per cent of agricultural output, contributing up to 3 per cent of GDP of the OECD by 2030. For developing countries this share is likely to be higher, and these proportions are probably conservative given the potential and knowledge 'spillover' effects on energy, health and farming where a wide range of R&D activities are maturing at a remarkably rapid rate (see Cooke, 2008, 2011) and form a major part of the 'green growth' agenda in OECD countries (see OECD, 2011).

The EU bio-economy, with its growing economic turnover and widespread employment potential, innovatively explores the intersections between agriculture, forestry, fisheries, food, marine, pulp and paper production, as well as parts of chemical, bio-technological and energy industries. In addition, its regional R&D and innovation impacts are considerable, with each euro invested in bio-economy research and innovation estimated to trigger ten euros of value added in bio-economy sectors by 2025. The needs and onset of the bio-economy, therefore, presage a new phase of 'post-carbon' development involving many industries, university research establishments and facilitative private–public sector partnerships.

The progress of the bio-economy has exploded in the past decade both in terms of scientific expertise and technical expertise. This growth comes as the world reaches 'peaks' in many of its resources and which is reflected in both growing price volatilities and the search for new land-based resources. The bio-economy has several narrow and broader definitions (as seen above), but it needs to be understood as both the science and practice of utilizing living things to produce a wider range of goods and services. It involves manipulating organisms to create new and practical applications for primary production, health and industry. McCormick and Kautto (2013: 2594) distinguish between green, grey, red and blue bio-economies:

Industrial bio-technology or white bio-technology uses enzymes and micro-organisms to make bio-based products in a diverse range of sectors, including chemicals, food and feed, bioenergy, paper and pulp, and textiles. In turn, grey bio-technologies – once under white bio-technology – encompasses technological solutions created to protect the environment, like the case of oil spills and purifying sewage water. Green biotechnology is applied to agriculture for instance to develop genetically modified crops or improve plant-breeding techniques using life science knowledge. Blue bio-technology is a term used to describe the marine and aquatic applications ... while red technologies relates to health sector, for instance, pharmaceuticals. Finally modern bio-technology is used to distinguish newer applications, such as genetic engineering and cell fusion, from more conventional methods, such as breeding and fermentation. ... Biofuels and bio-refineries are closely related priorities to the bio-economy.

Hilgartner (2007) argues that the established and variably institutionalized definitions of the bio-economy are deliberatively framed in economistic terms, thus placing the risks and ethical issues of the bio-economy as secondary. A generic feature is that it implies a massive transformation of current production and consumption systems. Some argue that, as such, it requires 'specialist political husbandry' (Parry, 2007), because of its distinctive and transformative features. Others argue that this distinctiveness is overhyped and that the bio-economy is no different than electricity or aeronautics (Parry, 2007). In its framing there is also a significant element of anticipatory knowledge assumed, or, self-fulfilling 'future making' (Levidow, Birch and Papaioannou, 2012). There are arguments for wider and more socio-economic definitions of the bio-economy and critiques which suggest its restricted technocratic agenda. Goven and Pavone (2014) locate the dominant OECD framing within a Polanyian critique of neo-liberalism whereby it creates a particular prospective vision based upon the furtherance of international competitiveness and a particular brand of neo-liberal techno-science. They argue that

> just as a market system is distinguishable from markets, the bio-economy is more than just a repackaging of bio-technologies or a re-branding of biotechnology strategies. Whereas markets can be found in societies characterised by a variety of economic systems so – in principle, at least – biotechnologies could be developed for and from within a wide-range of political-economic settings. But just as the market system required state action to eliminate alternative modes of meeting needs and organising the economy, so the bio-economy aims to embed biotechnology, and science in general, in a neo-liberal logic that eliminates alternative scientific and political-economic pathways, including alternative ways of (defining and) meeting needs with the help of bio-sciences. (p. 12)

It is this elimination or, at least, marginalization of alternative bio-economic framings – what I call, for instance, the variant of the bio-economy as eco-economy – which we will explore further in subsequent chapters. Here, it is necessary to examine how, so far, the bio-economy has been understood by varied bodies of scholarly work, as well as how various nation states are seeing its potentiality.

Theoretical integrations and spatial development

Clearly, because the bio-economy is based upon the exploitation and production of a wider range of biological resources, these have to be found and produced/

processed *from somewhere*, and so the onset of its development holds important, yet so far underresearched, spatial and sustainability questions (see Bridge and Smith, 2003; McAfee, 2008a,b). These questions in turn require new theoretical insights and development, starting from a multi-theoretical basis. This needs to incorporate and develop:

Multilevel transitions theories and socio-technical systems (Geels, 2004; Kemp, 2000; Grin, Rotmans and Schot, 2010). Here transition from a carbon regime to a bio-economy is based upon a function of regime members, the resources needs for the change to be enacted, and the coordination of responses and actions (Smith, Stirling and Berkhout, 2005). Landscape pressures (including climate change, population growth and volatile food and fuel scarcities) can trigger system-based transitions, with actors looking to (bio-economic) innovative technological 'niches' as enablers for this change (Geels, 2002). Transitions can often be crisis-led or initiated by 'disruptive-innovation' whereby social change is often an unintended by-product (Christensen et al., 2006). There are also strong forces of inertia, driven by investment in status quo local, regional and national power structures and institutions which focus more on specific product innovation rather than system-changing 'catalytic' innovation.

Questions of panarchy, resilience and vulnerability (see Folke, 2006; Gunderson and Holling, 2002; Eriksson et al., 2010; Peck, 2005) whereby panarchy is a framework to account for the dual characteristics of all complex systems stability and change, reflecting on how economic growth and human development depend upon eco-systems and institutions, and how they interact. Here the concepts of *pre-adaptation* – taking existing innovations from one industry and adapting to different solutions in another – and *adjacent possible* – whereby proximity to one innovation can lead in the same space to their novel proliferation in other areas given certain levels diversity in the economic web – can lead to systemic change. We can begin to see this co-evolution in the clustered developments of bioenergy, bio-refining and biomass production, and the renewable use of household waste streams. In some places these are becoming interlinked components of public–private innovation networks (see Alberta and Finland examples below). This also suggests a significant extension to the social-ecological systems perspective, whereby science-based university research is linking to new and more sustainable product development based upon, in many cases, speeded-up, production processes (such as fast growing Willow).

Complexity science, the analysis of complex adaptive systems (Kauffman, 1995) and *evolutionary economic geography*. This (see Frenkin, van Oort and Verburg, 1995; Martin, 2010) takes concepts from spatial economics and technological history and focuses on how 'related variety' in different regions and places can create knowledge spillovers and innovative deviations from path dependent 'lock-in' technological systems like carbon-based agri-food systems (see Garud and Karnoe, 2001; Arthur, Durlauf and Lane, 1997). New spatially based conceptions of innovative forms of relatedness across traditional production and processing sectors like intensive agriculture, forestry and renewable forms of energy can come together to create 'transition regions' (Cooke, 2011).

Finally, theories of rural and regional development (see Murdoch et al., 2003; van der Ploeg and Marsden, 2008; Marsden, 2010) are emphasizing the contingent social, economic and political regionalization and differentiation of rural areas and the reactions of their production and consumption networks to their city regions and new 'equations' between the roles of the city and their surrounding countryside (Morgan and Sonnino, 2010). Here new nested 'webs' of intersectoral economic activity are based upon grounded knowledges and practices of novelty, endogeneity and sustainability as active arenas of innovation. The rapid development of the bio-economy thus provides a rich opportunity to link and develop these current bodies of innovation and sustainability-thinking around the goal of sustainable growth. In particular, these approaches are highlighting the varying degrees to which different variants of the bio-economy emerge in different rural/regional spaces, and how these begin to operate as change agents for wider aspects of rural and regional change (Kitchen and Marsden, 2011; Marsden, 2012). What is becoming clear is that the development of the bio-economy and its various eco-economic variants and oppositions is becoming an important axis around which local and regional social and political interests are forming and acting. We will explore this process more fully below.

Here, it is difficult to predict the speed of uneven development of the bio- and eco-economic variants. And public and consumer reaction to these variants becomes a major factor in the uneven process. Also a key question concerns how rural regions can utilize bio-economy in ways which add local and regional value to their primary and secondary economic activities. With a new primacy being placed especially upon land resources, with whom and where will the increased value of the bio-economic premium be located?

Competing and hybrid strands of the bio-economy

The uneven development of the bio-economy is being shaped then by a number of key drivers so far underresearched by social scientists. They include

- The rapid uptake of biotechnologies in agricultural production and related processing industries;

- The rising demand for sustainable renewable biological resources and bio-processes as feedstocks for these new industries;

- The construction of eco-industrial clusters and technology parks that produce sustainable and eco-based goods and services, jobs and value-added income;

- The opportunities to 'decouple' industrial growth from environmental degradation through more sustainable production methods, using industrial-scale biotechnology;

- The need to respond to global challenges such as energy and food security with the increasing constraints of water, soil and productive land and carbon emissions;

- The variable social and political opposition to some of the new technologies and the parallel rise of eco-ecological alternatives at the producer and consumer levels;

- The variable facilitative role of multilevel governance in fostering innovation;

- Regulatory frameworks for stimulating market entry for the bio-economy over different spatial scales.

These drivers and applications are now in need of serious social science investigation around the twin objectives of examining how bio- and eco-economical development can also deliver sustainable development goals. *How can real 'green growth' be built around the bio-economy and its eco-economic variants? What is the specific role of social science in shaping the understanding and delivery of these twin objectives?*

A critical theme that underpins this research agenda concerns the options between different pathways towards more sustainable places that are being proposed, and which embody contrasting variants of the bio-economic paradigm. Clearly, lying outside of this paradigm we have to incorporate what we might call 'business as usual' *carbon-based approaches* which rely on resource intensification and extracting greater economic and social value from existing environmental resources, especially land (see Chatham House, 2009). These tend to be technologically intensive and reflect a 'Promethean' approach (Dryzek, 1997), and critics tend to view them as adopting a too-instrumental concept of nature, which tends to further intensify unsustainable twentieth-century patterns of exploitation of natural resources and eco-systems. However, it is important to recognize that this arena is far from static as it, on the one hand, seeks new exploitative technologies such as gas-fracking and tar sands removal and, on the other, partially accommodates the bio-economic paradigm through, for instance, testing out bio-refining and biomass demonstrator projects.

Moreover, volatilities in the price of oil and related commodities, variable national and supernational targets on biofuels, among others, are setting an uncertain investment context for many resource-based industries. These relative volatilities (such as those governing the relative price of oil vs. bio-ethanol) are central to appreciating the degree of innovative investment and potential transformation of existing carbon-based business models (Tyner, 2012; Passmore, 2012).

The *alternative bio-economy paradigm* may be rooted in a 'stronger sustainability' framing which entails reconfiguring innovation and economic activity around a series of 'socio-technical niches' to make it more consistent with 'nature's metabolism' (Huber, 2000). In terms of the theoretical basis of the work this needs to build upon ecological modernization (Murphy and Gouldson, 2000; Horlings and Marsden, 2011), reflexive governance for sustainability (Feindt, 2012) and transitions theory for sustainability (Schot and Geels, 2008; Smith, Voß and Grin, 2010; Spaargaren, et al., 2012). It is important to explore the different strands of the bio-economy paradigm with regard to its management and exploitation of resources and the relative degree to which it is embedded in different spatial contexts. It includes biofuels, biotechnology, genomics, chemical engineering and enzyme technology, all fields which are experiencing significant growth internationally and which are attempting to provide solutions to the resource- and food-scarcity problems by promoting forms of 'sustainable intensification' (see Foresight, 2012; Garnett and Godfray, 2012; Marsden, 2012). Alternatively, more eco-economical strategies are also appearing and proliferating. These focus more on place-based social and economic innovation, and the development of new types of businesses and production and consumption networks (see Goodman, DuPuis and Goodman, 2012). It has been argued that the eco-economic model as part of the bio-economic paradigm depends more upon the emergence of more complex networks or webs of viable businesses and nested markets (van der Ploeg and Marsden, 2008; Oostindie et al., 2010), many of them small or medium sized, and economic activities that utilize ecological resources in more harmonious and efficient ways (Marsden, 2010; Kitchen and Marsden, 2011). Examples in Europe, North America and Brazil include new types of firms involved in renewable energy, agri-tourism, amenity management and local food processing and catering.

Eco-economic strategies have the potential to realign production–consumption networks in order to capture more local and regional value while better protecting and articulating a wider vector of eco-system services and resources. These innovations embody the process of re-localization as well as externalization and over time the boundaries between these strands of the bio-economy may become much more blurred and hybridized. What is clear is that we are now witnessing an unprecedented, new political and economic emphasis upon land and water resources to deliver a wider range of eco-system goods and services, some of which remain within the food sphere, but many others which transgress the traditional resource-based sectors of food, energy and health. This is raising important questions about the capture of value added and its distribution across the main actors in supply chains and their spaces of production and consumption.

- Will the development of the bio-economy lead to new regional and rural opportunities for the capture of economic value?
- How far will the economic and social benefits of the bio-economy stretch? What sort of new business and supply chain models will this create?
- How will it recast the former divisions between production and consumption and urban and rural relations?
- What will be the new spatial coordinates and drivers for maintaining these developments?
- How will national and regional institutions and governance frameworks either facilitate or hinder these developments?

Some key research questions and the emerging research agenda

There is then a clear need to develop a critical and multi-theoretical contribution from the social sciences to enable a better understanding of the bio-economy in the second decade of the twenty-first century. The approach will be interdisciplinary within the social sciences and it will also make a wider contribution to the rapidly expanding interdisciplinary field of sustainability science (see Clark, 2007; Ziegler and Ott, 2011; Marsden, 2012). More specifically the objectives need to:

- Explore the economic, social and spatial implications of the variable and contested development of the bioeconomy in different regional, rural and urban settings;

- Develop a new interpretation of the position of the agri-food and forestry sector in advanced and newly emerging countries in the context of the rise of the bio-economy;

- Map and delineate the variants in the bio-economy in relation to alternative developments in the fields of the eco-economy and agri-ecological and consumer movements and networks;

- Assess the implications of the above or of sustainable rural and regional development and new theories of urban–rural relations;

- Generate new theoretical developments and research-based tools to contribute to the potential transformations and adaptations needed in pursuing the 'green growth' agenda;

- Create a detailed international comparative regional analysis in order to identify ways of stimulating more sustainable forms of bio-economic innovation in rural economies.

Progressing the research agenda: Developing the sustainability science approach and methodology

Currently, the social science contribution to this emerging field is lagging behind other sciences, market trends and policy agenda. While there are some in-depth studies of the global food crisis now appearing (see Lawrence et al., 2013; Ingram, Ericksen and Liverman, 2010; Marsden et. al., 2010; Marsden and Morley, 2014), these have been restricted to the current architecture of the post-2008 food price hikes and its connections with the interactions between food and energy security and sustainability (see special issues in *Journal of Agrarian Change*, 2010; *Journal of Rural Studies*, 2013). There is a critical need to readdress the position and structural shifts in agri-food and forestry and its now-related energy, health and community fields through a new interpretation (see Mol, 2008a,b). This needs to contribute to and adopt a critical sustainability science (SS) perspective (see Marsden, 2012). SS is now developing rapidly as a major and urgent scientific endeavour in its ambition to be post disciplinary, and to engage more innovatively in the co-production of knowledge that will assist global and local transitions and adaptations required over coming decades (Turner, 2010). There is a need to move beyond current scientific barriers so as to develop a more effective and dynamic understanding of interlinked socio-ecological systems. This, it is argued (see Ness, Anderburg and Olsson, 2010; Kates, 2001 and Clark, 2007), means that SS is more 'defined by the problems it addresses than by the disciplines it employs'. This asks: (i) how can the dynamic interactions in socio-ecological systems better incorporate emerging models that integrate earth systems, social development and sustainability? (ii) how are long-term trends in environment and development reshaping nature–society relations? (iii) What factors determine the limits of resilience and sources of vulnerability for such interactive systems? (iv) What systems of incentive structures can most effectively improve social capacity to guide interactions between nature and society towards more sustainable trajectories? (v) And, how can science and technology be harnessed more effectively to address sustainability goals? The current contested and, in many ways, competitive transitions associated with the agri-food system and bio-economy are ripe for study from this SS perspective.

The development of this more wide-ranging but integrative and cohesive perspective is timely given the quite rapid speed of innovation in the bio-economy sector (see Bressler, 2012), and the need for social scientists to subject these innovations to critical SS scrutiny. This is an ambitious challenge which now goes significantly beyond the earlier research works of the author on tracing agri-food and rural and regional developments in a series of consecutive research texts over the past 20 years. There is a need to develop a new thesis about the bio-economy and the more unstable and vulnerable phase in which agri-food, and rural development specifically, finds itself. This involves evolving a new critical sustainability paradigm which will examine and delineate weaker and stronger forms of ecological modernization as they are practised and promulgated by sets of private and public actors in different regional settings.

Regional approaches to bio-economy framings

Several countries are currently leading the development of the bio-economy by creating concerted strategies for developing biomaterials, biochemicals, bioenergy and biofuels as part of their future-focused strategy for economic development and diversification. This is increasingly seen as a cornerstone of a parallel low-carbon economy with the continued development of the carbon economy. In the United

States, $877 million is committed in support of the Bio-economy Blueprint (2011–14). The new EU 877 billion euro R&D programme (Horizon, 2020) includes 1.8 billion dedicated to bio-industrial development and related work on eco-system services (EU, 2012). Within Europe, member states are supplementing this. In Denmark $2.21 billion by 2015, and Norway $370 million by 2015. Finland is one of the largest member state investors having started early in 2008 and planning to spend over $554 million between 2012 and 2020.

Bio-economy developments are strongest in those places where there is a strong historical agricultural and/or forestry base. In Finland it is seen as a new panacea and paradigm for regenerating its marginal agricultural base and its weakening forestry and paper sectors. Taking a cross-cutting, multidisciplinary approach, Finland's Funding Agency for Technology and Innovation (TEKES) has been funding projects in biomass, bioenergy and bio-refining. Public–private partnerships have created the Finnish Bio-economy Cluster since 2007. Competition for raw materials and energy/foods will increase and will have an upward pressure on prices. It is recognized that policy actions will be needed in building up stable and affordable markets and fixing consistent standards for the bio-based fields.

A recent Finnish Innovation Agency and funder (SITRA) identified the need to examine the possibility for joint business models in the bio-economy, arguing that there is a need for local medium-sized biofuel plants collecting the local biomass and producing value-added main and by-products such as biofuels, fertilizers and medical products. A bio-economy that is distributed has greater viability and is generally more sustainable, as there are less transport costs involved. Another characteristic that, according to Sitra (2012), should belong to the Finnish bio-economy is a tight connection to waste management, ensuring that there is a 'double' benefit coming from utilizing waste for value-added applications (Sitra, 2012). The Natural Resource Strategy for Finland and the more recent 2014 strategy (Ministry of Environment Finland (2014)) is acknowledging that the country has significant amounts of biomass and the base for developing expertise in its efficient and high-value application. There are four key strategic goals:

• Finland has a thriving bio-economy generating high value added;

• It utilizes and recycles material flows effectively;

• Regional resources generate both national added value and local well-being;

• Finland takes initiatives and leads the way on natural resource issues.

Finland is seeing the bio-economy also as a knowledge export opportunity, which currently needs new integrated business models based on a local and regional basis. A key objective is the development of rural communities through cross-sectoral integration and the development of bio-economy value networks. These value networks have the capacity to link: Water-based resources: wastewater treatment, fish farming; with land-based farming, biogas production to energy arena of wind power, the electricity grid and bio-chips. Here, a key feature is the integration of flows across social/industrial sectors and a design that meets multiple social/environmental/economic needs, with a constant goal of increasing ecological efficiency and the elimination of waste. These concepts are being taken up in Canada – for instance, in the British Columbia bio-economy strategy.

In Alberta, Canada, despite the dominance of the carbon-based 'big-energy' sector, there has developed a strong collaborative network of public–private organizations to steer and develop the bio-economy sector. This is linking the traditional agricultural and forest sectors to bio-solutions networks, and it comes together in the recent bio-economy strategy report (2013). While in contrast to the established agricultural and forest industries, the current contribution of the newly developing areas of biomaterials, biochemicals and bioenergy to the Alberta economy are relatively small, there are over 50 companies working on biomaterials, 7 in biochemicals and 14 in bioenergy. The province's renewable biomass resources include 64 million tonnes from agricultural sources, 2 million tonnes of underutilized forest biomass and roadside residue, 4 million tonnes from municipal waste and 78 million tonnes of slowly renewable peat.

Major contestations and fault lines in the bio-economy

It is clear from the preceding discussion that the onset of focus upon the bio-economy is far broader, more contested and profound, than earlier and more specific discussions on the genetic modification of plants and animals. Rather, these are part of the developmental story but by no means the only or dominant part. The more turbulent world since 2007–8 has meant that the 'turn' to the bio-economy by governments and their agencies and corporate firms has been associated with the increasingly recognized need to generate post-carbon solutions to the combined energy and food crisis. This by necessity is placing a re-emphasis upon the 'horizontal' exploitation of plants and animals and, more broadly, their ambient natures. Somewhat inevitably, even if often denied, this exploitation will place a renewed premium upon the demand and use of rural land (and crucially water resources) in order to satisfy these new horizontal demands. Moreover, given that much of the land and water resource is in the hands of farmers and peasants to varying degrees, and in a global context where the majority of the population are detached from this resource because they are residing and working in cities, will place a renewed emphasis upon the role, structural position and political-economic power of landholders in the urban-dominated but rural-reliant bio-economy.

This suggests that we need to reconceptualize the structural position of rural land resources (human, physical, ecological) within this more contested context. In doing so a significant lens on these contestations surrounds the quest for control and coherence of the rural land resource. We can give two examples of this related to (i) the controversies associated with control over seed varieties, and (ii) the contestations between different governance arrangements associated with harnessing the bio-economy.

Islands and empires: Producers and users of seeds

Transgenetic agri-biotechnology is clearly viewed critically by political ecologists as a radical and 'third-nature' break with established agro-ecologies (see Wield, Chataway and Bolo, 2010). As the food and fuel crisis has deepened, the debates about the use of these technologies has intensified, especially given their alleged potential for reducing plant diseases, water shortages and farmers' input costs. These innovations are still regarded by many scientists as being in their infancy and 'first generation', in that they mainly deal with rearranging input traits associated with herbicide, insect, pest and disease resistance. The second- and third-generation biotechnologies, yet to be commercialized and being developed by a rapidly concentrating private sector, are associated with quality traits such as flavour enhancement, better processing and feed quality, including animal feed crops tailored to nutritional requirements of different species; improved nutrition in crops such as vegetables and rice (e.g. rice with additional vitamin A and iron); or traits that might lower the incidence of heart disease and other human health problems described as functional foods or nutraceuiticals. By 2008 field trials in these areas had increased to 30 per cent of total field trials (up from 3 per cent in 1990). Moreover, the third generation of GM innovations involves plants being used as 'factories' to develop a wider range of chemicals, including pharmaceuticals.

The intellectual property rights surrounding seed varieties has been a major battleground between, on the one hand, those 'empires' (like Monsanto) insisting through the courts on tightening rights as new molecular GM traits are incorporated into products and, on the other, those place-based 'islands' who are fighting for conditional 'open-source' systems and the protection of local and traditional seed varieties (Kloppenburg, 2010; Deibel, 2013). The privatized patenting of seeds and plants and, in particular, the restrictions placed upon producers in not being allowed to re-seed or reuse these seeds has been a major driver of their intensive commodification and reductions in seed and plant diversity.

For example, Deibel (2013) quotes the following conditions of Monsanto's Canola for producers:

> The grower shall use any purchased Round-up Ready canola seed for planting one AND ONLY ONE crop for re-sale and consumption. The grower agrees not to save seed produced from Round-up Ready Canola seed for the purpose of replanting nor to sell, give, transfer or otherwise convey any such seeds for the purpose of replanting. (my emphasis)

This reproduces economic and ecological scarcity rather than diversity, and enhances the power of the input suppliers vis-à-vis producers. In this sense it privileges the new owners of Deoxyribonucleic Acid (DNA) seeds rather than the land-based users. Plant breeder rights, open variety rights and 'creative commons' movements are attempting to counter this dominant tendency. It is essentially a battle over land rents and seed varieties, and local farmer organizations are attempting to exert a new influence over the already changing internal dynamics of the dominant commodity system for plants and the commercialization of the life sciences. The eco-economic reaction to the onset of these controls is, as Negri and Hardt (2004: 110) argue, to realize that

> every agriculturalist is a chemist, matching soil types with the right crops, transforming fruit and milk into wine and cheese, a genetic biologist, selecting the best seeds to improve plant varieties, and a meteorologist, watching the skies. ... This kind of open science typical of agriculture that moves with the unpredictable changes of nature suggests the types of knowledge central to immaterial labour rather than the mechanistic sciences of the factory.

Thus the place- and land-based knowledge, ability and skills that sustain the diversity of seeds and their usage are critical, yet, as Kloppenburg (2010) observes, the particularly limiting and parameterized application of GM seeds by the large corporate turns the farmers into their main (land rent) competitors.

The creation of 'protected commons' and seed conservation networks can assuage this appropriational process by corporates and bio-science, and as, Kloppenburg (2010: 17) argues, needs to be supported by 'institutionalised recognition of genetic resources and associated cultural/indigenous/ community knowledge as a broadly social product, a collective heritage of farming communities that is to be freely exchanged and disseminated for the benefit of all'. As Deibel (2013) argues, there is no reason why associations of seed conservation networks, farmers and retailers could not proliferate and disseminate more shared conditional open-source arrangements, and, indeed, incorporate DNA-adjusted plant material as well. Their usage could be conditional upon supporting and maintaining farmers' land and property rights, as well as the exercise of their skills in maintaining plant diversity.

Several Non-Governmental Organisations (NGOs), like the Centre for Sustainable Agriculture,[1] Deccan Development Society,[2] Navadhanya,[3] Green Foundation,[4] Annadana,[5] Timbaktu,[6] have created seed banks in crop cereals (minor millets), oil seeds and pulses at village level. These banks focus on selection and reuse of quality seed by the farmers, with a focus upon maintaining crop and varietal diversity (Centre for Sustainable Agriculture, 2013[7]). Guidelines for creating such seed banks include (i) identifying groups which can conserve and revive traditional varieties, characterize and share with others; (ii) develop value for cultivation and use visual data for existing traditional/improved varieties and hybrids in different agro-climatic and growing conditions using participatory varietal selection; (iii) develop newer varieties/hybrids based upon their pollination/breeding behaviour using participatory plant breeding; and (iv) establish community-managed seed banks at village level which can be federated with an effective decentralized production, procurement, storage, distribution and marketing network in which community-based organizations at village level can play a role.

Land- and place-based open-source methods of seed production and use are thus a key axis of contestation as bio-economic generational transformations take place. Wield, Chataway and Bolo (2010) argue that research is currently limited in understanding the class-based differentiation of producers, and, more specifically, how small-scale producer networks could be formed to cope with the wider range of demands. They argue (364):

> There is a serious lack of evidence on the class-differentiated nature of GM technology take up and benefits. The critique of GM is typically limited solely to bio-technology in agricultural production and homogenises 'farmers' versus the myriad ways in which different classes of farmers organise their production and reproduction. A second weakness is the need to address the ways in which changes to intellectual property rights and other regulatory issues might open up innovation in GM and related technologies to broaden both the range

of GM crops available and their delivery and accessibility to various categories of farmers. ... Our evidence suggests that GM technology is not determined into some indefinite future, that its control and direction can be changed as it evolves into new generations.

The case of control over and use of seed varieties is thus one critical axis of contestation developing around the bio-economy which will act as a major driver of social and structural change in rural regions across the globe. While this is particularly affecting early adopters – big commodity (soya, maize) and innovating countries like the United States, Canada and Brazil – it is also now becoming a major focus of debate in newly developing countries. The onset of output/product-led, second- and third-generation bio-tech seeds and plants also have large implications for the less developed countries as climate change effects and food shortages become more common. A key research concern here, so far largely overlooked, is how and by what types of institutional means are bio-technological innovations to be organized, and how inclusive of local and regional producer and consumer interests and actors with this level of organization be. Those with land-occupier interests are of particular concern in this regard, and the ways and powers that they will have to define this organization will be important in shaping how bio-economy is spatially and socially configured. It would seem that so far we are only at a relatively rudimentary stage of assessing the complexities of the new relationships between bio-science and its land-based consequences and social and political contingencies.

Institutionalizing the bio-economy in the sustainability agenda: UK and Wales

While there is increasing recognition of the potential for the bio-economy in the UK, the current approach by the UK government is less purposeful than in some other European countries (e.g. Scandinavia and the Netherlands). Research and development funding through research councils is starting to be coordinated around the theme. There have been recent statements from ministers and DEFRA to support GM research and development and there is an increase in field trials. However, the links between agriculture and energy generation are limited by the EU bans on the current commercialization of genetically engineered crops which is in danger of also affecting private sector investment in research and development. The UK government produced an agri-tech strategy on the back of a recent report, *Feeding the Future: innovation requirements for primary food production in the UK to 2030* (Parliament UK,

2014). This embraces the now-established mantra of 'sustainable intensification' which promotes increases in the intensity of production while also ameliorating environmental risks. This is now the dominant bio-economy philosophy in England at least (see below the case of Wales), and it is attempting to not only stimulate neo-productivism in UK agriculture but also assuage the variety of environmental interests.

The recent policy statements are clearly embracing the bio-economy even though there are clear public and EU restrictions upon overall acceptance and commercialization. There is an assumption shared by the minister for DEFRA (Owen Paterson) that the EU restrictive framework will eventually break down and that public acceptance is increasing. As he argued in a speech (DEFRA, 2013) at a leading plant experimental and research station (Rothamsted) in June 2013:

> While I acknowledge the views of other member states, I want British researchers and farmers to have access to the latest technologies so that they can reap the economic and environmental benefits. At the moment we are expecting them to respond to the challenges of global food security with one hand tied behind their backs. The current situation is deeply regrettable. It means that the prospects of crops coming through which offer solutions to UK problems are some years away. We risk driving scientific and intellectual capital away from Europe for good. This will reduce our ability to develop and deploy crucial tools which could help ensure European agricultural production meets future demands while protecting the environment. We need evidence-based regulation and decision-making in the EU. Consumers need accurate information in order to make informed choices. The market should then decide if a GM product is viable. Farmers are also consumers but right now that market is not functioning and they are being denied choice. That's why I want to explore ways of getting the EU system working, as this will encourage further investment and innovation.

In England, however, there is a far less integrated strategy being adopted with regard to the potential linking of the food, fuel, energy and biomass nexus. This is partly because of the lack of government support for small-scale biogas and related projects and the restrictions in feed-in tariffs which are acting as an obstacle for producers such as farmers. Also big corporate players, while originally investing in biomass conversions, are rethinking their strategies (*Farmers Weekly*, July 2013).[8] In this sense, food, energy and water are still set in sectoral and different governmental silos, and, perhaps even more significantly, there is little recognition of the local and regional value added the bio-economy nexus can bring; rather there is a more generic faith in technologies, somewhat divorced from their spatial roots. Hence, provenance and the bio-economy are not being linked so far in the UK government thinking.

In Wales, this bio-economic stance is less strongly adhered to by the devolved government. Being more pro-European and realistic about the continued high level of financial dependence of its farm population on EU subsidies (even after the agreements to reform of June 2013 and Brexit 2016), the political and policy stance is more embedded in an eco-economic paradigm which supports multifunctional agriculture as a key element in the provision of a wide range of eco-system goods and services (see Marsden and Sonnino, 2008). While there are strong neo-productivist pressures from the farming unions and some related business interests, especially around the intensive dairy sector, there is a growing consensus around developing a revised 'sustainable land management approach'. This is emerging through the setting up of the merged Welsh environmental agency – Natural Resource Wales. This has brought together three preexisting bodies: the Forestry Commission, the Countryside Council for Wales and the Environmental Agency Wales. This body now has a broad remit covering the land, coastal and water regulation policies of Wales, biodiversity, amenity and forest resources, and management of a wide range of protected areas. It is an independent advisory body to government, as well as now a significant land manager in its own right, with 7 per cent of the land area.

Unlike in England where there has been an abolition of many of the environmental agencies and advisory bodies (like the Countryside Council, Royal Commission on Environmental Pollution and the Sustainable Development Commission), the new more integrated Welsh body is centrally adopting a broad eco-system paradigm to resource management and governance, following the results of the UK National Eco-System Assessment (NEA). In January 2012, the Welsh government published proposals to develop a new framework for managing natural resources which aimed at embedding this integrative approach so as to 'ensure that Wales has increasingly resilient and diverse eco-systems that deliver environmental, economic and social benefits now and in the future' (Welsh Government, 2012: 4). With a professional staff of 2000, the new body will be supported by forthcoming legislation on sustainable development obligations, environment and planning bills.

We can witness here, then, a growing divergence of resource governance approaches between England and Wales, coming at a time when the rural land base is under increasing pressure to deliver at some real or imagined cost a wider range of environmental goods and services. While the idea of payment for these goods and services is becoming more accepted, it is by no means clear who or how they are to be paid, especially in the amenity area. CAP subsidies are likely to continue to pay for some of these for some time, but it is uncertain how new market-based incentives to manage the land for public goods is going to develop. Nevertheless, in Wales there is more of a concerted government commitment to do this through purposive legislation and institutional building.

Farmers and foresters, under these conditions, either reluctantly or proactively are being repositioned as primary providers of a wider range of publicly demanded environmental goods and services, including food and energy production, amenity, tourism, wood and fibre. We see here, then, how in England and Wales the bio-economy is being framed by governance systems in different ways. In the former, a more neo-productivist model is emerging based around the notion of sustainable intensification based upon unlocking market distortions. In Wales, a more state-led approach is framing resource governance in the context of valuing and accounting for a wider range of land-based multifunctional environmental goods and services in a context where agriculture and forestry are more historically dependent upon state support.

In both countries, however, we see the rising significance of rural land as a basis for delivering both environmental sustainability goals and new or neo-productivist goals. In this sense we are moving far beyond our earlier conceptions of the 'consumption countryside' in the UK (Murdoch et al. 2003). Now, sustainability concerns of the public and state sectors are confronting again food and energy security concerns. Rural land is no longer seen as a backwater to macroeconomic concerns. Rather, it begins to emerge as a foundation for multifunctional 'green growth' in an increasingly populated and urbanized society.

Discussion: Shaping and spacing the bio-economy

The further uneven development of the bio-economy is requiring significant and more integrated forms of both technological and market development (value network thinking). This is the case, for example, in Finland, with new industrial processes affecting production and consumption patterns, as well as shifts in market, trade and development policies. The OECD, among others, argues that government policies and support will be critical and indeed decisive in shaping the bio-economy, with a major challenge facing policy makers being how to *design* policy schemes which promote innovation and development without 'locking into particular systems of technologies, or locking out future opportunities' (McCormack and Kautto 2013: 2601). Foresightful policy frameworks are thus critical within a strategic policy framework. Innovation and research are seen as central in the EU framework. This needs to be guided by principles of sustainability, trade-offs and precaution; and there are serious questions about how the current policy and scientific optimism can be qualified with aspects of public involvement, participatory and reflexive governance and sustainable development.

The growing and recent literature is providing alternative visions to the dominant development paths in the increasingly interrelated fields of energy, agriculture biomass and the role of the social and the natural. And indeed what the 'natural' means and how it is re-configured socially and spatially. There needs to be much more debate about whether the bio-economy is seen as just the next new 'technological fix', driven by a narrow and corporate-interest conception of 'greener economic growth', or whether it can be managed to deliver a range of interconnected sustainability goals which benefit not only local but global society. In particular, there is a question mark over how and by what means rural areas could benefit from bio-economic development, and the degree to which they can capture value by carefully designing policy frameworks which stimulate a diverse and place-based bio-economy. This is particularly relevant due to the fact that, whatever the technological advances over the control and design of nature, the onset of the bio-economy means that its origins and, in part, its pathways of development are conditioned by land-based and essentially local factors and production (e.g. associated with the relative provenance, economic rent and scarcity of initial endowments and feedstock). Hence, the onset of the uneven development of the bio-economy in different regions and national settings and the variable approaches adopted by governments and policy makers to it need to reignite a place-based scrutiny of its potential sustainable rural and regional development benefits.

Clearly, then, some regions, aided by systemic and value-networked thinking governments, could capture the benefits of bio-economic growth, and place their land-based sectors in new comparative advantageous positions relative to more traditional 'carbon-thinking and dominated' areas. If the residential public community can also be persuaded of this, then real green growth could become a social and economic multiplier. Hence, the new spatial transitions could not only take different place-based pathways of development, but also travel at different speeds in relation to (i) their relative degree of local and regional public acceptance; (ii) the dominance or relative decline of the carbon-based model; and (iii) the degree of local and regional bio-economic social and technical knowledge, skills and capital available in the particular region. Thus, there are new spatial transitional variables which come into play with regard to the bio-economic developments and their applications, which are linked to social and organizational capacities as much as they are to the rapid technological progress which is currently being made.

Fragmentations and integrations

We started this analysis of locating the uneven development of the bio-economy by placing it in the context of four contingent arenas: sustainability, security, sovereignty and governance. We can see from this analysis that these spheres will condition the pathways and the viability of the economies of the bio-economy now and into the future. These essentially grounded social, spatial and political arenas have so far only partially been assessed in terms of tracing the links between them and their role in shaping the levels and types of innovation, the types and shapes of markets, the levels and types of regulation needed, and the degree to which there is public value capture and support for these bio-economy developments.

We have seen how different countries and regions are framing the bio-economy in different ways. The United States generally sees no contradictions in developing or co-evolving the fossil-based economy alongside the emerging bio-economy. The EU takes a more transitional and anticipatory knowledge approach, seeing it as part of a wider post-carbon transition within a dwindling carbonized economy. Scandinavian countries see it both as improving their global competitiveness and, at the same time, as creating a more spatialized 'distributed' economy which could particularly benefit their vast rural regions.

The conceptual model outlined and explored to some degree in this chapter currently, then, raises more questions than it answers. One tension within it is the twin and somewhat contradictory processes of integration and fragmentation. The emerging bio-economy creates more headroom and innovation around the concept and reality of integrated value-chains and networks (as exemplified by the Finnish and Swedish models). More generally, and especially since the food and fiscal crisis of 2007–8, we are recognizing that our traditional sector specialisms between, say, food, energy and water are clearly breaking down under this new paradigm of nexus thinking and integrated business model development. One problem here is to assess how flexible existing sectoral-based policy programmes are to these developments and innovations. Moreover, this integrationist and interdisciplinary dynamic is also set in some sort of distinction with progressive forms of fragmentation, for instance, around the role of some key political actors like environmental groups and civil society groups. This means that there needs to be space and opportunity for new coalitions and alliances often, although not exclusively, based around place-based mobilizations. Network integration, therefore, is meeting aspects of network fragmentation and reformation as Castells (2012) records.

Increasingly, we are also witnessing a period when the conceptualizations of appropriatism, substitutionism and, more recently, expropriation are at best only partial explanatory tools in our conceptual toolbox for understanding questions of control and transition. As we see above, this necessitates a multi-theoretical approach which takes these concepts as starting points but broadens and opens them up for more uneven and differentiated application. As we see with the open-source seed movement, and in the development of alternative food and agri-ecological movements, the concepts of place-based empowerment and associationalism is also of significance, as are concepts of reflexive governance and eco-economy. The allocation of local and regional control over the development of the bio-economy is a critical dimension as is the degree to which 'alternative' modes of dealing with it can build up resilience and sustainability over time and space. It will be important to track the development of the various national and regional strategies to see how these co-evolving and competitive models play themselves out.

So far we can see the dominant framings of the bio-economy as in many ways 'crowding out' a variety of alternative models of development which would engage places and communities more proactively in its development. As Goven and Pavone (2014) argue, the dominant framing is based upon assumptions of advancing neo-liberal international competitiveness even at a time when it is in crisis and, indeed, facing severe global ecological limits and vulnerabilities. However, partly because of these crisis tendencies, it is also providing, especially in the agri-food and rural development field, new bases for alternative eco-economic models to take root, as we shall see in the forthcoming chapters.

Notes

1. http://csa-india.org/
2. http://ddsindia.com/
3. http://www.navdanya.org/
4. http://www.greenfoundation.in/
5. http://annadana-india.org/
6. http://www.timbaktu.org/
7. http://csa-india.org/
8. http://www.fwi.co.uk/blogs/livestock-and-sales-blog/2013/07/

Chapter 4

An alternative model: Exploring the 'new rural paradigm' and the rural eco-economy in Europe

We have argued in recent years that despite the macro-bio-economic and technological trends outlined and analysed in the previous chapter, many rural regions in Europe are undergoing a more diverse and dynamic place-based eco-economic transition.

The dominant discourse of bio-economic competitiveness portrays a narrow focus on the growth of a region rather than the development of a region (Markusen, 1994). Not surprisingly, as a result, orthodox regional economic development strategies are littered with the Darwinian language of 'winning'; of gaining some form of competitive advantage over other regions, and of measuring competitive performance against 'rivals' in the form of indicators and league tables (Bristow, 2009). This bio-economic competitiveness imperative mirrors the dominant thinking across many places and scales from cities and city-regions, to nations and even supranational powers, such as the European Union (EU), where regional competitiveness is now deeply embedded. Indeed, the neo-liberalized bio-economic model assumes that nations, regions and cities have to be more competitive to survive in the new marketplace that is being forged by globalization and the rise of new information technologies, and, indeed, bio-technologies (Buck, Gordon and Harding, 2005). More generally, competitiveness has effectively become a dominant framing for broad neo-liberal economic development and policy, and the resulting imperative is the pursuit of globally competitive firms. Furthermore, in the recent global economic recession (post 2008), the economy has been prioritized over environmental and social aspects, partly transparently and partly behind the veil and rhetoric of balanced sustainable development (Jauhiainen and Moilanen, 2011).

As a response to the 'place-less' discourse of bio-economic competitiveness, new, more sustainable, place-based strategies have been developed, which embody multifunctional agriculture and the construction of identities, brands and images around new and redefined rural goods and services. Territorial and place-based approaches have recently also become more important in the view of some EU member states (EU, 2007), in European policies for territorial cohesion (EC, 2010a), in the development strategies and practices for the EU programming period after 2013, and in the Green Paper on research and innovation funding (EC, 2010b). The response of place-based development reflects a discourse of 'reconnection' (Ilbery and Maye, 2007: 507) and incorporates a shift from homogeneous agricultural commodity markets to more segmented and diversified markets (Winter, 2003: 506).

In particular, the reconnection between specific foods and specific places is a form of reterritorialization, which attempts to reverse the intrinsically aspatial order of globalized production and concentration, as the heterogeneous properties of food become celebrated outcomes of different places and natures (Winter, 2003). Reterritorialization emphasizes the role of agriculture not only as an economic sector and food producer, but also in maintaining multifunctional green amenity space and landscape quality.

Reterritoralization is an important dimension of what major development agencies such as the OECD, as well as scholars (van der Ploeg and Marsden, 2008) postulate as the New Rural Paradigm (NRP) in Europe. According to the OECD, this paradigm includes a new, multisector, place-based approach to rural development that claims a need for closer linkages between the rural and urban economy, and sees rural European urban development as a close interplay with regional development more generally. Key elements are the re-valorization of local assets, a shift from subsidy-driven development to more variable development through investments, and the exploitation and redefinition of hitherto unused resources (OECD, 2006).

We can witness many expressions of this new paradigm, especially in those places where the rural domain is no longer exclusively tied to food production but is being transformed into a 'multifunctional landscape' to meet wider and more diverse urban consumer demands. Here the aesthetic–consumptive functions of places become as important as the utility and productive functions. These developments create opportunities for multifunctional agriculture to produce a wider array of new products and services linked to local and regional assets and identities (Marsden and Sonnino, 2008). These can create new synergies in utilizing the *same set* of factors of production to make a wider (and expanding) range of place-based products and services. Marsden (2010: 124) defines this process 'as the relative capability for the local rural economy to do more than one thing at the same time from the same (and necessarily restricted) resource base'. *Synergy* involves doing this in such a way that the economic effects grow more than proportionally. Horizontal as well as vertical networking together with variable levels of reciprocity can create the conditions for these rural eco-economies of scope and synergy.

Some scholars argue that these trends now recast our conceptualizations of rural development practices with a much more stronger focus upon the social organization of actors and networks (van der Ploeg, Ye and Fu, 2015: 25). It is argued:

> Rural development practices are usually (but not always) autonomously generated. More importantly, they are a strategy for regaining and/or enlarging autonomy. Even when there is considerable state support, the unfolding of these practices represents a search for the *enlarging of autonomy*. This search for autonomy subsequently translates into a *search for endogeneity*, building as much as possible (but not exclusively) on locally available resources in order to avoid getting entrapped in new dependency relations. It also translates into *novelty production*, the search for local and original solutions which helps to avoid dependency on externally developed innovations.

In conceptual terms, scholars have developed a more robust and, as we shall see, empirically viable model of 'the new rural paradigm'. Here it is important to also incorporate ecological considerations into this more multifunctional and actor-oriented approach, given that it is centrally and intentionally mobilized by a redefinition of place-based ecological as well as human assets. Hence we introduce and develop it here as the eco-economic paradigm.

The eco-economic paradigm and sustainable place-making

We can conceive of this eco-economic paradigm (EEP) as an alternative and more diverse and fragmented arena for the development of new production and consumption chains and networks. It partly develops its vibrancy in creating a more autonomous but also oppositional status to the neo-liberalized bio-economy paradigm. It places an emphasis upon the recalibration of microeconomic behaviour and practices that, added together, can potentially realign production–consumption chains and capture local and regional value between rural *and* urban spaces. The EEP involves the rise of complex networks or webs of viable businesses (many of them small- and medium-sized new businesses) and economic activities that utilize ecological resources in more sustainable and ecologically efficient ways (e.g. new renewable energy firms, agri-tourism, food processing and catering, and social enterprises). Importantly, these do not result in a net depletion of resources, but instead provide cumulative (more than proportional) net benefits that add value to rural and regional spaces in both ecological and economic terms. Kitchen and Marsden (2009: 289) suggest a definition of EEP that captures these characteristics:

> The effective social management of environmental resources (as combinations of natural, social, economic and territorial capital) in ways designed to mesh with and enhance the local and regional ecosystem rather than disrupting and destroying it. The eco-economy thus consists of cumulative and nested 'webs' of viable businesses and economic activities that utilize the varied and differentiated forms of environmental resources of rural areas in sustainable ways. They do not result in a net depletion of resources but rather provide net benefits and add value to the environment and to the community.

The important implications of this definition are a revised socio-spatial understanding of both production and consumption spheres and the basis for new understandings of sustainable communities which are more rooted in (and reliant upon) rural regions.

We can argue that the EEP is rooted then in a 'stronger' form of ecological modernization (EM). The connections between the EEP and (strong) EM, and hence sustainable communities, become tangible if we adopt a conception of sustainable communities that encompasses two interrelated types: communities of interest and of place. First, we suggest that communities of place with the capacity to support the EEP are more likely to be in rural spaces. Primarily, this is because rural spaces tend to possess an abundance of ecological resources, which can be turned into a variety of embedded ecological goods and services. In addition, the idea of the EEP thriving in rural spaces may be further developed by association with rural geographies and rural development, specifically the concept of multifunctionality – defined as the degree to which farms and other economic enterprises contribute, beyond their primary function of producing food and fibre, to environmental benefits such as land conservation, the sustainable management of renewable natural resources, the preservation of biodiversity and the enhancement of the socio-economic aspects of rural life. McCarthy (2005) observes that, while EM has been applied principally to manufacturing (viz. weak EM), its core elements appear in rural multifunctionality, and that a number of authors have articulated this point (e.g. Wilson, 2001; Evans, Morris and Winter, 2002; Marsden et al., 2003, Marsden, 2004).

These core elements consist of the internalization of former ecological externalities, the promotion of inter-generational equity, reflexivity among EM actors and a clear role for the state. Although McCarthy (2005: 804) argues that rural spaces have been and remain prime, even archetypal, sites of capitalism, he notes that the characteristics of alternative economies and commodities often tend to overlap with the characteristics of rural spaces and products: for example, close and interactive communities, short supply chains and the embedding of economic processes in local cultures and communities (e.g. Renting, Marsden and Banks, 2003; Lamine, 2005; Kirwan, 2006). Secondly, and in a reciprocal relationship with communities of place, we may envisage communities of interest, where eco-ecological processes (interests) are sustainably more embedded in communities of place and connected in interrelated webs to their regional and urban hinterlands. Thus, the EEP, indicative of a deeper and stronger EM, potentially realigns production–consumption chains and captures local and regional value between rural and urban spaces. The importance of the rural–regional–urban nexus should not be underestimated, as the relationships and linkages between rural and urban spaces and their regions are important elements of sustainability. Although, globally, populations are becoming more urbanized, as Taylor (2000: 28) argues: 'It is research and action designed to make this modern and urban way of life more environmentally sustainable which will contribute most to the cause of sustainability.' Paradoxically, as urban spaces become more prominent, so rural spaces assume even greater importance as repositories of natural resources and potential hubs of eco-ecological processes and the EEP.

The aim of the rest of this chapter is to critically investigate the rural eco-economy as part of 'new rural development paradigm' in a comparative European regional context, by describing and analysing the various strategies in rural regional development. An important issue is how promising these strategies are in terms of eco-economic development (Kitchen and Marsden, 2009). Are some of them just short-term survival strategies of an agricultural sector that is doomed to fade away in urbanizing regions? Or can they contribute to more viable, resilient and sustainable regions? This leads to the central question to be addressed here: What types of strategies and pathways for eco-economic development can be witnessed in rural regions in Europe? And how sustainable are they likely to be in the long term?

This question is addressed using an analysis of sixty-two rural development cases, in which the analytical framework of the 'rural web' (see below) has been used to understand the dynamic interplay between different domains of rural development. The first section deals with some of the key theoretical questions: What are the main driving forces of rural transformation? How can the complexity and dynamics of rural, regional development be understood? How can this complexity be analysed using the model of 'the rural web' as a heuristic device? The second section describes the methodology, after which pathways for sustainable rural regional development in Europe are identified. The final section reassesses and elaborates on the conceptual parameters for the NRP.

Understanding the complexity of sustainable rural regional development

The establishment of new and more diversified markets is one of the building blocks of the NRP. This can be regarded not only as a rural but also a new regional paradigm, which stems from a re-localization or reterritorialization process, resulting in new linkages among sectors, businesses, producers and consumers and markets. But what are the driving forces involved in rural development that stimulate the search for new markets? Three main motors can be identified.

First, the continued 'cost-price squeeze' in conventional agriculture (as well as other land-based activities, such as forestry, as discussed in Chapter 2) requires new and radical remedies. This refers to the ongoing rural debate where rural economies are described as being caught in the process of a continuous squeeze between the prices and costs associated with land-based production and the growing market and consumer expectations of high-quality or natural rural resource-based goods and services.

The 'cost-price squeeze' refers to the endemic economic pressures facing landholders and farmers, who are caught in the context of the conventional and corporately controlled upstream and downstream sectors, face constant pressures to accept higher input costs (feeds, seeds, fertilisers, pesticides, machinery and financial credit), and pressure to reduce farm-gate prices from the food processors and retailers. This has traditionally been a main driver for further farm intensification and scale enlargement, as well as the continuous adoption of labour-saving technologies. However, now faced with these far-reaching concerns and issues, farmers and other landholders are also being encouraged towards more 'value-adding' and multifunctionality (see, for example, Marsden and Sonnino, 2008; van der Ploeg and Marsden, 2008). Some rural economies respond to this squeeze by attempting to raise their competitiveness in order to realize improvements in quality of life in rural areas.

A second driving force is the continued crises in conventional agriculture, such as foot-and-mouth disease, swine flu, bovine spongiform encephalopathy and food scandals. These have set the momentum for transition. Environmental problems in agriculture, animal diseases and food scandals have influenced the image of agriculture such that the agricultural 'licence to produce' is no longer undisputed.

The third factor concerns the growing urban demands for rural goods and services with the entry of new (often ex-urban) actors now both demanding and providing these. New functions, inhabitants and practices are taking root in rural areas. While decreasing the power of rural actors, these changes are also diversifying and complicating the rural arena, raising questions about more traditional conceptions of rural space (Frouws, 1998). As a response to these challenges, there is no single, exclusive path for sustainable rural regional development. However, in the search for new models of sustainable development, different trajectories can be identified: the bio-economy and the eco-economy, each of which underpins alternative models for economic growth and sustainable development. Both models include different views on 'green investments', have their own sustainability claims and can be analysed in the context of the overarching development theory of EM. We argue that the ecologically modernizing agenda has been too narrowly interpreted as bio-economic development and should be based on a more diverse theoretical base (see Buttel, 2000; Gibbs, 2000; Horlings and Marsden, 2011a,b; Mol, 2000; Murphy, 2000).

One consequence of a political choice for an eco-economic regional development path is a stronger institutional embeddedness of activities in specific spatial contexts of space and place. The 'place-based' eco-economy does not result in a net depletion of resources, but instead can provide cumulative net benefits that add value to rural and regional spaces in both ecological and economic ways (Kitchen and Marsden, 2009; Marsden, 2010). Stimulating sustainability is this sense is not merely creating vertical linkages (agricultural or bio-energy chains), but combining horizontal and vertical innovation facilitated by new governance arrangements. The choice of a bio- or eco-economic development trajectory is specifically urgent for those rural economies currently dealing with the challenges of continued peripherality, agricultural decline, low levels of economic activity and expectations, and volatile and variable consumer demand. The NRP referred to by the OECD incorporates what we identify here as both 'bio-economic' and 'eco-economic' features as a result of adopting either 'weak' or 'strong' notions of ecological sustainability. The next section describes how different trajectories for rural eco-economic development can be analysed by using the model of a 'rural web' as a heuristic device. The rural web provides a way of harnessing diversity and 'photographs' the configuration of six dimensions in regional rural development (Van der Ploeg et al., 2008). Rural development in this model is the unfolding of a rural 'web' in the regional context. Responding to the 'squeeze on rural resources', the model empirically describes rural resources, actors, activities, linkages, transactions, networks and positive externalities. Theoretically, the model captures the interrelations between six conceptual domains: endogeneity, novelty, production, social capital, market governance, new institutional arrangements and sustainability (Table 4.1). In this model sustainability is territorially based. As such, rural development is viewed as a dynamic web of linkages that reshapes the rural while enlarging its competitiveness and enhancing the quality of life (Table 4.1).

We can develop the model further by conceptualizing eco-economic strategies as part of broader regional pathways – which emerge through the different mobilizations of the rural web – and their influence on rural change (see Figure 4.1).

Table 4.1 Domains of rural development (Marsden, 2010). Adapted from van der Ploeg and Marsden, 2008

Endogeneity	The degree to which rural economies are (a) built upon local resources; (b) organized according to local models of resource combination; and (c) strengthened through the distribution and reinvestment of produced wealth within the local/regional constellation.
Novelty	New insights, practices, artefacts and/or combinations (of resources, technological procedures, bodies of knowledge, etc.) that carry the promise that specific constellations function better.
Social capital	'[T]he norms and networks that enable people to act collectively' (Woolcock and Narayan, 2000) or, more specifically, the ability of individuals, groups, organizations or institutions to engage in networks, cooperate and employ social relations for common purpose and benefit.
Market governance	Institutional capacities to control and strengthen existing markets and/or to construct new ones.
New institutional arrangements	New institutional constellations that solve coordination problems and support cooperation among rural actors.
Sustainability	'[T]he existence of the social and ecological conditions necessary to support human life at a certain level of wellbeing through future generations' (Earth Council, 1994)

Methodological aspects of the comparative case study analysis

The empirical material was gathered in the context of a large European research project, (ETUDE[1]) Enlarging Theoretical Understanding of Rural Development was carried out by research institutes in six European countries (UK, Germany, the Netherlands, Italy, Latvia and Finland). ETUDE aimed to acquire a better understanding of the dynamics, scope and regional economic impact of rural development processes, while reflecting on the large heterogeneity of rural areas and activities.

ETUDE analysed sixty-two project cases and twelve in-depth case studies. This chapter is based on an analysis of the project cases, described by researchers of the six country teams. For the analysis of the twelve in-depth cases we refer to Milone and Ventura (2010). The rich empirical material shows a broad overview of strategies on rural, regional development in Europe and the emergence of new rural–urban linkages. We will describe here methodological aspects of the case study research, the selection and inventory of cases and the analysis (Marsden, 2007; Marsden and Sonnino, 2007).

Each case focused upon describing economic activities or initiatives in rural areas responding or attempting to respond to the squeeze on rural economies by raising their competitiveness. The cases were based on primary and secondary data regarding the actors involved in the rural development, the institutions involved and the social and economic impacts (direct or indirect) of the

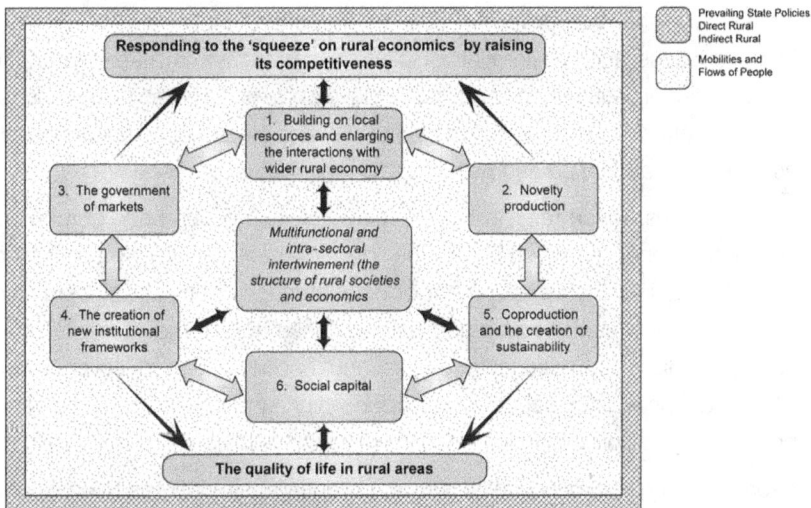

Figure 4.1 The rural web (Marsden, 2010).

development. The inventory contained rural projects on agricultural production, tourism, education, energy, nature and landscape care and regional branding, but also included research projects, partnerships and grass-roots movements.

The aim was to demonstrate in the separate cases (1) to what extent each domain was related to the others and (2) how these domains were combined and created, or did not create, quality of life benefits for the rural areas.

The case studies were reanalysed in the context of exploring eco-economic regional strategies for regional development. The goal was to identify the variety of development pathways that emerged through the different mobilizations of the rural web.

Comparative analysis: Pathways for sustainable rural regional development in Europe

Based on the analysis of the sixty-two cases, Horlings and Marsden (2010, 2014) later identified different eco-economic pathways in European rural regions. These findings deepen the insight in the interplay between the 'governance of markets' and the other domains of the rural web (see Figure 4.2). They also reflect the ongoing struggles for diversification of agriculture as well as a shift to a broader, more integrative regional approach, including an increased role of non-agricultural actors. In the next sections we will describe the following three pathways:

- *(niche-) innovation*, which specifies the different ways in which the relations between 'governance of markets', 'novelty' and 'sustainability' take shape, especially in the area of food. Social capital often functions as a lubricant in this process; the proliferation of place-based niches is a key feature of multifunctional agriculture and rural development, whereby the 'niche' becomes attached and promoted by its novel and place-based features such as breeding, landscape and growing and rearing qualities.

- *new interfaces*, which refer to the interplay between governance of markets and institutional arrangements. The development of new place-based markets requires the development of new interfaces between farmers and a variety of new stakeholders and actors. These, for example, include new trading bodies, promotional agencies and cooperative and collaborative consortia. These often set new rules upon which land-based production and processing are conducted.

- *re-orientation of territorial capital,* which (potentially) strengthens the relations between governance of markets, endogeneity and sustainability. This reterritorialization process can be seen as an attempt to integrate markets on the regional level, and potentially leads to a more integrative regional development process. Here, territory, despite the rigours of EU competition law and trading regulations which attempt to 'smooth-out' differences between products and trade between places and regions, becomes an active parameter in creating novelty and marketing products. This means that local and regional actors (including farmers) need then to become more territorial and to practise place-based skills and knowledges in ways which embody their products and services. This takes on new innovative forms of entrepreneurship (see Morgan et al., 2008), which in itself becomes more place-based in that it relies upon a deep knowledge of local and regional practices.

(Niche-) innovation

(Niche-) innovation refers to the development of new product–market combinations, mostly in the area of food, based on novelties and linked to sustainability as a basis for eco-economical regional development. This strategy specifies the different ways in which the relations between governance shape, often lubricated by social capital, 'novelty' and 'sustainability' through cooperation between producers and individual leadership. Innovation in itself does not lead to sustainability, but it can be linked to the sustainability domain by (a) developing certification schemes (e.g. organic agriculture), (b) production and quality guidelines, (c) new and re-invented animal breeds/products or varieties, (d) European labels, (e) environmental farm management or (f) the use of renewable rural sources (such as wind energy or biomass). Four dimensions of sustainable (niche) innovation can be identified, along the two axes of products and markets (see Figure 4.3).

1. The improvement and marketing of existing products in existing food markets

Examples include a large variety of initiatives and projects in Europe. This strategy seems to be dominant in alternative agri-food networks described in the cases. In terms of innovation, the focus is on developing, and in many cases 'retro-innovating', quality products and marketing tools as a response to the cost-price squeeze and crises in conventional agricultural markets. The main constraint concerns the competitiveness and regulation in already established markets, which often tend to be dominated by corporate retailers and well-known, powerful, industrial brands. Organic production, especially,

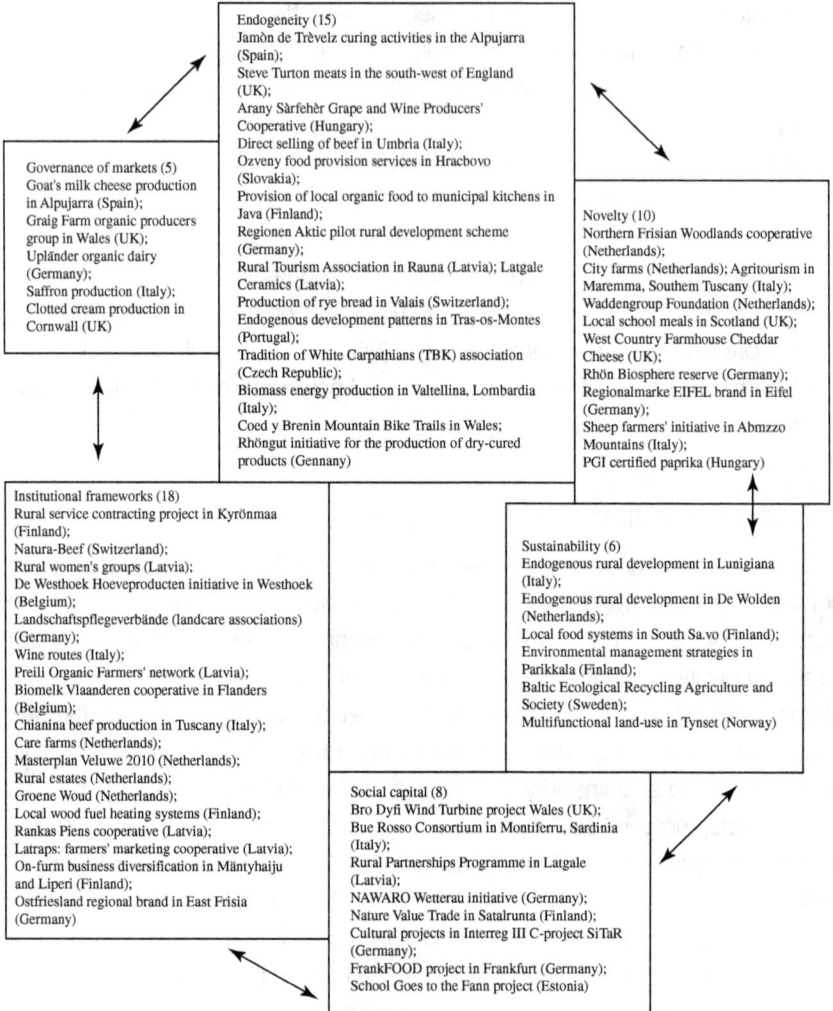

Endogeneity (15)
Jamòn de Trèvelz curing activities in the Alpujarra (Spain);
Steve Turton meats in the south-west of England (UK);
Arany Sàrfehèr Grape and Wine Producers' Cooperative (Hungary);
Direct selling of beef in Umbria (Italy);
Ozveny food provision services in Hracbovo (Slovakia);
Provision of local organic food to municipal kitchens in Java (Finland);
Regionen Aktic pilot rural development scheme (Germany);
Rural Tourism Association in Rauna (Latvia); Latgale Ceramics (Latvia);
Production of rye bread in Valais (Switzerland);
Endogenous development patterns in Tras-os-Montes (Portugal);
Tradition of White Carpathians (TBK) association (Czech Republic);
Biomass energy production in Valtellina, Lombardia (Italy);
Coed y Brenin Mountain Bike Trails in Wales;
Rhöngut initiative for the production of dry-cured products (Gennany)

Governance of markets (5)
Goat's milk cheese production in Alpujarra (Spain);
Graig Farm organic producers group in Wales (UK);
Upländer organic dairy (Germany);
Saffron production (Italy);
Clotted cream production in Cornwall (UK)

Novelty (10)
Northern Frisian Woodlands cooperative (Netherlands);
City farms (Netherlands); Agritourism in Maremma, Southem Tuscany (Italy);
Waddengroup Foundation (Netherlands);
Local school meals in Scotland (UK);
West Country Farmhouse Cheddar Cheese (UK);
Rhön Biosphere reserve (Germany);
Regionalmarke EIFEL brand in Eifel (Germany);
Sheep farmers' initiative in Abmzzo Mountains (Italy);
PGI certified paprika (Hungary)

Institutional frameworks (18)
Rural service contracting project in Kyrönmaa (Finland);
Natura-Beef (Switzerland);
Rural women's groups (Latvia);
De Westhoek Hoeveproducten initiative in Westhoek (Belgium);
Landschaftspflegeverbände (landcare associations) (Germany);
Wine routes (Italy);
Preili Organic Farmers' network (Latvia);
Biomelk Vlaanderen cooperative in Flanders (Belgium);
Chianina beef production in Tuscany (Italy);
Care farms (Netherlands);
Masterplan Veluwe 2010 (Netherlands);
Rural estates (Netherlands);
Groene Woud (Netherlands);
Local wood fuel heating systems (Finland);
Rankas Piens cooperative (Latvia);
Latraps: farmers' marketing cooperative (Latvia);
On-furm business diversification in Mäntyhaiju and Liperi (Finland);
Ostfriesland regional brand in East Frisia (Germany)

Sustainability (6)
Endogenous rural development in Lunigiana (Italy);
Endogenous rural development in De Wolden (Netherlands);
Local food systems in South Sa.vo (Finland);
Environmental management strategies in Parikkala (Finland);
Baltic Ecological Recycling Agriculture and Society (Sweden);
Multifunctional land-use in Tynset (Norway)

Social capital (8)
Bro Dyfi Wind Turbine project Wales (UK);
Bue Rosso Consortium in Montiferru, Sardinia (Italy);
Rural Partnerships Programme in Latgale (Latvia);
NAWARO Wetterau initiative (Germany);
Nature Value Trade in Satalrunta (Finland);
Cultural projects in Interreg III C-project SiTaR (Germany);
FrankFOOD project in Frankfurt (Germany);
School Goes to the Fann project (Estonia)

Figure 4.2 The 62 ETUDE projects and dominating domains.

faces difficulties in the marketing of products. A clear example is the Preili organic farmers' network in Latvia. The lack of economic, human and social capital, inadequate state support for small-scale cooperatives in this country, the lack of commitment and trust among cooperative members and the lack of appropriate management (institutional aspect) were among the most relevant limiting factors. In other cases regulation is a constraint, such as in hygienic sanitary norms for food in direct selling, for example, in Umbria in Italy. Farmers in this region adapted to the regulation by following a strategy of vertical integration, first by developing cooperatives through collective contractual integration with the distribution system and, second, by more autonomously internalizing the slaughtering activity and marketing of beef.

Entrepreneurs often cope with the above difficulties by strengthening the domain of social capital. They form cooperatives or associations aimed at collective marketing, vertical integration in the production chain, new product branding by developing quality guidelines to distinguish the product from others or by applying for and achieving European PDO and PGI labels. In some cases the initiative of 'wilful individuals' or ecological entrepreneurs plays a stimulating and key orchestrating role (e.g. in the case of ham production, Jamon de Trevelz in Spain, and in several UK cases, such as Rodda Creamery, Graig farm producers' group and Steve Turton Westaways sausages).

2. The production and marketing of new products for existing food markets

Here, innovation is focused on the production of new varieties or breeds, or the (re)introduction of agricultural products or non-food products. Most projects are initiated by private actors but sometimes also by public actors (e.g. production of rye bread in Switzerland and wine routes in Tuscany in Italy). The main constraints include the necessary investments for product and market development. A strategy to cope with these difficulties is collective action, upscaling and networking, searching for support from governmental authorities or European programmes (such as LEADER) and non-governmental organizations (such as the 'slow food' movement). In some cases innovative new products have been developed with the initiative of visionary individuals (e.g. saffron production in Tuscany, the dairy group Rankas Piens in Latvia, the food producers organized in the Waddengroup in the north of the Netherlands and the food initiative Tegut/Rhongut in Germany).

3. The production and marketing of agricultural products for new markets

Here, innovation is focused more on finding new groups of consumers on the local or regional scale, which can contribute to local food sovereignty, the strengthening of producer–consumer relations or reducing the 'ecological footprint'. Some of the projects are initiated by women's groups, whereas others are the result of policy initiatives (such as local school meals in Scotland) or European projects such as Interreg IIIB (e.g. the project Food for Municipal Kitchens in Finland).

Some innovative initiatives (e.g. city farms in the Netherlands) face the constraint of no institutional procedures for support or policy programmes available for their stimulation. Another problem for food producer initiatives is the search for new consumer groups such as schools and municipalities, which can create difficulties in networking and in breaking into established supplier networks.

	Current Markets		
Current products	*Improved products in existing markets*	*New products for existing markets e.g. specific breeds*	**New products**
	Examples are the Rhöngut initiative (production of dry-cured products) and Upländer Diary in Germany; direct selling of beef in Umbria; cooperation of organic entrepreneurs in Järna in Sweden; goat's milk production in Alpajurra; improvement of 'Jamon de Trevelz' (ham businesses) in Spain; the production of Tuscan Chianina beef; UK initiatives such as West Country Farm House Cheddar, Cornish Clotted Cream, Steve Turton's Westaways sausages and the Graig farm producers' group. In Latvia the Latraps marketing cooperative, cattle breeding and the Preili organic farmers' network; Biomilk in Belgium; the entrepreneurs' cooperative in Het Groene Woud (the Netherlands). The tradition of White Carpathians association (marketing of regional fruit products) in the Czech Republic, Hungarian paprika, Natura-beef in Switzerland and the wine producers' cooperative in Hungary.	Examples of new products are Gregoriano cheese and smoked ricotta from sheep farmers in the Abruzzo Mountains, the development of the almost extinct breed Bue Rosso in Sardinia, reintroduction of the Saffron spice in Tuscany, some of the products of the Waddengroup in the Netherlands, wine routes in Hungary, rye bread in Valais (Switzerland), Dairy Rankas Piens in Latvia	

Figure 4.3 Dimensions of product – market innovation.

New markets	New products for new markets
Examples are school catering in the FrankFood project in Germany; delivery of products from Ecological Recycling Agriculture (ERA) to Municipal kitchens in Finland; the School Goes to the Farm project (Estonia); ERA products for schools and other institutions, restaurants and private consumers in Sweden; city farms in the Netherlands; the provision of local school meals in East Ayrshire in Scotland; direct sales of Westhoek Hoeve products in Belgium; provision of food services for pensioners in Ozveny Slovakia; and Nawaro Wetterau in Germany (crops for bio-energy and industrial use).	Examples are Landcare ('Landschaftspflegeverbände') in Germany; local bio-energy heating systems in Finland; nature value trade (protection of nature values by forest-owners) in Stakunta, Finland; energy production based on biomass of forests in Valtellina in Lombardia (Italy); off-farm income generation in the Wolden in the Netherlands; non-agricultural products in the Green Forest; care-farming, rural estates and paid nature/ landscape conservation in the Netherlands; wind energy production (Bro Dyfi) in Wales; mountain trails ('Coed y Brenin') in Wales; and Artisan Ceramics in Czech Republic.

New Markets

Figure 4.3 Continued

4. The production and marketing of new products for new markets

The focus here is on finding completely new product – market combinations often by crossing the boundaries between different sectors (i.e. the fourth, lower-right, quadrant). This implies a more radical break with the past and establishes entirely new eco-economic practices. Most initiatives are focused on horizontal networks, started by private or public initiatives. An example is the 140 voluntary 'Landschafts-pflegeverbände' in Germany, which engage farmers in conservation work with a reliable source of additional income and help them market products that are typical of their respective regions. This fourth strategy is the most innovative but also the most risky and difficult, combining the constraints of the second and third strategies above.

With regard to these four subcategories we can see that most projects are focused on the first strategy: the renewed and remade marketing of existing food products for existing or new markets. An important challenge for the future is to strengthen also the other two strategies described below. The re-orientation on local assets especially, can integrate different rural and urban interfaces and be linked to broader notions of quality of life.

New interfaces

As part of a process of eco-economic change, new interfaces are established between (public and private) actors, between producers and consumers, within the production chain, between sectors, functions, city and countryside or between domains of regional development (see Figure 4.4). These interfaces refer especially to the web domain of institutional arrangements in the sense that new institutions are formed that enable cooperation between actors. New interfaces as such do not contribute to sustainability automatically. However, linkages between the domains of the web strengthen the coherence of the rural web and create synergy and dynamics within the web, which can then create possibilities for sustainable regional development. Within this strategy different dimensions can be distinguished along the axes of individual and multi-actor and market versus public goods. We can witness

- individual and more direct interfacial market relations within the chain (shortening the chain) between producers and consumers, for example, by direct selling of products (upper-left quadrant);
- rural services in the form of public goods such as health, nature and landscape offered by individual farms, for clients, tourists or consumers (upper-right quadrant);
- market products by multi-actor groups, cooperatives or communities (lower-left quadrant); and
- public goods produced by associations, communities or cooperatives such as the agricultural nature and landscape associations in the Netherlands, the 'Landschaftspflege verbände' in Germany, educational activities by rural women's groups in Latvia, multifunctional land use in Tynset (Norway) and the use of locally available commons ('baldios') in Tras-os-Montes in Portugal (lower-right quadrant).

Especially interesting are interfaces that contribute to new rural–urban linkages. In Cardiff (Wales, UK), for example, a new model for local food production has been implemented (see Box 4.1)

Individual actors			
Market goods	*Shortening the chain and new relations between producer and consumer*	*Rural services by individual firms*	**Public goods**
	Examples are the direct selling of a variety of products in European regions	Examples are the care farms, city farms and rural estates in the Netherlands; agri-tourism in Maremma, Southern Tuscany; the Rural Tourism Association in Rauna (Latvia); protection of nature values by forestry owners in Satakunta in Finland and contracts for rural services in Kyrönmaa in Finland.	
	Market goods produced by collectives	*Rural services by collectives*	
	Examples here are the wind turbine owned by a local community in Wales and the family-based production of Latgale Ceramics in Latvia.	Examples are the landscape care associations in Germany (Landschaftspflege Verbände)	
Multi-actor			

Figure 4.4 New interfaces in rural regional development.

Box 4.1 Riverside Market Garden; local food production for the city of Cardiff (Wales)

Riverside Market Garden is a new ethical model for sustainable local food production, developed by RCMA Social Enterprise, to make more fresh food available to the local community. A new food production site has been located on 10 acres at St Hilary, 10 miles west of Cardiff, and work has already started – the first crops were produced in July 2010 and sold at the farmers' markets in Cardiff. The garden will produce a wide range of organic vegetables; offer training, care placements and educational visits for schools; and contribute to landscape management. Citizens can become shareholders in the new farm, involve themselves as customers or volunteers, or become co-investors for a minimum of £50 a year. The goal is to develop the Market Garden within five years as a self-financing community-owned business supplying high-quality seasonal vegetables to local people.

Re-orientation on territorial capital

This refers to the web domain of endogeneity in the sense that it is based on the valorization of local/regional assets or rooted in social cultural notions of regional identity. These strategies can (potentially) strengthen the link between governance of markets, endogeneity and sustainability. The aim here is not only to develop agriculture or agri-food networks but to integrate different sectors. Most projects are initiated by public actors or research projects (see Figure 4.5).

This final category shows a gradual shift from agricultural diversification to a more integrative rural and regional development, including non-agricultural actors. This is especially interesting because of the potential for combining horizontal (in areas between sectors) and vertical (between actors in the production chain) linkages. Different dimensions can be distinguished along the axes of product versus culture ('experience') orientation and agriculture versus multisector/region orientation

We can make a distinction between

- the development of new/old breeds, food products, production guidelines or collective marketing action (upper-left quadrant);
- culturally embedded agricultural products that aim to tell the 'story of the region' (upper-right quadrant);
- new product–market combinations based on local and regional assets (lower-left quadrant); and
- experience- and multisector-based branding of multiple sectors or entire regions (lower-right quadrant).

Producer–consumer relations can be linked to cultural capital (examples are the regions of Lunigiana in Italy and Devon and Shetland in the UK), thereby using symbolic capital that functions as a cement to align people around the cultural storyline of the region. This strategy emphasizes the role of place identity in development, 'to evoke the meanings which are attached to particular places by different groups of people who experience places in different ways – as residents, business people, policy makers and tourists for example' (Kneafsey, 2000: 36).

Part of this strategy is the production of culturally embedded products that reflect place identity and aim to tell the 'story of the region' and offer experiences to citizens. Many of these products have a European PGI status. An interesting example is the development process in Lunigiana in Italy (see Box 4.2).

Agricultural products			
Product-based	*Specific agricultural products (breeds, guidelines)*	*Brands of products rooted in cultural identity*	**Culture-based**
	Examples are direct selling of beef in Umbria, goat's milk production in Alpajurra (Spain), cattle breeding in Latvia, fruit production in Czech Republic, biomilk in Vlaanderen, and initiatives on marketing of organic production	Examples are 'Jamon de Trevelz' (Spain), Chianina beef in Tuscany, Hungarian paprika and wine, West Country farmhouse cheesemakers, Cornish clotted cream, Bue Rosseo in Sardinia, rye bread in Valais (Switzerland), Waddenproducts (Netherlands) and specific cheeses in Abruzzo Mountains (Italy).	
	New product–market combinations based on natural regional resources	*Place branding*	
	Examples are bioenergy from forests in Lombardia, local bioenergy heating systems in Finland and Nawaro Wetterau in Germany (crops for industrial use or the production of energy).	Examples are rural transition in Lunigiana (Italy), Regionen Aktiv, regional brand Ostfriesland and the Rhön Biosphere reserve (all three in Germany).	
Regional products and services			

Figure 4.5 The degree of re-orientation on local/regional assets and identity.

Attempts to link agriculture, landscape, biodiversity and identity partly stem from, and are aided by, branding-based activities (Ilbery and Maye, 2007: 508). Branding can (potentially) function as a vehicle to market regional products of different sectors.

A brand can be described as 'a consistent group of characters, images, or emotions that consumers recall or experience when they think of a specific symbol, product, service, organization or location' (Simeon, 2006: 464). It can, in general, refer to destinations, corporations, products and services (Balakrischan, 2009).

Box 4.2 Cultural capital in Lunigiana in Italy

Lunigiana is a historical region with rich cultural capital (churches, abbeys, pilgrimage route, book festivals and medieval rural villages). The inhabitants have a strong 'sense of place' and feel they are neither 'Liguri' (people from Liguria Region) nor 'Toscani' (people from Tuscany Region). In this region, since 1990, new informal, hybrid and locally controlled networks have been constructed that comprise a wide range of regional and local institutions. This has fostered new locally controlled markets for typical food products and rural tourism, whereby the regional image is connected to the local agro-food products. As a result, there are, for example, now seventy-two local agro-food products, such as lamb of Zeri, bread of Caosola, the PDO honey of Lunigiana, some wines and the mushroom 'fungo di Borgotaro'. However, the risk here is the symbolic overexposure and the consequent generation of conflict among lived, perceived and conceived ruralities (e.g. you can only find the onion of Treschietto during the specific period of the local 'Festival of the onion of Treschietto').

Place branding is the deliberate planning of the image and identity of a region. In some places a narrow definition of branding is used, limited to marketing of the existing situation. In this sense, referring to Pederson (2011), place branding is about strengthening the legibility of the region in a pragmatic way: it sees no potential of social development that is not marketable. Anything particular and authentic is an asset. Yet, Pederson (2011) also argues that place branding has a creative and affirmative potential which the literature on creative spaces bore witness to (Florida, 2002). It is driven by an explicit intention – in line with organizational branding – by suggesting organizational changes of the place in question. It is about constructing territorial ideas, signs and practices. It devises new ways for a local society to identify itself (Pederson, 2011: 78). As a consequence, place branding concerns not only what a region is, but also what it aims and desires to be in the future. This can lead to new ideas, images, products, alliances, organization forms and services. Based on a comparison of six European regions, Árnason, Shucksmith and Vergunst (2009) state that the process of branding in networks can be divided into three aspects: (1) increase visibility, (2) develop new products and (3) reorganize activities. We can add to this by stating that increasing visibility can increase people's awareness of the qualities of their places, which encourages new innovations. An interesting example of regional branding is the Regional Marke Eiffel (see Box 4.3).

> ## Box 4.3 Regional branding: the Regional Marke Eiffel
>
> The Regionen Aktiv (RA) is a pilot programme in Germany and an example of an innovative support scheme that tries to generate new economic activities, linking them to the enhancement of environmental quality. A jury chose 10 'model regions' out of more than 200 applications for regional plans. The Regional Marke Eiffel, a region with a high potential for tourism, was developed as the first regional brand in 2003 within this RA competition. The brand stands for quality products and services from agriculture, forestry, crafts and tourism services originating in the Eiffel, such as a large variety of food products, spirits from traditionally managed orchards, wood, heating wood and furniture, as well as services in tourism. Brand users in tourism have to prove a minimum quality classification and are, among others, obliged to offer up to 30 per cent of 'Regional Marke Eiffel' products. The 165 brand users produce 180 products for the cities in the Rhine area. Target groups for the sale of Eiffel products are food retailers and the local gastronomy; some farms also do direct marketing.

An important question remains concerning the role of more 'place-based' types of governance and planning facilitating eco-economic development. Promising changes for an eco-economic development can be created by stimulating horizontal and vertical linkages, leading to new urban-based consumption chains and inter-sector networks. These networks can be strengthened by an overarching regional storyline based on territorial capital, which can mobilize networks of entrepreneurs as well as citizens. Governments can facilitate local agency and entrepreneurial networks and embed these in coherent regional development plans and European programmes.

Eco-economic clusters also require spatial planning mechanisms that include the facilitation of new rural–urban relations. This not only includes rural interfaces and arrangements but also creates space in cities themselves. An example is an integrated rural–urban food strategy developed by several city-regions that can encompass a range of activities such as home gardens, (specialized) food markets, city farming, children's education, and consumer-supported agriculture and 'experience-based' activities such as food fairs.

Conclusions: Exploring and qualifying the new rural development paradigm as the eco-economy

This chapter has, through a brief comparative empirical analysis (see also Horlings and Marsden, 2010, 2014), begun to unpack some of the key developmental processes involved in what has been termed the 'new rural development paradigm' in Europe. This represents, we can argue, an entirely radical break from the dominant modes and framings of the bio-economy discussed in Chapters 2 and 3 so far. It is clear, given the parameters and workings of our dynamic rural 'web model', that while these developments may be seen as significant 'niches' in rural regions, the potential to scale up and out are indeed considerable. Overall, however, as we shall see in the next chapter with reference to two UK cases, they struggle because of the relative lack of consistent state and scientific support. Indeed, we might characterize them as finding their energy and vitality outwith and, indeed in some cases, in opposition to dominant state policies. They are, indeed, as we indicated in the introduction to this chapter, partly characterized as 'quests for autonomy'. They are thus fragile entities and pathways which require constant and multifarious types of encouragement and varied forms of institutional support. Here, a recognition by state authorities of the empowerment of local endogenous knowledge is an important factor outwith and, indeed in some cases, in opposition to dominant state policies.

Vihinen and Kull (2010), for instance, examined the state and policy supporting mechanisms across the European case studies outlined here. Their conclusions point to the need for innovative forms of local, regional, as well as national support for rural web developments. This extends beyond traditional jurisdictional boundaries and sectoral support mechanisms to cover novel forms of institutional and market development support. Encouraging participatory and cooperative working is often crucial. In the Netherlands, for example, utilizing participatory approaches, such as LEADER, has been of fundamental importance. The approaches enable, empower and motivate different actors to move towards shared ideas. In Finland, nationally funded local participatory projects have developed alongside EU LEADER programmes, and the Regional Councils (*Maakunnan Liitto*) and the Employment and Economic Development Centres (*TE_keskus*); located at the regional level are important mediators, functioning as a link between the local and the national levels.

Vihinen and Kull (2010: 208) conclude their comparative analysis of stakeholder and policy workshops across EU member states by emphasizing:

Cooperation among actors from the public sector, private companies and entrepreneurs as well as civil society and their common search for and realisation of goals, clearly have a positive impact on local and regional development policy. Their concerted activities towards fostering the economic situation of their region are also significant. ... Policies do not function in a vacuum. They need the active involvement of endogenous knowledge and rely on it being actively linked across sectors and domains. Contextual endogenous knowledge and expertise is needed in relation to most stages of the policy cycle and not only when it comes to the implementation of rural development policy. At the point of policy formulation, decision making and policy evaluation, bottom-up mechanisms should already be trusted and more extensively relied upon.

We have also witnessed (see Marsden and Sonnino, 2008) that many of these eco-economic developments tend to cluster in those regions which historically have been relatively marginal to the dominant intensive model of agricultural modernization, as practised in the most agriculturally fertile regions of Europe (such as East Anglia in the UK and the Paris Basin in France). We may well, then, be seeing something of a spatial bifurcation occurring with regard to the current processes of the bio-economic and eco-economic framings and practices, whereby the latter, indeed, as we see in the next chapter with regard to Devon and Shetland, tend to cluster in what were regarded as the remoter and 'more peripheral' agricultural regions.

More specifically, however, differentiated eco-economic strategies have been distinguished and shaped along different axes of products and markets that express the variable responses to the conventional cost squeeze in agriculture, agricultural crises and increasing urban demands. The three specific pathways of (niche-) innovation, new interfaces and re-orientation on territorial capital give more specific insights into the dynamic ways in which the governance of markets takes shape within the rural web. Although different strategies are expressed, the cases indicate a gradual shift from an agricultural-based development to a more integrative, place-based approach, including a wider vector of non-agricultural actors. We can postulate the following parameters in understanding these transition processes.

First, regional strategies are rooted in different and competing trajectories, referring to, and expressing, weak and strong notions of ecological modernization. These trajectories express themselves in dynamic bio- and eco-economic patterns of development and shape notions of time, space and place in different ways. Most of the sixty-two cases create new social and economic spaces in which more sustainable actions and practices are given the capacity to develop. However, they continue to face the problem of competition within a market dominated by mass-produced, cheap products and the emergence of the bio-economy, and, therefore, their long-term sustainability is often in potential jeopardy. Yet, in terms of new, more eco-economically based forms of competitiveness, promising pathways of development can be created by combining horizontal and vertical linkages leading to new production–consumption chains and networks. The emerging pathways can potentially function as a counterforce, challenging the dominant but weaker form of ecological modernization.

Second, and as we shall see in the next chapter, the understanding of more integrative rural and regional development requires the use of a dynamic and longitudinal analytical model that shows the interrelated domains of rural eco-economic development and the interactions between the domains (i.e. the rural web). However, we also have to realize that external factors such as counter-urbanization and commuting, climate change and globalization should be also accommodated as influential factors in rural development. One aspect that was not sufficiently built into the earlier rural web model was the influence of the specified driving forces of rural transformation on the domain interrelations. The empirical analysis showed, however, how the continued cost squeeze in agriculture can lead to new eco-economic strategies, which, in turn, influence not only the domain 'governance of markets', but also change the relations between the web domains.

Third, an important parameter of a place-based integrative regional approach is the interconnectedness of cities and with their hinterlands. New urban–rural interfaces, once established, can function as lubricants and new drivers for eco-economic strategies, leading to more multifunctional forms of land use. For example, in regions in Germany and the UK, rural–urban relations in the form of new agricultural rural products and services for urban citizens have emerged, linked to other sectors such as leisure, energy and health. Furthermore, new networks and interfaces have been created, which can, in turn, reinforce the mobilization of the web and its eco-economic development (see OECD, 2013; Horlings and Marsden, 2010).

Finally, we need to explore the contestations that underlie the NRP. The concept of NRP itself is not uncontested: it is situated in the context of weak and strong forms of ecological modernization and the models of bio- and eco-economy. The scientific quest to understand the diversity, context dependency and complexity of its practical expressions and, more ambitiously, its conceptual dynamics, has only just begun. This chapter has attempted to define some consistent and comparative parameters for understanding this complexity, but it has done so by acknowledging that the development of the NRP has to be seen in a context in which bio-economic as well as eco-economic models are being actively progressed.

This raises the question about how control will be exercised over the bio- and eco-economy in different regional contexts as ecological modernization continues to evolve and mutate. This last question is clearly not just a scholarly one, for it also has important implications for, as an example, the development of EU rural and regional policy. This is supposedly becoming more 'place based', and therefore spatially integrative, but it is unclear how it will align itself to the broader, post-carbon demands of EU policies on the one hand, and the relationships with wider regional innovation (largely urban- and polycentric-based) systems on the other. It is not clear, for instance, how many city-regions' ambitions to compete on the international competitiveness agenda will incorporate or contradict the eco-economic developments analysed in this chapter. It can be argued that these current discussions need to be informed by the concepts contained here, especially how a more vibrant eco-economy can be stimulated by forthcoming policies in Europe.

Note

1. http://cordis.europa.eu/result/rcn/49629_en.html

Chapter 5

Evolving webs of agri-food and rural development in the UK: The case of Devon and Shetland

Introduction: Changing places

Noting then the emergence of alternative and re-embedded sets of production chains and networks, we saw in the last chapter how these place-based initiatives can provide new stimuli for scaling out sustainable rural development. They begin to mobilize the rural web, so as to multiply the economic diversity of rural regions. In this way, it is suggested that the relocalization of agri-food plays an important integrative function in the development of what we call rural and regional 'webs' of interconnection (van der Ploeg and Marsden, 2008). In this chapter – the second largely empirical chapter in this book – we focus on two longitudinal studies we have conducted in the rural regions of Devon, England, and Shetland, Scotland. This has involved three phases of place- and network-based longitudinal study, exploring the challenges and continuities in the unfolding of the rural web (see Chapter 4), paying particular attention to the role that agri-food initiatives play in unevenly mobilizing distinctive rural and regional development processes. Crucially, the intervening period since the first phase reported by Marsden (2010), based on data collected in 2007/8, has witnessed wide-scale political, social and economic change under the 2010 administration of the Conservative/Liberal Democrat Coalition government. Drawing on interviews with the same respondents interviewed in 2008 and 2010 (reported in Marsden, 2010; Horlings and Kanemasu, 2015), we find that agri-food plays an increasingly peripheral and marginalized role in rural and regional development across these regions. That is, with state retreat from strategic engagement with rural development, a process of further concentration of resource in urban areas to the potential neglect of more distributed rural services, and a concomitant squeeze on rural – and especially land-based – ways of life and livelihood, making diversifications that were previously considered new novelties move to the fore. Indeed, we might imagine that these novel diversifications were welcomed by the European Commission in its Sixth Framework Programme, given their reformed focus, away from a living countryside underpinned by agricultural activity towards a more integrated rural development strategy focused on 'increased diversification, innovation and value added of products and services, both within and beyond the agricultural sector' (EC, 2005: 32). However, we argue now with some hindsight that trends in this direction raise serious questions for governing transitions towards a more sustainable and food-secure future for the UK, particularly in the context of global environmental challenges associated with climate change and biodiversity loss.

The chapter takes, therefore, a more dynamic and longitudinal approach to rural and agri-food change than Chapter 4, and it begins by outlining the concept of the 'rural web' (Van der Ploeg and Marsden, 2008) by pointing to its continuing utility as a heuristic tool for the longitudinal study of continuity and change in rural and regional development processes. The work started in 2008 and ended in 2014, indeed, spanning the wider FFFF crisis discussed in Chapter 2. We begin by introducing each of the case studies, beginning with an overview of advances and challenges across the Devon Farms Co-operative – a farm tourism network of over twenty-five years – as an example of an initiative pursuing an eco-economic development pathway, before exploring the unfolding rural web in Shetland. Here, the advances of the oil industry and the burgeoning development of wind energy now suggest a more bio-economic rather than eco-economic trajectory. In each case, having interviewed and re-interviewed many of the same key actors over the period, we note a sort of constructed peripherality and marginality of agri-food as a novel and creative industry aligned to the support of tourism. The bio-economic and living countryside is, in both cases, certainly no longer based on agriculture alone, and it would seem that there is a significant lack of direction regarding agri-food and rural development policies. It is one which assumes more responsibility for the land-based actors to develop their own forms of resilience and sustainability, despite the recent alarms made about food security (see Royal Society, Poppy et al., 2014) and House of Commons Environment (2014).

Methods

In 2014 semi-structured re-interviews were conducted with a total of eight members of Devon Farms as well as two key development actors working for the Devon Local Authority. In Shetland, a further seven re-interviews were conducted with farmers, food processors and development actors to include the Local Authority as well as both protagonists and opponents to the proposed Viking Energy wind farm. Guiding this process are key research questions: How is the rural web configured? Have there been any changes since 2010? How is the rural development agenda framed at an institutional level and how is it understood by actors 'on the ground'?

In this way, our methodological approach is both qualitative and longitudinal, pursuing an in-depth understanding of development processes rather than statistical inferences and measurements. Our goal is not to achieve a statistically accurate description or explanation of development processes in each case, but to arrive at a greater and deeper understanding of their complexities. An important part of this pursuit is an ongoing refinement of theoretical devices such as that of the rural web. Quantitative methods such as a questionnaire survey were thus deemed unsuitable for these purposes, while not precluding the potential benefit of more statistically oriented approaches in future research. Indeed, through 're-interview'(Thomson and Holland, 2003) we are able to consider the development of narratives around rural development, food and farming over time as related to a particular locality. During interviews, an aide-memoire guided discussion, leaving considerable freedom for the interviewees/interviewers to digress to capture new insights, issues and themes. All of the interviews were tape-recorded with the interviewees' permission and later transcribed. Questions typically put to interviewees pertained to discussion of changes since 2010 – any opportunities, new novelties or challenges that have arisen. All interviewees were invited to speak of their future development vision for their business as well as their county and region, as a means to garner their insights, hopes and fears for their future.

The rural web: A dynamic analysis of the eco-economy paradox

As we saw in the last chapter, the rural web concept acts as a heuristic tool to highlight the differing responses to the squeeze on rural economies in order to maintain quality of life and some level of sustainability in rural areas at different times and places. This tool suggests that at the heart of each region's response are the intertwined institutions of society and economy of public and private life that draw differently on local resources in interaction with the wider economy, novelty modes and means of production, markets and market governance, the creation of new institutional frameworks, the co-production of sustainable ways of life and, finally, the benefits of social capital. Rural development is thus grounded in and driven by a varied 'set of internally and externally generated interrelationships that shape the relative attractiveness of rural spaces economically, socially, culturally, and environmentally' (van der Ploeg and Marsden, 2008: vii). These sets of relationships and transactions create synergies as they come to mutually reinforce one other. That is, rural development processes are not considered the result of direct policy interventions, but are informed and shaped by the unfolding of these creative patterns that we call the rural web, as illustrated below.

To explore these very rural development processes, we revisit participants, actors and their networks of the 2007–8 and 2010 studies, eliciting accounts of continuity and change, of the private tensions of their 'contested countryside' (Cloke and Little, 1997) as they connect with their milieu and come to form a larger structure of social, political and economic life that is their development pathway. Indeed, reversing C. Wright Mills's (1959) consideration of the city as an example of a private problem and public issue requiring unpicking by the sociological imagination, we consider the structural fact of the rural by examining the political and economic issues that affect innumerable personal and individual milieu – what Mills (ibid.) calls the social setting that is directly open to her or his personal experience. In Devon, we find the rural web unfolding and struggling in ways that are more aptly characterized by eco-economy, which we define as an alternative and diverse spatial arena for the development of new endogenous production and consumption chains and networks. On the other hand, in Shetland there are clear tensions arising over the development future, with a current trajectory set to a pathway characterized by the bio-economic mode, characterized by exogenous development through corporate-controlled production of biological products (fuels, mass, technology, enzymes, genomics) for global markets. In both cases, agri-food initiatives play an increasingly peripheral role, – a new agri-food 'squeeze' – which we suggest will have a calamitous effect on the potential for the UK to secure its sustainable food futures, and for the broader co-evolution of rurality and rural development. The conceptual and policy implications of this new agnosticism to the agricultural and the rural are occurring just at the time that society needs to consider the future sustainable resilience of its rural land-based infrastructures and resources. This paradox is explored in the conclusions to the chapter.

Pathways of development – the struggling eco-economy in Devon

Devon is the third largest county in the UK, sparsely populated by just under 754,000 residents in 2008 (Devon County Council, 2010: 9). Moreover, there is a lower proportion of people of working age compared with the rest of the UK, and a higher proportion of people aged over fifty. Thus, Devon has an ageing population, while the numbers of young people are in decline. The population is concentrated in the south of the county, with urban areas such as Exeter providing home to over 33 per cent of Devon's population, while urban areas in the north of the county account for 11 per cent of the county's population. However, more than half of the population live in rural areas, villages and small towns. Administratively, the landscape of the county is complex, being split into eight districts, 357 parish and town councils with nine parliamentary constituencies. Two national park authorities – Exmoor and Dartmoor – act as planning authorities for protected landscapes. Noting the uniqueness of their economy, Devon County Council (DCC) report that the most significant contribution to the increase in Devon's output between 1998 and 2008 were in industrial sectors – construction (7.8 per cent), distribution (13.7 per cent) and business services (30.4 per cent). These three dominant sectors together contributed some 52 per cent of the increase in total output for the county. The agricultural sector, to include crop and animal production, hunting, forestry, fishing and aquaculture, has the lowest labour productivity in Devon. It is also less productive when compared to the UK, with output at 83 per cent of the national average. This may be partly accounted for by the topography that lends itself best to livestock, dairying and lowland cattle and sheep and upland hill farming, which tends to be more labour intensive. While the outbreak of foot-and-mouth disease in 2001 marked a low-point, the share of output contributed by the agriculture and forestry sectors grew in this period up to 2008, which DCC notes was the result of diversification.

Not only has the growth of the agricultural sector outstripped the overall growth for the Devon economy – increasing its relative share – it has also outstripped the national growth rates. The national economy grew by just 5.4%, the Devon economy grew by 6.2% but the agricultural sector in Devon expanded by 12.5%. In Devon the agricultural sector expanded almost six times faster than the sector nationally (growing by just 2.4%). In the ten years to 2008 agriculture was the fastest growing sector in the Devon economy. As a result the relative contribution made by the agricultural sector almost doubled – from 2% to 3.6%. Whilst agriculture makes an important contribution to the Devon economy in terms of critical natural capital, the sector is the least productive in terms of output per worker. (DCC, 2010: 58)

Moreover, food and drink contributes just 10 per cent of the total manufacturing output (around 1 per cent of total output), a share that DCC report as falling over the ten years to 2008, while DCC report that agriculture in Devon 'contributes *four times more* to output than it does in the national economy' (DCC, 56). With such a decline in agricultural output, alongside an increasing focus on diversifying agricultural output towards value-added products and services, what is the development destiny for rural ways of life? To explore this question, in February/March 2014, we revisited the same members of the Devon Farms Co-operative interviewed across the intervening periods of 2008, 2010 and 2014, asking them to discuss the changes and continuities in the challenges they face operating a farm business, as well as the diversified aspect to their business; farm tourism. This retreat from mainstream agricultural productivism is characterized by the shift towards multifunctionality, extensification and diversification marking a new period for farming that is less well understood.

In 2010

Participation

Devon Farms adopts a notably participatory approach to decision making. The cooperative consists of seven local groups, each of which represents the views and interests of the individual members of the area. All local group representatives inform their members of the main committee meeting agendas and collect their views prior to the meetings. All decisions must be unanimous. For instance, one local group recently decided against organizing the Open Day, an event held for the purpose of attracting new members; and this decision was accepted by the main committee. As for cooperation between individual members, sharing of knowledge and ideas often takes place, while the members also keep marketing channels to themselves due to competition.

Commitment

Devon Farms' ability to mobilize social capital is demonstrated by its members' strong commitment to collective goals despite their diversity and differences:

> I think Devon Farms has worked because of the people, and the commitment of the people. There is a great diversity of farm sizes, types, etc., but the very reason for Devon Farms' existence overcomes that, which is to allow members to work together to market their businesses as a whole. And in doing that, it doesn't matter where you are coming from. What you are trying to do is to achieve that goal.

Human resources

Almost all of Devon Farms' work is carried out voluntarily. There is only one paid secretary, with the committee members paid only to cover their expenses. Consequently, Devon Farms struggles to secure adequate human resources. The current chairperson has accepted the position for the reason that no one else would; the members have less time to devote to the cooperative's tasks. Devon Farms has been driven by a number of committed individuals willing to sacrifice their own time, but this seems to be beginning to present new challenges.

While establishing a full-time staff position may be a possibility, the membership is not large enough to cover such costs. In addition, our respondents observed that such a move may lead to a division between paid and unpaid members, leading to a loss of the sense of collective ownership: 'Then it would lose the input of its members; that is how Devon Farms has developed. It is always listening to its members. If you have someone who is in control, who is paid, they are going to make the decisions. The Devon Farms members think they are the bosses.'

Social networks and support

Devon Farms does not only function as a marketing tool but also strengthens social capital. A purely rational, economic motive is balanced by a willingness to sacrifice time and to give each other social, not just economic, help: 'Some local groups have a lot of social activities. For instance, one member has lamas on her farms, and the others are visiting her to see her farm. There are such events once or twice a year. This helps to get to know new members. Some groups do Christmas meals, summer outings, etc.'

Devon Farms' function as a social network benefits not only the cooperative as a whole but also the individual businesses:

> You do networking, you share your problems, especially during the FMD. You can come and talk to other people, find out what others' experiences are. It is a social network as well as a financial one. You are talking to people with a similar background, you have the same objectives, so you share your experiences. If you can't help someone with a booking you pass it on to another member.

The members visit each other's farms, share their challenges, exchange new ideas and support each other, based on trust. As noted earlier, Devon Farms organizes events/training for members (cooking, writing adverts, web training, etc.) and social events, all of which facilitate such bonding between the members.

There also seems to be a link with community support. Those who are active in Devon Farms tend to be active members of their local community as well. Social networks become more important when viable farming has become more difficult and farmers have fewer opportunities to interact with each other: 'We have a decline of (livestock) markets in this county, so people don't take their livestock to meet people. You don't have the social network that you did 25–30 years ago. It is important that you hold on to some of these organisations because of the support it gives to people, when times are bad.'

What was not identified in our previous studies were the differences among Devon Farms' local groups. Some play more significant social roles than others. There are also individual differences: to some members Devon Farms is a social space where friendships as well as professional contacts are cultivated, while others see it merely as a business relation: 'For some members, joining Devon Farms is purely for advertising and they don't gain much. However, for others, it is also about networking and development. If one member encounters a bad customer, their experience can help the others who might have similar situations in the future.'

Gender

Devon Farms was originally run almost entirely by women. However, as farm-based tourism has become economically more viable, more men have become involved in the cooperative. About a third of the main committee is now male:

> There are quite a few men involved now, originally it was all women. Tourism was thought of as a bit of pin-money for the wife. It wasn't considered as important, but now it has become really important. A lot of farms are actually running because they get the extra money from tourism. Tourism on the farm has expanded a lot, and men are accepting that and are becoming more involved.

Yet women remain in charge of Devon Farms. The cooperation between members has a gender-related aspect in that women are generally considered to be better skilled at cooperation. According to some respondents: 'Women will work often closely together to achieve this sort of objectives. Males are somewhat insular and don't have that type of social networking. It is not in their make-up, being a man. Whereas the female side has more flexibility; it is in the nature of their person to work together.' The social aspect of networking is also more important for women than for men. A respondent observed that women share business information with others more willingly: 'Women share more easily than men. NFU, in comparison, is dominated by men. They are very reluctant to share where they sell their beef cattle, milk, whatever, which in Devon Farms, we don't find.'

Skills development

Another important characteristic of Devon Farms is the manner in which the committee members and, particularly, the chairperson have cultivated necessary skills. Building up confidence, empowerment and developing skills such as public speaking are all benefits of being part of Devon Farms. This was especially important in the early days when farmers' wives had less formal education and training than today. The group has been able to 'nurture' members with lower-standard accommodation, stimulating them to become more professional.

Integration of 'incomers'

Among Devon Farms' strengths is their ability to encompass and integrate a diversity of members in a pragmatic way: 'They are going to be there anyway, operating. It's better to have these people join your group and channel them to the way of thinking and bring their ideas into the group and share business than be in competition.' There is great diversity among the members, in terms of the size of their tourism businesses, the nature of the tourism activities they provide and the scale of their farms. However, any potential tension caused by such differences is overcome by the collective marketing goals: 'We have the whole range from 5 acres till 600 acres. But they don't have different interests in terms of tourism. They get together and do what it takes. The chairman with more 60 acres is keen on getting tourists, as someone with 5 acres would. It doesn't matter, the objectives are the same.'

Over the last ten years, the number of 'incomer' members has increased, resulting in a greater mix of famers from different backgrounds. The tension between 'traditional' farmer and ex-urban 'incomers', which had been reported in the last report, seems to be more or less overcome in the last few years: 'People coming in from other professions, which is what brings us up to speed, because they know what is going to be the next thing. Like, we're doing on-line booking. That's going to be quite exciting.' Some traditional farmers seem to be somewhat cynical about the farming skills and experience of the incomers and feel that they should not take over Devon Farms. But they also realize that these members have more time to commit to Devon Farms, which is beneficial to the cooperative. The general feeling is that incomers contribute to the variety of services and offer new useful skills, such as internet skills: 'You need "outside blood" so you know what the visitors want. Farmers' wives have always lived on the farm, so they see things from the farmers' perspectives and don't necessarily know what visitors want. That's where incomers really help us.' In a broader sense, the integration of incomers into Devon Farms contributes to an amalgam of agri-ruralist views of traditional farmers and more post-productive views of incomers.

A challenge to the future cohesion of the cooperative is the question of 'working farms'. There is ongoing discussion as to whether businesses without a 'real' working farm should become members of Devon Farms. The current situation is that the cooperative devolves the decision to individual local groups, but this could change in the future when Devon Farmers needs more members to cover their costs:

> We have had a few people who wanted to join Devon Farms but who were not really farming. They might have a country house, with 2 acres and a few chickens, but then you have to decide they can't join, because we are selling our organisation as a stay on a farm, these are our criteria. It is up to the local groups to decide.

Governance of markets

The history of Devon Farms indicates positive developments in the domain of governance of markets. The cooperative initially developed out of the ten farm holiday groups which were operating under the umbrella organization Farm Holiday Bureau, now Farm Stay UK. The members at the time felt that county-level marketing was the most appropriate approach, as visitors were usually not able to distinguish between parts of Devon but would know where Devon was. Added to this was the need to achieve economies of scale. With a collective pool of money, the members were able to produce a better-quality, more professional and coloured brochure to be provided to tourist information centres. The members also wanted to produce a free tourist brochure to replace the 'Stay on a Farm' booklet which was sold for £6 and was perceived to be out-dated. The neighbouring county of Cornwall, with access to much European funding, was producing brochure in colour, and the members felt that Devon needed to keep up. The formation of Devon Farms also helped spread bookings, which shows a sense of solidarity between the members. 'Some areas were getting a lot of bookings and others hardly any. It helped to spread that trade to areas which weren't that well positioned in the county. It became a marketing tool.'

In Devon as a whole, farm tourism is of great economic importance today. It plays a synergistic eco-economic role with farming. For instance, one of the member farms has 120 acres, yet would not survive without the B&B business. For others, agriculture remains the most important source of income, but in general, the two businesses are economically intertwined: 'One sits on the other really. One without the other wouldn't work. People are interested in the animals. Without that we would have to market the accommodation in a different way. One rides on the other. And also without tourism we couldn't cope with another family here, with only agriculture.'

There are large differences among the individual farms. Some attract a lot of repeating visitors, while others 'who started farm tourism years ago, now face more difficulties in tourism but have to keep doing it'. Some incomers seem to be doing very well in attracting visitors by offering novel 'farm experiences', such as hands-on experiences with a variety of rare animals, farm education and workshops. Farm tourism is a durable economic strategy in Devon which is, together with Cornwall, the most important holiday destination for UK visitors. Farm tourism is also a unique product; individual farms can distinguish themselves from others and offer a large variety of products and services. Some Devon Farms members use the services of booking agencies, but most undertake all work themselves: 'We left English Country Cottages, a big farm tourism company, as soon as we could because they charged a 25% commission on the deals plus other costs. We were also not allowed to turn down bookings.'

Devon Farms is not the only farm tourism organization in Devon, but it displays some unique and novel characteristics such as low costs, cooperation, individual freedom and voluntary work. Its marketing strategy is to attract a large variety of visitors. Some members also try to extend the season by attracting couples outside the traditional holiday period. There is, however, scope for improving the existing marketing strategy. One respondent observed, for instance, that B&B businesses should charge more at peak times: 'They now have fixed prices throughout the year. They need to market themselves better.' One of the questions that Devon Farms is currently trying to resolve is the type of marketing tool to be employed by the members; for example, whether the cooperative should concentrate on printed brochures, online marketing or both. While its website is operating successfully, Devon Farms faces the challenge of improving the quality of its brochures.

There is also an ongoing debate over the new online booking system. Many members feel that it is important for them to be 'in charge' of their bookings, and not hand them over to an electronic system or an agency. Upon the introduction of the online system, however, many B&Bs accustomed to telephone bookings will need to adjust their routines. Online booking is expected to present some challenges as it will take away some of the personal contact associated with more traditional booking methods, such as opportunities to inform visitors in advance of what may be expected from a stay on a farm: 'You have to give visitors information: farms smell, its noisy etc. You have to get across that it is a working farm.' Participation in online booking is entirely voluntary. Members can choose whether to use the facility or not. Operation and collective pooling of skills and resources may facilitate this process.

Endogeneity

Farm tourism is in itself an endogenous development initiative insofar as it mobilizes, redefines and reconfigures local resources in ways that enhance the livelihoods of participating farms and their control of these resources. Farm tourism, as developed by Devon Farms, also indicates another defining characteristic of endogeneity: it is organized according to local models of resource combination. The cooperative has embraced and incorporated Devon's long-established local/ organic food culture. For many B&B members, for instance, farmhouse breakfast (and occasionally evening meals) alongside the physical/environmental assets of the farm and the locale, is the crucial selling point.

To many Devon Farms members, farm tourism also crystallizes their sense of connectedness with the land. Some traditional farmers have lived on their farms for decades and generations. At times religious feelings may also play a part:

> You farm with nature and you treat everything as you want to be treated. I am not a religious fanatic, but it is just part of my life. ... If I get out for a walk and see all God's wonderful creatures, there has got to be a purpose. I have often said, when I come here, I leave my mark. You can leave it better, you look after it as well as possible and perhaps leave it for the next generation.

There is also a new trend of visitors showing interest in experiencing traditional skills connected to the land, such as making home-made products, gardening and cooking with local products. At a time when more people face uncertainties, economic crises and fast (technological) development, there is a need for a sense of belonging. As one respondent pointed out:

> Maybe technology is too fast, and they don't have their roots, but they want to come back and find their roots again. They want stability and comfort and maybe it is the feeling that we are in this economic recession; people want to have 'the food that granny used to make', it is comfort, things that make you feel good and warm and secure, all these factors. [Contemporary life] is an emotional rollercoaster. ... The world is so fast that we don't belong anymore.

Agri-environmental subsidies have allowed some farmers to reconvert some parts of their farm assets to the late-nineteenth-century structures, which strengthens the link between endogeneity and sustainability: 'We created a new orchard, looked at the maps of 1880. Where there was small woodland, we cleared it and fenced it off, replanted it and fenced some fields that have gone amalgamated; we have gone back to where they were in 1880 and put on fences. Those areas we graze with native breeds.'

Sustainability

The success of Devon Farms represents the explicit interweaving of sustainable and eco-economic motives. Promotion of renewable energy, for example, is encouraged by public-relations-related motivations and used as a marketing tool. Devon Farms 'gently' encourages members to work more sustainably, by giving tips on such initiatives as the use of photovoltaic cells, which also provides a financial pay-back: 'We don't push it. There is nothing more irritating as to tell a farmer he should be green, because he is as green as you can get. He recycles everything. But what we do is give examples – Green Tips.'

The more traditional farmers, who did not go the route of intensification and specialization, tend to shift towards more sustainable agriculture, encouraged by agri-environmental schemes, which also has the effect of decreasing potential differences between them and incomers: 'Even the most traditional farmers appreciate how important the landscape is. They have been attracted to an entry level scheme, payments you get for basic things for the environment. Farmers have joined that as a bit of extra income. So this has slowly brought things around to a fairly common view point as well.'

Incomers seem to have a special interest in sustainable agriculture by, for example, contributing to biodiversity, using less inputs, restoring the landscape or producing special breeds or varieties. One respondent describes it as: 'Farming the land that is available to you in such a way that you are able to continue to undertake farming without resources being drained so that your inputs and outputs are equal.'

Novelty

Devon Farms tries to keep abreast of the latest developments in tourism by using a website for marketing, developing an online booking system and updating its brochures. The novelties focus more on collective aspects, which means improvement of the joint marketing strategy than on tourism innovation on the level of individual businesses, which is considered the responsibility of the entrepreneurs themselves.

As discussed earlier, many new (and some old) members have developed new *experiences* for guests, and there are ample examples to attest to this. One incomer has developed a visitor centre that facilitates educational visits such as school visits by children with learning disabilities. Another tries to educate visitors by taking them out to the farm and talking to them about the 'realities of farming, sheep breeds, government agricultural policy, how to cook meat', as part of their effort to re-establish the connection between people and farms. One of the old members turned a part of their land into woodland and developed a farm walk. A young member intends to provide nature education for children, give bird-fly demonstrations, courses for pig keepers, knitting and natural dying workshops, etc.

There is further scope for novelty production, such as the development of new activity packages, and especially cross-sector activities that respond to the retro trend where (young urban) visitors may learn traditional farm-related skills such as jam making and cream making, bread baking, knitting, traditional cooking and gardening. Traditional farmers' wives in particular possess many of such skills, which they are not often aware of, yet which can be marketed and packaged into new tourist products. 'We could do workshops, we could extend our seasons, get more people. I had a group of ladies in their thirties in my self-catering; they just wanted to knit in the weekend. They love the wool shop here. They got inspiration from colours of the countryside. We could do more, we are missing something here.'

Novelty production is thus linked to endogeneity, in that both involve a creative recombination of territorial resources, farm activities and land use. However, the potential of these new connections has not been fully developed to date, and a lack of local labour seems to be an ongoing constraint.

Institutional arrangements

Devon Farms does not have a consistent working relationship with Visit Devon or the DCC, and has little contact with farming unions, although individual members may be actively involved with organizations such as the NFU. This is partly explained by the fact that the cooperative does not aim to become a political organization. Its prime objective is for farmers to get together to market their businesses and to influence legislation, regulations, grant schemes, which impact on the members' businesses (such as the EU tax legislation that treats cottages as taxable investments). Individual members participate in different networks; for example, one member participates in the Council of Rare Breeds Survival Trust; another is actively involved in Uplands Farming Group of Dartmoor NFU and in the Moor Skills Project whose aim is to educate the next generation of farmers about the skills of Dartmoor farming.

Several members expressed concern over the bureaucracy of the public sector and the amount of 'red tape' that interferes with their businesses. Examples include the requirement for sheep tagging, which could cause infection when the tags are ripped off by bushes, and the increasing hygiene and safety regulation, which restricts on-farm activities such as the production of home-made cream: '25 years ago, all the farms made their own cream and sold it to the neighbours in the village. But you are not allowed to do that unless it is all tested and inspected. It makes it hard, it is overregulated and then it dies.' The planning restrictions for new rural development are also perceived to be too strict: 'The restrictions on land and building use have been tough really. It is very restrictive. It needs to be reviewed in some ways to help the sustainability of the countryside.'

Devon Farms has received minimal assistance, financial or otherwise, from outside bodies to date. Grants for new tourism activities have recently been discontinued in Devon, and, consequently, there is no public funding to assist organizations such as Devon Farms. Individual members may receive assistance from different farming organizations such as the NFU, but this has not happened at the cooperative level. Our respondents observed that tourism is not a priority on the DCC's current development agenda. Visit Devon, for instance, encountered a number of operational and organizational problems, which eventually saw the departure of the former chief executive. Devon Farms members feel 'let down' by such lack of public/statutory support in Devon, especially in comparison to other rural areas such as Cornwall and Wales where greater support for farm tourism initiatives is available: 'Devon seems to miss out. I don't know why. We've had Foot and Mouth; we've had all sorts of problems. We just seem to miss out on a lot of funding. ... We try, but we don't seem to get support from the public sector at all.'

Devon Farms and the mobilization and 'turning' of the rural web by 2014

In the follow-up research it has become apparent that in the last few years Devon Farms has experienced a number of developments which has led to strengthening of some rural development dimensions and weakening of the others. This has caused some change to the dynamics of the emerging rural web, as explained below.

The relationship between endogeneity and sustainability

As noted earlier, farm tourism as operated and envisioned by Devon Farms is not only a market governance initiative but an explicit endogenous development strategy for farmers to counter external forces and to achieve and assemble greater control of their place-based resources and circumstances (Kanemasu et al., 2008). In this context, the relationship between endogeneity and sustainability has been strengthened by European agri-environmental schemes, an increased focus on local food, the existence of planning regulations which protect the landscape, and a variety of measures to promote green tourism. The branding communication strategy discussed earlier is, though, not sufficiently specific or coherent with this development trajectory.

Rural–urban relationships

Devon's many and diverse 'deepening' activities (to enlarge value added though alternative food networks) and 'broadening' activities (to pursue multifunctional rural enterprises through farm tourism) present significant scope for reshaping rural–urban relationships (see Kanemasu et al., 2008). By 2014, we found that the continuing influx of incomers (especially from urban areas) as well as the return of farmers' children with experience of working and living in urban areas, presented a notable potential for the development of innovative services and products to meet urban demands such as education, workshops or nature walks, which potentially strengthen rural–urban relations. Tourists were coming from further afield, with more specific time and niche demands, and were expecting to view the full countryside 'offer' online before they became committed. That offer was becoming more place-differentiated and, indeed, more demanding.

The relationship between social capital and institutional arrangements

There have been a number of developments in the recent years that have impacted on the scope and effectiveness of public–private cooperation. As a result of the recent change in the Local Authority's approach towards development initiatives – giving a stronger emphasis to urban-based economic development initiatives in concentrated locations – and a large budget deficit (austerity), policy support for rural networks such as the Devon Rural Network and the Devon Food and Drink group has been considerably down-sized and centralized. This seems to have undermined the possibilities for public–private coordination, and it has become more difficult for development actors to influence policy through such networks. Cross-sectoral cooperation, which could potentially benefit from regional networks of entrepreneurs, is also hampered by these recent developments. In addition, public grants for new tourism activities have been recently discontinued in Devon. These relatively small levels of distributed resource were often critical for seed-corn rural development initiatives. Consequently, farm tourism initiatives like Devon Farms face a difficult situation where no substantial public/statutory support is available to them.

The relationship between socio-economical conditions, eco-economical developments, institutional arrangements and competitiveness

As a result of the changing and intensifying international market conditions for food, the continued cost-price squeeze on agriculture (especially dairy and beef), and the continuous upscaling trend in conventional farming, food processing and distribution, Devon Farms members face some intense challenges in maintaining their competitiveness. On the one hand, the current socio-economic conditions favour large-scale commercial farming, and as noted above, the arrival of newcomers also contributes to the upscaling trend through selling or letting parts of their farmland to commercial farmers. On the other hand, the development of rural services, multifunctional land use and small-scale sustainable investments may favour a more eco-economical trajectory. Such a development trajectory is strengthened in Devon by institutional arrangements such as agri-environmental schemes and grants for diversification and green tourism promotion. Increasing urban demands for recreation, local food and organic products may also reinforce this trajectory, although the current economical crisis has negatively impacted on these demands.

In conditions where the maintenance of working farms becomes critical as a basic foundation for a more diversified eco-economical farm tourism business enterprise, the working farm comes more under threat due to the stringencies of ever more concentrated agricultural and agri-food markets. In this sense we need to recognize that successful forms of multifunctional agriculture rely upon the construction of relatively stabilized and, indeed, state-supported bio-economic markets, both in the food and wider socio-natural realms. Hence, the future direction of agricultural policies holds a potentially profound effect upon wider potentials for the multifunctional rural eco-economy, especially in the less intensively farmed parts of upland Britain.

The relationship between social capital, leadership, novelty and market governance

As we have seen, the active and ongoing cooperation among Devon Farms members has stimulated the development of new marketing tools such as online booking. While the scope for novelty production has not been fully explored to date due to a lack of labour, Devon Farms may mobilize its wealth of social capital to stimulate the exchange of ideas among members and to facilitate cooperation and training, which could in turn strengthen the cooperative's capacity for novelty production. Opportunities lie in the development of new 'farm experience packages' and cross-sectoral product–market combinations which can add value to farms, such as craftsmanship workshops, nature and landscape exploration, and activities in health and well-being. Devon Farms enjoys effective leadership, which may be usefully employed to accelerate this process through agenda-setting, development of new skills (with provision of specific training) or promotion of study visits to innovative farms.

Future threats and challenges

Devon Farms faces some future threats and challenges:

- *Maximizing the use of digital and related technology* is a key challenge to some Devon Farms members who are accustomed to more traditional methods of communication and administration. Devon Farms has begun to address this with the development of the online booking system.

- *Animal diseases and infections* may undermine farm tourism. One respondent mentioned, for instance, that educational activities for children had been put on hold because of an e-coli outbreak. The issue of TB spread via wandering badgers has also caused some tension between environmental organizations and some farmers.

- *Membership maintenance* may present a challenge in the coming years, given that not many young people are coming into the business while many current operators are expected to retire in the next 10–20 years. This creates problems of securing successors, despite some cases of farmers' children returning to and taking over their parents' businesses after working in a professional field for a number of years. Devon Farms could provide 'mentoring' to these young people where skills and experiences can be shared. Given the financial implications of membership, the cooperative may also need to explore a way of reconsidering the membership criteria without losing its unique identity.

- *Labour shortage* is a significant challenge which could have a large impact on the future of farm tourism. Most Devon Farms members juggle multiple tasks, working long hours to attend to care work (caring for children, older parents, etc.), farming, administration, household chores and community activities in addition to running their tourism businesses. This impedes the possibilities for developing new activities:

> Even with my daughter on the farm, we still have too less time to do the things we want to do. ... What we do is 24 hours a day, 365 days a year. We don't go off on weekends and holidays. It is a life style. That's what you are used to and what you have been brought up to do.

Given the *labour-extensive* nature of many farm tourism businesses (especially B&Bs), a likely future trend is a shift towards more incomers than traditional farmers taking up farm tourism, combined with a small-holding:

> B&B compared to self-catering is more labour-intensive, so it may not be an option for farmers' wives in the future. If children of farmers do return, it will be a matter of necessity rather than choice. But incomers will carry on farm tourism. Smaller scale farms will be sold off – farmland will be integrated into larger farms whereas farm buildings will be sold to incomers. In this sense, farm tourism as a traditional farmers' wives business will not remain in the future. Farm tourism will therefore become a business for smaller-scale, new farmers rather than traditional farmers.

- With the number of incomers steadily increasing within Devon Farms, it will be important for the cooperative to continue to cultivate the members' *skills* to draw heterogeneous interests and agendas together under a single umbrella (i.e. to draw traditional farmers and incomers together) to fully overcome the dangers of a 'contested countryside'. A key strength of Devon Farms is the unique and high-quality products and services that its members offer (e.g. home-cooked food, landscape, accommodation). This follow-up study found, for instance, that a member won an award for excellence in breakfast, and another member a farming magazine's award for the Most Beautiful Farm in the south west.

One of the key future challenges is to sustain this high-quality standard. At present Devon Farms does not have its own quality control system:

> Each group goes to visit farms, but we don't grade them. The visits are for new members coming in. The secretary will visit a new member and take on board the welcome they have, their ambiance, their approach, and check that it is a farm. And check that they have a grading. If they are not sure about something they have to discuss it at group level and get the majority vote.

In order to become a member, a business must be a member of one of Devon Farms recognized local farm holiday groups, be inspected by either Quality in Tourism or the AA, and operate accommodations on a farm with a source of income from agriculture (although this last criterion has been relaxed somewhat lately). The absence of an independent quality control mechanism is an area that Devon Farms may investigate further.

Devon Farms by 2014: Continuities and vulnerabilities

In March 2014, the Devon Farms Co-operative of 110 farms providing bed and breakfast as well as self-catering accommodation to visitors, celebrated their twenty-fifth anniversary. Over this period they have supported each other to develop the diversified aspect of the farm business, not least, advertising and promoting themselves as one cooperative. While they comprise separate businesses, the farm and the accommodation components complement each other in providing a unique landscape and experience for visitors, while the generated income relieves pressure on farm productivity and the widely noted 'cost-price squeeze' explored by Horlings and Marsden (2011), Darnhofer (2005) and van der Ploeg (2000). Indeed, the story of Devon Farms speaks to the persistence of a business form that has largely disappeared elsewhere (Whatmore et al., 1987), that is, the combining of family ownership of assets with managerial control as an institutional unit. Indeed, while Lobley and Potter (2004) find in their survey of agricultural households in England that the economic centrality of agriculture for the family farm business had declined, we also suggest that Devon Farms offers an example of the collective reconfiguration of the farm business towards an eco-economical form of endogenous adjustment and development to the cost squeeze in agriculture, echoing what has been termed the new rural development paradigm in Europe (Horlings and Marsden, 2012).

Indeed, Evans and Ilbery (1989) devise a conceptual framework for the investigation of farm-based accommodation and tourism in Britain, using a political economy perspective as advocated by Marsden (1984) that interrogates the interactions between market and family relations that coalesce around the family farm. Here, external institutions shape farm investment through the supply of capital for the development of farm tourism accommodation; from high street banks and heritage organizations to direct government influence in the form of grant aid for the establishment of alternative enterprise. Furthermore, the internal farm environment demands diversified activity to boost family income and farm profitability. As the external capitalist environments pressure the internal farm environment to restructure, Evans and Ilbery (ibid.) argue that a diversification to farm accommodation may not necessarily reduce reliance upon external capitals, but in some ways deepens this relation of dependence through loss of control over business assets and management rights. Here, they also note the emergence of farm-based accommodation and tourism as an important phenomenon for agricultural restructuring, one that received little serious attention, scholarly or otherwise. While this has somewhat been redressed by further studies in advertising (Evans and Ilbery, 1992a), marketing (Clarke, 1999) and in communication (Clarke, 1996), further work by Evans and Ilbery (1992b) has returned to the conceptual framework outlined above, arguing that outside organizations are increasingly involved with farm-based accommodation, thus facilitating the penetration of agriculture by private and public capitals.

These trends mark commentary on the resilience of the family run farm businesses, one that we seek to develop by means of revisiting the conceptual framework of the 'rural web'. This section now draws upon the experience of a number of respondents as related to the thematic categories derived from the analysis of each interview. We focus here on a common thread that permeates each narrative: (i) the growing economic centrality of the tourism aspect of the farm business, (ii) the travails of meeting the demands of a shift towards the novelty-driven customer-facing service sector, and (iii) the perceived and real retreat of the state from the support of family farming agriculture as a mode of commodity production. These shifts, when taken together, we argue, represent a devalorization of food and food production as a centrifugal force in rural economies that will serve to undermine the balance of a sustainable rural web of interconnections now and in the future.

Novelty as economic centrality in diversified family farming

Speaking of the bookings that returning customers make annually, Jan (pseudonym) reflects upon the intertwining and co-production of the farm and service aspects of the farm business. Crucial to note here is that the agricultural aspect is not only called into question in the first instance in terms of its profit-making potential, but is considered only in terms of its capacity to generate income and profit for the tourism aspect. Agriculture is *itself* the value added.

> For instance, Easter is fully booked and has been, well, apart from the fact that the schools have messed up and they're going back Easter week this year, but the two weeks before Easter, the school holidays if you like, have been booked for a year, because people book before they leave, because they want their children to experience lambing. So therefore from a research point of view, or a cost analysis thing, how do you work out how important the sheep are? Is that profitability for the sheep, or is that profitability for the cottages? And inevitably, it's very interlinked.
>
> Jan: X acres, livestock

Indeed, Jan and her husband began as dairy farmers, working with 100 acres of land. Recognizing the somewhat limited capacity for productivity with this size of farm – 'It's going to make you money but you're not going to live on it' – Jan developed the cottages for farm-stays. The cottage business then became 'absolutely key in providing our family with an income', which was not necessarily noted at the time as being quite so central to the business. Rather, farming 'was the most important thing', and the cottages were considered a bonus, as a little 'pin-money for the wife'. Noting a considerable shift in emphasis since what she describes as the 'most amazing agricultural downturn', Jan says:

> Those bits of cottages on the side were probably the only things making any money on a lot of farms, and certainly hugely important in the farm income, and that has changed the way that women have run them, because I think women if you like, I think I'm being very rude and very categorising, but I think women went from something they did and, you know, the husbands were pleased that they did it and it was quite nice and everything – to actually realising how important it was, and also when really it didn't particularly matter if they sold 20 weeks or 22 or 18 or 30, then suddenly it really did matter, so those women became much more professional in what they wanted to achieve, because they needed this business to make money, because it was a key part of the farm, and as such was being respected as such by the farmers.
>
> Jan: X acres, livestock.

The professionalization of service provision on Devon Farms thus also points towards an often underappreciated and less well understood aspect of the farm business as an ecological entrepreneurship – the contributions made by women (Gasson and Errington, 1993). While many women are not perceived to consider themselves entrepreneurs, and, as noted by Little (2002), are therefore less likely to apply for Local Authority grants to support the development of their business endeavours. Indeed, with the shift from government to governance, the sorts of project funded at local partnership levels tend to focus on masculine interpretations of development centred upon the 'bricks and mortar' projects with literal concrete outputs, rather than those focused around community development. This is not to even mention the competitive and corporate-style application, a process found to be unfamiliar and typically uncomfortable for women. It seems worthy to point towards the benefits of the eco-economical trajectory of endogenous development that has brought recognition, professionalization empowerment for women who begin to see centrality of their contribution to the business as more than a fringe activity. Another participant had this to say:

> I mean, there's a long way to go for all of us [women], in various – you know, we all have our different strengths, but I would say over the fourteen years, I've seen a lot of people realise that they are actually running a successful

business, and that it is a business, it's not pin money, it's not something you do on the side, it's integral to the business of the farm.

Jan: X acres, livestock

Moreover, interviewing husband and wife farmers, Ron and Joan, they go further in emphasizing the economic centrality of the tourism aspect of the farm business. Crucially, it is the farm that provides the building block for the success of the tourism business:

> R: And I think lots of the men farmers have realised that their wife's got a lot of input into their farm industry combining them both. The farm might have been struggling and then suddenly they've got these barns that they've converted and two things; the value of the farm's gone up because they've got not just a shitty old barn, they've got another house sort of thing and it's supplemented the income without using up any land in a way. So we've never really relied on the land as income. It's been more what I call an attraction, that's why we've got the sheep and so the guests can see it. We did have outdoor pigs and that's why we put in the woodland, 40 acres of woodland, and that was all to –
>
> J: Make it more attractive for our visitors.
>
> Ron and Joan: X acres

Developing further this narrative of economic centrality of the diversified aspects of the farm business is the growing sense that the family business and its resilience as a whole suffers, still, from the widely recognized problem of succession (Gasson and Errington, 1993).

> How are you going to get the next generation in? Which you know, if you're doing agricultural things, you'll know. The trouble with these businesses, they're so capital-intense. My husband and I are both in our middle fifties. This business is very profitable, it's a nice business, it's a lovely place to live and all the rest of it. There's not room for one of our children here. We have three children. We employ, effectively, we did a study the other day on it, we worked it all out – we effectively employ one full-time person, by the time we've contracted out the cleaning and painting, you know, you have a contractor to come and bale the hay or a contractor to cut the hedges or whatever it might be. If you add up all the hours of people that help us run the business, it's almost one full-time person. Well, it probably is one full-time person. Probably 50, 60% of that on minimum wage. Well, our children don't want to work for minimum wage! (Laughter). Well, you know, they don't. I mean, they're all university-educated. Ruby, get down! It's a shame, isn't it? So, I mean, although this business has

made us a good living and has brought up three children and helped them through uni and all the rest of it and we're making a nice living, it requires us both to work full-time and there's no way that any of our children could carry it on, which is a challenge, isn't it, if you like, in the rural community?

James: X acres, livestock

Indeed, these challenges are exacerbated by those of meeting the demands now of a service industry defined and led by consumer demands for services to be delivered at digital pace. Speaking not only of the shift to online booking, the use of card payment terminals and the provision of wireless internet, there is also the growing sense of demand for high-spec fittings, furnishings and decoration;

From our business perspective it's how I keep abreast of everything, and how you have the energy to keep abreast as well, because I think that not only have you got the changing electronic market, I think people's expectations have massively changed over the last fourteen years. When I was a child, we used to go on holiday to a holiday cottage, and you were delighted that you were away, and whoever owned the cottage, it was all great-granny's old furniture and it was all mix and match and it was just chaos, but that was fine. And then it became that that was completely unacceptable, and now it's really ... better than home, almost. It's meeting that balance of not going down the iPad route, but providing them with access. ... Because if you just say, 'Well, this has been good enough for all our guests up until now', you'll drift backwards, and I don't want to drift backwards, but sometimes I don't like to be dragged forward!

Jan: X acres, livestock

Meeting more specific and novel customer demand is similarly a struggle for Lynne and Catherine, whose farm cottages undergo continuous refurbishment and investment. Painting, updating bathroom suites and increasing access to digital services through the provision of wireless internet and flat-screen televisions are but only the beginning in the potential for the growth of the farm tourism business. Indeed, they find a market for the provision of childcare on the farm, corporate retreats and team-building trips as well as cooking holidays for groups of friends and families celebrating holidays and special events such as birthdays and anniversaries. Indeed, catering to these events requires further investment in specialist cooking equipment as requested by customers, time to be spent in party planning and decorating, all of which they provide without increasing prices, in fear of the loss of custom. This, we argue, represents a second squeeze upon the diversified resource of the family farm:

L: We're finding that people are asking more and more and more and we don't quite know how we need to package it or. … Because, you know, it's spending more time doing it but 'Oh yeah, course we'll dress it', but then that's taking you …

C: Well that's right, we had find somebody who makes gluten free cakes, that was the last one, birthday cake, we had to find those sorts of things.

L: We were thinking about what to do because this is ridiculous that we spend all these hours …

C: But it's hard because somebody just asks you, 'Could you hang up some balloons?' Well, yeah, I could really. But course then it's, 'Can you do the balloons and can you find me someone who and can you …?' and then it adds up. But is that the best way, though, because of the experience, is that the best way to optimise a second booking? You know. The experience will far exceed by me hanging up some balloons than it would to be petty and charging £5 for hanging up some balloons.

Lynne and Catherine: X acres, livestock

Trepidation over raising prices to cover the cost of inputs to the farm tourism business is not unique to Lynne and Catherine. Indeed, this sentiment resounds across interviews with each of the participants revisited in this round of study, with concern expressed over the potential loss of custom if one was to charge for an evening meal, charging a premium for local and farm produce sold directly to farm stayers, to reflect the costs of refurbishing converted farm buildings to such high specifications, or simply raising prices to cover the costs of services now charged to individual businesses such as recycling and rubbish collection.

I think more people are more aware of being customer driven, rather than, 'I've got a nice house and if you don't like it, well that's up to you.' Now it's actually, more people are saying, 'Okay, if you don't like my house like this or you want me to put in whatever, or you want me to provide meals or get the shopping in for you, of course we will,' sort of attitude, I think.

Jan, X acres, livestock

This customer-driven focus, we can argue, represents an added form of self-exploitation that has been widely noted as unique to the family farm business. Here, individuals may be more exposed to exploitation within the privacy of their own family business than anywhere else in the economy. Indeed, while the flexibility of primarily family-owned and family-operated farm businesses afford the weathering of hard times better than other business models typical of the wider economy, farm tourism adds a further string to this bow of resilience. However, the further restructuring of the agricultural business towards the provision of not only accommodation, but the tourism services associated with entertaining, add a further labour burden, without immediate remuneration, thus complicating the strong vision of leadership presented by Horlings and Padt (2013) in their comparative analysis of farm diversification initiatives across Europe. That is, while the additional labour associated with entertaining is treated as a trade-off for the long-term profitability of the business, or as a benefit to be repaid through inheritance of the farm business in the longer-term future, without the concomitant rise on price charged to the customer, this restructured farm business is figured, we argue, in a further exploitative relation that adds to the devalorization of agriculture, rural ways of life and the services and benefits that can be derived from it.

Crucially, this cost-price squeeze on the tourist service aspect of the farm business, as has been the case with the agricultural dimension, is coupled by a decisive retreat of state investment and support for development. While the Local Enterprise Partnership (LEP) is presented by DCC as a means for such rural business development, it is widely perceived by farmers, and more specifically the Devon Farms Network, as being biased in favour of capital-intense businesses with direct employment returns, amounting to an urban bias. From an interview with DCC, it is clear that future pathways for development for the county as a whole are focused upon attracting new businesses in the 'knowledge economy and digital services sector' as outlined by the Heart of the South West Local Enterprise Partnership's Strategic Economic Plan 2014–30 (Council, 2014). Better transportation links are considered key to bringing employment to rural areas, as rural dwellers may commute more easily to take up employment in the towns and cities across Devon. This is far removed from an endogenous rural development policy or strategy; and it is left to farm families and other rural entrepreneurs to create their own endogenous developments. Moreover, speaking of his experience of the dwindling institutional support for family and more diversified farming, Richard says,

> Because you certainly don't get any sort of help from institutions in terms of Devon County Council now. That's all gone. I've had a go with the LEP as well and they're not particularly … I mean they're interested and they pretend to be terribly … oh yes, but you don't get anywhere. Because we're not a high sort of capital type job which could create employment.
>
> Richard, X acres, livestock

Furthermore, speaking of the deterioration of the local village amenities, Lynne speaks also to the feeling of isolation as a rural business:

> L: Yes, I mean, there is so much really deprivation in the rural areas in our villages reflected in that. Like we only have now, you know, one bus a week, we don't have a shop anymore, you know, it is becoming ... and the roads – it's only going to get worse. It's all getting worse because the investment is not happening in the rural areas at all. So you're becoming even more isolated within rural economies actually.
>
> Lynne X acres, livestock

While as a cooperative, Devon Farms continues to demonstrate its use of considerable collective social capital, and its capacity for diversification through the introduction of new novelties, while also drawing upon endogenous resources afforded by the Devon landscape to boost their resilience in the aftermath of agricultural downturn. However, the wider (post 2007–8) financial crisis, a more neo-liberal governance regime, especially from 2010 (Bevir, 2013) and the provision of more centralized knowledge services as a key strategic development focus, alongside growing disaffection with food and agriculture in the context of apparent plentiful global supply, combine to significantly erode support for agri-food, rural development and the distributed services it struggles to provide. Marsden (2010) has suggested that the relocalization of agri-food plays an important potential integrative function in the development of what we call rural and regional 'webs' of interconnection. There is little confidence now however among Devon Farms members that food represents more than a side-line role in supporting a business focused on the provision of tourism-related services.

> There are lots of issues within the agriculture industry, like food security I think is something that the Government never addresses, never thinks it should invest in sort of a structured agriculture sort of kind of policy at all really; it's just from hand to mouth.
>
> Lynne, X acres, livestock

There are, then, clear new questions about the social and economic resilience of the infrastructures upon which Devon Farms has depended over its 25-year history of cooperation and development. These questions arise especially because the state seems to lack a strategic focus upon building the 'new rural paradigm'.

While Gasson and Errington (1993) argue that the family farm business will indeed survive, they note that it will not necessarily do so 'in the form that we know today' (ibid.: 305). Twenty years on, with increased diversification, innovation and value added of products and services within the agricultural sector, we are led to critically explore the implications for food security in the UK, as food production is increasingly relegated as a marginal and non-productive sector.

Pathways of development – Shetland: Wrestling with the bio-economy

The Shetland Islands are the most northerly Local Authority area of the UK, with a development history characterized by the rapid expansion of the petroleum industry since the 1970s. Given the unprecedented level of economic prosperity brought by the oil industry, Shetland remains relatively wealthy today, owing also to the continued success of a long-standing fisheries sector and a well-resourced system of public administration, which remains the largest employer on the islands (Shetland Islands Council (2012)). Indeed, according to data compiled by the Office for National Statistics (Statistics, 2014), Shetland has considerable lower unemployment rates (1.3 per cent) compared with the rest of Scotland (4.3 per cent) and the rest of Great Britain (3.8 per cent). Individuals who are economically active in Shetland also surpass the average figures for rest of Scotland and the UK, with 81.3 per cent economically active compared to 70.7 per cent in Scotland and 70.1 per cent in Great Britain. These figures are also higher than other island communities. Orkney, for example, has 79.3 per cent economically active, and an unemployment figure of 1.5 per cent. The number employed full-time in shellfish aquaculture across Shetland is growing each year, while there has been a steady increase in the number of fish processing firms and factories from 11 and 15 in 1977 to 18 and 19 in 2011.

While during our 2008 and 2010 research in Shetland we found considerable emphasis being placed, by the local council and bodies such as Sustainable Shetland, on endogenous and local food, fisheries, wool and energy, by 2014 the rise of a more externalized bio-economic approach had become more dominant.

Speaking, for instance, of the development and investment plans for Shetland in 2014, a representative of the Shetland Island's Council's (SIC) economic development branch states that support is now geared towards the development of business projects that 'bring value to the economy' (interview, SIC, 2014) rather than circulating 'what is already there' (ibid.). This support for exogenous (as opposed to endogenous) development is further demonstrated by its support for a wind farm proposed by a partnership between Viking Energy Shetland and Scottish and Southern Energy (SSE) Viking Ltd, which is a subsidiary of SSE plc. The proposed wind farm consists of 103 turbines, to be located on the central mainland, which they anticipate being the third largest wind farm in Scotland, and the most productive onshore wind farm in the world. Running alongside this proposed development are tensions between other development trajectories that have traditionally represented the mainstay of the Shetland economy: fisheries and agriculture. While the wind farm poses little known or direct threat to the fisheries sector, it tears a fault line through the heart of the agricultural community, and for many Shetlanders alike. A voluntary organization – 'Sustainable Shetland' – was set up to directly oppose the development of the wind farm. With a membership of approximately 870 to 900, they hold more support than the number of votes that Labour, the SNP and the Tories combined in Shetland.

Indeed, while Kanemasu et al. (2008) suggested that it was unclear in 2008 what role the Viking Energy wind farm project would play in the unfolding of the rural web – would the farm represent a bio-economical replacement of oil, or a mode of endogenous development on the basis of multifunctional use of land and resources? Indeed, the 50:50 partnership structure between Viking Energy Ltd and SSE Viking Ltd implicates considerable community ownership, for VE Ltd is 90 per cent owned by the Shetland Charitable Trust. However, differing interpretations over the use of these charitable trust funds lie at the heart of the controversy and we suggest are representative of competing and contested ideas as to the pursuit of a post-carbon *bio*-economical or *eco*-economical development trajectory for a sustainable Shetland. That is, the future is undecided, with clear support from the SIC to continue on the bio-economical mode; but with considerable trepidation on behalf of communities, particularly those represented by 'Sustainable Shetland', over the use of the reserve community funds for investment in what they consider a risky project, that may not deliver the returns for further community investment. In other words, there is fear that the wind farm will lock Shetland into one bio-economical pathway of development that will disable potential for a more multifunctional eco-economy. Seeing the wind farm as a potential to replace oil as its primary industry, Viking Energy speak to the view that the wind farm will bring long-term community benefits.

Looking ahead we have got renewable energy, a wind farm looking to be built towards the end of this decade which will be quite a lot of investment and work as well, and big income. Because the wind farm is going to be 45% owned by the Shetland community itself it is going to be a huge amount of money coming in to help the community build its future. A lot of that money will be able to use for our economic development potentially. Nobody has decided what the money will be used for yet, they won't discuss it because it is not in the bag yet. And humans have got this aversion to count their chickens before they are hatched I suppose. But I see that money which could be £20/£30 million pounds a year coming into the public ... into this trust charity that is owned by the community ... so we can use it for developing industry. And no other community in Britain will have that sort of vast amount of money for such a small number of people to use to build a stronger future.

Interview: Viking Energy

Opposition, however, arises from severe scepticism over the financial statements made by Viking Energy. Indeed, while they suggest there are long-term community benefits to be derived from profits, due to the unique ownership structure of this wind farm, they anticipate only a successful outcome for the project. Furthermore, there is perceived to be little discussion of the high risk and other community-based opportunity costs involved in investing £180 million of Shetland Charitable Trust resources in the project. Sustainable Shetland emphasize that the best-case scenario publicized by VE is based on financial conjecture, as the final build costs, cost of energy transmission to the mainland, and the final price of electricity to be sold are all unknown. In this case, conflict over two differing potential outcomes are sorely debated, and divide communities and families across Shetland. This painstaking process has been met with sustained opposition, starting with a petition to the Court of Session in Edinburgh to review consent granted by Scottish ministers under section 36 of the Electricity Act 1989. This process culminated in judicial review in September 2013, wherein the application made by the Viking Energy partnership was found to be 'incompetent', for they did not hold a licence to generate electricity. Furthermore, ministers were found to have failed to address issues under the Wild Birds Directive as concerning the whimbrel. During this phase of fieldwork, the project strived to meet concerns and awaited approval, while the opposition suggested the VE wind farm project is 'dying a slow death' (interview: Sustainable Shetland). The explicit undercurrent of this conflict is the debate over competing sustainable and post-carbon visions and pathways for Shetland's development. Will the rural web unfold in ways that support a bio-economical trajectory through the export of energy, as wind power gradually comes to replace oil as the mainstay of Shetland industry? Or, will the VE wind farm project create new sets of relationships and transactions that create synergies as they come to mutually reinforce one other? Indeed, while revisiting interviewees from the previous round of study, it is clear there is thirst for the latter mode, which, if the wind farm were to go ahead, would be seen to stifle any such opportunity for the creative unfolding of these patterns and interactions.

> But I'm thinking smaller. If something big comes along fine, but not to the exclusion of all else. I think we're not big enough to sustain failure on a big scale but we can manage lots of small ones, lots of small failures and lots of small successes. It's not going to be headline news but it creates a really healthy diverse economy. [The wind farm project has] also stopped sensible renewable things going ahead.
>
> Interview: Sustainable Shetland

Speaking of future challenges and opportunities, there is clear local pressure for Shetland's development strategy to be hinged upon endogeneity and multifunctionality.

> I think it's a kind of reality check in that we're a lump of rock in the middle of the ocean. We can't change geography no matter how much we pretend we want to. So I think recognition of transport links and where we're physically sitting and making use of the assets that we've got. We've still, despite the cuts and closures, we've still got a relative egalitarian society compared to a lot of places so that regardless of someone's background there's a good chance they'll get reasonable care and attention through the education system.
>
> Interview: Sustainable Shetland

This is similarly echoed as we revisit a local business and branding consultant, who has been active in building Shetland's brand 'Pride of Place' in order to advance the reputation of Shetland across the rest of the UK and worldwide, boosting the attractiveness of Shetland as a place to live as well as for tourism. While reflecting upon changes and challenges arising, the bio-economical pathway of development in Shetland is subject to further trepidation.

> I think I would want to try and realise … I'm quite wary of lots of eggs in one basket. And I think we've suffered to some extent to that in some ways, in relation particularly to oil. But I think it would be good to … and I know everybody says this, we need to diversify. But I really think we need to make more of some of the things we do at the moment which we're not doing enough of. And I'm thinking particularly about the food sector away from fishing. I think there are things we need to do in terms of fishing as well. Mainly to do with value adding, provenance, there is more to be done there. … But we need to do more in terms of other kinds of food production. Certainly the agricultural sector, the sheep, cattle.
>
> Interview: Consultant

Large-scale oil and, indeed, renewable energy projects are thus considered to be detracting potential to realize a more multifunctional eco-economy characterized by the social management of the reproduction of ecological resources in ways designed to 'mesh with the and enhance regional and local regional ecosystems' (Kitchen and Marsden, 2009). This not only presents a picture of a contradictory and contested development landscape, but is the site of struggle and tension over the potential to become *locked into* the bio-economy to the exclusion of all else. Again, as with Devon, the Shetland case is most acute in the apparently growing peripherality of agri-food initiatives, which, as van der Ploeg and Marsden earlier argued (2008), play a crucial role in mobilizing distinctive rural and regional development processes in the unfolding of the rural web. Indeed, efforts to develop agri-food initiatives by the Shetland Livestock Marketing Group (SLMG) are now (by 2014) found to have been met with some disinterest from the SIC, who instead focus on what they call 'big projects' synonymous with the bio-economy. Indeed, while the wind farm project presents in such potential development, the singular focus upon fish and fisheries is frustrating to those with a more holistic view of a rural development landscape that embraces also an agri-food dimension:

> Well, the food and farming is … unless you're into fish you don't matter anymore. The SIC don't do agriculture anymore, they've removed all the support payments that they had for various grant schemes and they have no development officer dedicated to it, so as far as agriculture's concerned that's a dead stop and … so any development that goes on now we'd basically have to try to do it ourselves and so as chair of the cooperative then I try to if possible foster schemes that I think may have potential that we might be in a position to persuade people to help fund. I mean we're involved in a couple of projects at the moment which Development weren't interested in at all. One project on climate mitigation and carbon sequestration in sheep production on the peat moorland and we've been involved with the University of Aberdeen in a knowledge transfer partnership and the figures suggest that if livestock management is maintained at a certain level the whole system can be viewed as being carbon benign, can actually sequester carbon as well as producing lambs and wool, which is probably a first anywhere in Europe for an agricultural system to be showing a positive balance in climate change mitigation, so we've tried to do things like that, things that no other agency is willing to take on, but obviously we have no resources at all, so whatever we do we basically have to cheat and swindle our way. We have to be very quick and very shrewd in going about any kind of development, it's just simply not something that's encouraged.
>
> Interview: SLMG

Development concentration focused around oil and fish results in a fragmented experience of Shetland's economic 'boom'. Indeed, the volatility of Shetland's oil industry since the 1970s is thought to be forgotten with the boost to the construction, service and transport sectors since decisions were made to build a new and refurbished gas terminal. The benefits of which are therefore enjoyed by only particular sectors of the Shetland community.

> That bit is booming, but you go out to the villages here and you look through the streets and you try and find where it's booming down there. It's not booming with your average person. There's huge disparity there, so if you are told that Shetland's economy is booming – only for some.
>
> Interview: SLMG

This exogenous focus is, moreover, considered by a representative of the SLMG as damaging to the potential to develop initiatives that have impact within the wider community, for a pound spent locally through traditional industry circulates within the local economy for a longer period of time.

> I mean that's the frustrating thing about the Shetland example at the moment is … some years ago I learnt the use of the word synergy, there's no synergy here. It's all pigeonholed. The same as if you ever get into battles with the Civil Service you'll find that Civil Servants all sit in their own little pigeonholes and they're basically not interested in anything else outside their realm and the consequences of that are ridiculous legislation, ridiculous regulation and that's what's happening here. You have people who, 'Oh fishing, fishing, fishing, fishing', and ignore everything else. The multiplier effect was on spending a pound within a local economy on a local product because it went around and it stayed within that local economy for a long period of time before it disappeared out, whereas the pound spent on imports was like giving it to Tesco, it was bye bye. You'd think a Development Agency, be it either the Development Department of the SIC or the HIE would grasp that and be actually saying, 'Hold on, why not do this? Why do you persist in doing something that's obviously costing the local economy lots of money?' Nobody does it. Nobody does it.
>
> Interview: SLMG

The profits gained by the oil industry are understood to be leaving Shetland. This focus upon one development pathway is met with further exasperation, compounded by what is perceived as an obstructive attitude on behalf of the SIC towards the continued development of traditional industries on Shetland, including agriculture in particular. This is exacerbated by not only the expense of imported food, but the profits that do not circulate in ways that boost the local economy, evolving rural webs and eco-economic volatilities in a post-carbon setting.

By 2010 it was clear that Shetland's rural web had yet to take full shape with its future dynamics and direction largely indeterminate. In short, it was argued (Kanemasu and Horlings, 2010) Shetland stood at a crossroads and was in need of collective action and decisions to develop a more coherent collective vision as to whether and how it could balance both an eco-economical and bio-economical path. There were significant potentialities to develop endogeneity through mobilizing branded food, knitwear, tourism and seafood (both coastal and deep sea) into high-quality niches. We argued that despite the significant history and tradition of public sector leadership and not insubstantial funds for these development initiatives, there was a sense that the large-scale wind farm development was casting something of a shadow over these initiatives. In essence we concluded that it has never been more important for Shetlanders to make creative use of their unique assets – not only their natural, social cultural and ecological heritage, but also their unique bonding as an island community bound by its common history and future.

Four years later (2014) there is at best statis, and, in some cases, a process of fragmentation and fragility of the rural web (Paddock and Marsden, 2015), for a variety of exogenous and endogenous reasons. Let us now explore these in more depth, as they demonstrate something of the struggle between the eco-economic and bio-economic pathways.

Exogenous factors and the local web reactions to these

Our earlier models of the rural web, (with the hindsight of 2014) did not take sufficient consideration of the powerful (bio-economic) non-agricultural and rural influences affecting its main domains. These have become more significant over the recent past as the post-carbon economy has exhibited through both the eco- and bio-economy framings that have played themselves out. These exogenous forces have melded with internal social and political relations in ways which have shifted some of the foci of the domains analysed above (and based upon 2010 data).

Despite, and partly because of, since 2010, a renewed mini-boom in the oil sector, and the prospect of significant community and regional revenues emerging from the Viking wind energy project, neither have been able to fend off significant public sector cuts in budgets, a reallocation of existing budgets (i.e. towards a more spatially concentrated and scale economy approach), and, more profoundly, a shift from a state paternalist role towards, specifically, a neo-liberal framing of the role of the public sector and, more generally, sustainable development pathways. Consider the following quotations which sum up this trend:

> For development on Shetland, it's still the same general ethos although from the council point of view, the council's cut quite a number of services, just generally I suppose with UK public sector cuts. But in Shetland the new council came in two years ago and it felt that the council before and subsequent councils had overspent. And it had possibly put some Shetland's reserve into, not quite a danger zone, but into a position that it would want to try and reserve some of that. So it instigated a number of cuts across services and economic development. And so we took quite a significant financial budget hit this last year.
> SIC representative.

> The priorities however are still generally the same. We're looking at quite a narrow economic base in Shetland and the focus is always on projects that are going to take money into the Shetland economy so we're not supporting projects that are circulating money in the economy, but import substitution where we'll only take things in at the moment if there's a service that can be provided or a product provides that, we can support those kind of things. (SIC representative)

This is also creating more emphasis upon commoditizing land:

> We had various ideas where we might be able to derive some kind of income from that, but they (SIC) want to be in a position where they can sell off the land which I pointed out to them if they do they'll close the loop because it can't operate without some land and ... but big argument, raised voices and it wasn't very pretty, but they were determined that basically they own this land and they will sell it off for development if they can get anybody to buy it, so yet again no big picture. All they see is the edicts coming from the town hall where, 'Make money where you can. We need to save money, we need to make money', and if you're of an industry like agriculture, OK, it's not one of the big generators of wealth, but it keeps folk in Shetland and it uses a resource that otherwise would be unused and it's always going to be there, so ... but no vision.

> R: Five years ago what we had was a very forward looking, things are looking great, things are going to be better and most folk were kind of on board with that message and there was a kind of vitality in the air but it's very changed since then. There's a lot less trust and there's a lot less willingness to take things at face value but that's to the detriment of everyone. If you can't trust your local officials and if you can't trust the Councillors to do the right thing, you then get less engagement with them, especially through the school closures thing, there's

public meetings, huge turnouts and I think after the event folk realised it would have been better not to attend because the fact there was a bit attendance gave those wanting to close schools say, 'We consulted with 300 people.'

The pivotal aspect of it would be the Council. Historically, probably since the 70's, the Council's played a kind of paternalistic role and with power and financial muscle then that's been a strong factor but that's increased in recent years as well. Simple things like if there's something happening the Council feels partly obliged it should be involved but partly driven to be involved to make sure that it goes the way it wants it to go. So I think the Council playing more of an enabling role. If there's initiative, happily supporting it or playing a role but not taking charge of it and I think given sort of the grass roots community and business or whatever initiative a chance to flourish under their own steam. There is an element of like the dead hand of bureaucracy and it's not even bureaucracy but a major bit of the Council's Development Department operates as a Council within a Council because it's got an enormous budget of its own which stands slightly separate from the Council.

This shift from a more paternalistic role to one of far more selective investment in those activities where beneficial external trading relationships can be 'enabled' and developed (large-scale fishing, tourism, some creative and cultural industries, and a new electric energy cable to the mainland via the Tidal energy development) has tended to centralize and scale up funding support. This has been a process of fostering externalization rather than endogeneity, with a strong emphasis not to invest in circular internal economies which cannot develop external trade links.

This is seen by many as reducing the support for agri-food and other smaller-scale activities and initiatives; and with other reductions in funding for schools and education outside of the larger settlements, this tends to lead to a continued distrust surrounding the use of funds for the large-scale wind farm developments. For instance:

So they're attracted to vanity projects or prestigious things or big things like big wind farms. They would have been a lot less interested if it was like, 'Let's have five wind turbines', and they would go, 'Yes, fine.' It's really big, all the energy focused in that area but if it doesn't work and often I think it's ... I don't know where it comes from but a focus more on celebrating the novel, the odd, letting folk have a go with it and while it's working getting these folk to tell other people, 'I had a go at this and it worked well but what I wouldn't do again is this bit here,' and sharing that experience directly. A flatter level of communication rather than everything having to go through different channels. But it still needs that centre just like go a little bit to be less fearful of the community. I mean the individuals live in the community, they're part of this but unless you're into fish you don't matter anymore.

The whole of Shetland is in a bad state because of the policies being pursued by the SIC and the sort of austerity policies. They seem to have this machismo culture in there where everybody is trying to undertake cuts fiercer than anybody else, so lots of rural schools being shut down.

So that's kind of where we're at, at the moment. I was thinking like the question of what's changed and it's difficult to say. The main thing I think that's changed is politically the atmosphere generally throughout Scotland is kind of going onto like a cuts agenda. In Shetland that's manifest by an obsession with making cuts. As long as something's being cut that's fine, it doesn't really matter what or how or why or what then follows from that. So as long as thing's are being cut that's fine.

In this less trustful policy context the opposition to the wind farm development has been increasingly fuelled by concerns about the domination of the project over support for other small sustainability projects. The case for the development has gone to judicial review, a process which has cost groups like Sustainable Shetland significant amounts of legal costs, and the charitable trust funds are also seen as being unnecessarily diverted towards such large-scale developments.

The process has continued to fragment the community:

Incredibly divided but it also stopped sensible renewable things going ahead because we can't think about a smaller scheme because we've got this one big one. So it stopped a new power station being built, because it could have been built five years ago and so our emissions could have been far lower five years ago but they didn't do it because they were waiting on this wind farm and waiting on this cable. So it's an opportunity lost. I think that's the biggest thing is the opportunity cost because it's difficult to measure. What we else have we really done with the time?

Alternatively, the representative from the wind farm development, with the SIC, sees the external and scalar implications of the proposed development in bio-economy terms, providing the start to a new renewable energy future for the island and facilitating its contribution to the rest of Scotland and beyond.

Yes. We have to get a cable connection to the grid because Shetland is one of the only places in the UK that is not grid connected. We just have a small local grid. So when we get this cable to the mainland yes we will be able to export our power to Scotland and further away. And Shetland might actually end up being a sort of crossroads for power cables coming from Iceland with geothermal electricity. From Norway with hydro and wind I suppose wave as well eventually and Shetland putting its wind power down and wave whatever in the future. It could be sort of a hub for the exchange of energy in the future which we are going to need. Yes so in Shetland at the moment or in the past it has exported, it has depended on exporting fish. Now we have got a much more recent industry exporting farmed fish, not just wild fish. So there is wild fish, farmed fish, exporting all our lamb goes out of the place, our knitwear goes out of Shetland. So we are going to export our wind power, we can now export our power. Good?

But the oppositional forces are rendered marginal to this process,

There is a tension between those people and the greenies shall we say who are not big fans of people, they prefer birds and they prefer wild land so called. And they don't like farmers, crofters, sheep, they don't like sheep, they don't like fishermen, you know? And they are intelligent educated people the greenies generally. And the more extreme greenies want, I think that they want at least quite a few bits of Shetland to be free of human development. And they see a different kind of Shetland than what other locals see. Locals don't want to be stopped from developing their island to improve their prospects for the future. Okay sure there is money to be made out of tourism and there is money to be made out of greenies coming here to do their studies and their twitching, you know? That is a big thing. We are getting loads of twitchers coming up from South England to race around after some stupid little birds. Sorry but I am getting a bit controversial here.

I am not sure what would happen if that consent was taken away and we couldn't produce a similar wind farm to get consent. We fully expect to continue with our project. And without the Viking project there will be no renewables of any scale in Shetland because the local grid can't take anymore renewable power because it has fluctuations. So we have to have this outlet to the mainland. And that cable to the mainland won't come unless Viking or something on the scale of Viking is built. Because basically building the motorway and then use the motorway. But there is no other project the size of Viking. And even Viking alone, would it justify the cable? I don't know. There are other smaller projects which are waiting for Viking to get the cable so they can develop. And that is everything from the crofter with its plan for a small 50 kilowatt wind turbine to sell some of the excess power to the grid. The local grid can't take anymore turbines so they can't develop their small scale renewable. And there is a wave farm and that is a big business wave farm plan which is waiting for Viking to get a connection a new local idea to build a wind farm in the north of Shetland – Energy Isles. Energy Isle Limited has just been formed in the last couple of months.

We witness in 2014, then, an escalation of the fault lines that are developing between different contested sustainabilities and place-making paradigms. These fault lines are, since 2010, beginning in some cases to undermine the already tentative linkages in our rural web model developed in 2008–10 (see Horlings and Kanemasu, 2015). It is far from completely broken, but its eco-economic elements are coming under new external pressures from a bio-economy paradigm based upon large-scale energy infrastructure developments, not only associated with the wind farm development per se, but also with new energy grids, cables and motorway links. These fault lines have also been exacerbated by a shift in more neo-liberal local governance which has become more centralized and financially constrained. These latter features seem to particularly marginalize agri-food, small-scale, local branding activities, and generally more distributed systems which are key to the co-evolution of the eco-economy of Shetland. The fisheries developments seem to be the exception here with considerable investment and support for large-scale deep water fisheries (subject to concerns over quotas) and smaller coastal fishery initiatives such as the mussels sector.

The decline of the previous and strong state paternalist role, coupled with the rise of the 'sustainable' bio-economy under more general fiscal conditions of austerity, seem to be further weakening the fragile links between endogeneity and social capital identified in the earlier phases of research. This suggests, in conclusion here, that rural eco-economical web development is both somewhat spasmodic over time and space, and highly vulnerable to changes in specific governance arrangements which tend to favour the bio-economy paradigm. Even so bodies such as Sustainable Shetland increase their broad support and membership, and continue to design alternative eco-economical pathways for the islands. Meanwhile state officials and bio-economical development interests stress the need for externalized forms of competitive advantage; seeing Shetland's future as an international player in energy production. Meanwhile, the social infrastructure and community is being 'hollowed out' despite previous support. Viking Energy obtained final planning approval to build 103 wind turbines in February 2015. It remains to be seen how this bio-economic development affects the wider development of the rural web.

Conclusions: A landscape of food insecurity; fragmenting the rural web in the post-carbon economy

Following the increasingly difficult and challenging longitudinal pathways and trajectories of the rural webs in Devon and Shetland between 2007 and 2014 has unearthed some significant generic as well as local results. The longitudinal (2007–14) research has allowed us to begin to assess how different 'pathways towards rural sustainability' are being shaped and articulated. A major finding in both regions is the realization that moves towards a more sustainable rural development trajectory under more post-carbon conditions is not necessarily likely to lead to more cohesive rural web developments. And, once formed, they are by no means highly resilient to the combination of state and market forces which have been unleashed during this increasingly volatile period.

Agri-food in particular can play a potentially leading and synergizing role. Yet left to their own state-led and governance devices, since 2010, both regions show that attempts at sustainable place-making is showing more signs of fragmentation, contestation and a diminution of cohesive rural webs built upon synergy, facilitative institutional arrangements and endogeneity. In both regions there has been a diminution of state support for agri-food developments – especially when it involves struggling multifunctional family and micro businesses (as in Devon), and the arrival of bio-economical mega projects in Shetland. In addition, the change of state policy regimes towards a more externalized, concentrated and, indeed, bio-economic approach has tended to severely restrain more distributed systems of eco-economic development.

In this context, and with the hindsight to be critical of our earlier conceptual formulations (see, for instance, Marsden, 2010), we have tended to underestimate the growing and powerful exogenous forces linked to both the bio-economy (such as expressed in the attractiveness of large-scale wind power developments in Shetland) and the shifts towards a more neo-liberalized and urban biased, spatial governance (in Devon), both of which tend to prioritize (and by implication devalorize) small- and middle-sized endogenous rural business development, especially in the multifunctional agri-food sector. These new exogenous factors, combined with those that we did incorporate in our earlier models of the rural web (such as the continuing and severe cost-price squeeze on agriculture) also now combine to marginalize and peripheralize small, land-based businesses and the networks (social capital, etc.) upon which they are based.

This does not necessarily devalue the conceptual power of our rural web model. Indeed, in many ways it tends to qualify it as a more dynamic heuristic barometer from which we can begin to assess the level and depth of contestation between the competing paradigms – the bio- and eco-economy outlined here. Also it shows that its very dynamic and contingent mobilization is indeed a site and a place of dynamic and increasing struggle over the control of rural natures: its land, biosphere and its livelihoods. A struggle we now see clearly in our Devon Farms Network; a network which has been developing over twenty-five years, but having to adapt and increasingly self-exploit itself and its members and families in ways which allow it to continue to innovate in ways of providing an increasing array of novelties to their growing and more demanding tourist consumers. These, indeed, are the new types of survival strategies upon which building the rural-based eco-economy depends, and are displayed more widely at the European level in the previous chapter. We see also that these practices and network-building activities are increasingly operating, and having to operate, *outside of the state* and its institutional and regulatory frameworks.

In the UK at least, current state policies are far less interested in encouraging endogenous rural and sustainable development – at least for the time being. In this sense the particular neo-liberal state response to the financial, fiscal, food and energy crisis which emerged in 2007–8, and which incorporates the time line of this research, has been one of divesting responsibility and, indeed, funding from rural and agri-food distributed systems. The competitive orthodoxy has been one of side-lining many of the smaller micro-scale agri-food initiatives which emerged in the late 1990s and early 2000s. The closure of regional development agencies in England in 2010, reductions in regional government offices and abandonment of local council initiatives in rural tourism have all cumulatively had a negative effect on the effectiveness of the rural web to maintain its vibrancy. Here we see the criticality of governance and state institutional arrangements to the vibrancy and continuity of the rural web. It is not, in this sense, a neo-liberal machine.

However, although the evidence points in both cases to the marginalization of agri-food and its potential centrality in rural development, it is clear that this fails to disappear completely. It is a central part of the construction of the eco-economic landscape value and tourism potential ('eco-system services') in both regions, and clearly a foundation for the maintenance of ecological biodiversity upon which the local and regional economy increasingly depends. *But it is not, at the moment, or indeed in the foreseeable future, being valorized as such.*

Indeed, quite the reverse in that it continues to be devalorized by dominant and corporate-driven food and energy markets with the neo-liberalized blessing of state agencies. Despite the rising concerns over food and energy security, we are still not creating markets which foster opportunities for small land-based businesses to prosper and grow. And, as we see in Devon, there is a demographic vulnerability emerging in organizations and networks like Devon Farms as a result of these trends. Thus, there are real generational and reproductive vulnerabilities on the social and economic fabric of multifunctional family farming in both regions, as family occupancy ages and actual farm-derived income continue to fall.

If we are in Europe to manage the post-carbon transition, we will have to devise ways of re-valorizing the nested socio-ecological infrastructures upon which it depends. The trends in these two rural regions, at either ends of the UK archipelago, suggest that the combinational effects of declines in multifunctional agri-food support, on the one hand, and a neo-liberalized retraction of non-agricultural rural development support on the other, are providing a potential and chaotic *new governance squeeze* which is likely to severely reduce the massive but latent adaptive capacity embedded in the rural eco-economy. One implication is therefore that we need to create new and more reflexive pathways for good governance so as to harness this potential if we are to protect and build resilient rural communities.

Indeed, a more multifunctional governance and policy-based approach, based upon creating conditions for the eco-economic rural web to flourish, needs to find ways of harmonizing different aspects of the post-carbon landscape such that its various segments (energy, tourism, agriculture, creative industries, etc.) can work in synergy with one another. This is very much what the Devon Farms Network is trying to do, but largely outside governance frameworks, and at considerable (potentially unsustainable) self-exploitative cost to themselves. Such fragmented and competing conditions as those revealed in both case study areas are unlikely to be sufficiently capable of meeting the new national and global demands for food security which have risen up the political agenda since our earlier phases of field work.

Chapter 6

Towards a sustainability science and place-making for rural and agri-food development

Introduction: From romanticism and modernization to sustainable place-making

This book has attempted to provide a fresh thesis with regard to the changing position of rural areas and agri-food and their rurality from the British and wider European experience. It has been argued that, unlike in earlier phases of development, it is now clear that rural areas, both in the UK and elsewhere in Europe, face new macro challenges of development as we move, contestedly into a post-carbon world. Such a shift is playing havoc with the old and established cherished notions of rural romanticism and then an overlaid modernization we have depicted in the nineteenth and twentieth centuries (see Murdoch, et al., 2003; and Chapter 1). While these may still hold some historical value as a recourse to some past rural idyllic state, increasingly they are giving way to more instrumental visions and models of development which are now more conflictual, contested, prospective and forward looking. Indeed, we can begin to see this as a major structural shift in thinking and locating the countryside. Whereas, for instance, we have depicted the twentieth-century countryside very much as a retrospective opposition between the forces and ideologies of romanticism and modernism, now these two oppositions sit somewhat uncomfortably betwixt a more fluid and contested prospective articulation which is being contestedly progressed by competing scientific, private and public sector interests. We argued then in 2003 (Murdoch et al., 2003: 3):

> Pastoralism and modernism provide two contrasting perspectives on the
> countryside yet both have been influential in shaping not only how we see

the countryside but how we act towards it. Each perspective prioritises certain values and actions: on the one hand, we might aim to maintain the countryside as an exclusive and preserved space, one that should be free from industrialism's corrupting influence; on the other hand, the countryside should be brought inside modern patterns of development so that rural resources can make a full contribution to national wellbeing. Put in these terms, it is clear that in vital respects these two perspectives are in conflict with one another. The romantics and the pastoralists see the countryside as areas to be protected from modernity, as a place that should be maintained as a pre-modern space; the modernisers see the countryside as inherently backward, as needing reform if it is to achieve the levels of dynamism that are integral to capitalist society.

The outcome of this conflict, then, was high levels or rural differentiation based around the playing out of these two dynamics in different places and spaces. Today, nearly two decades on, when deeper questions about the types of modernization and environmentalization have been raised, these questions become a backcloth to the more urgent agenda associated with the questions of what type of ecological modernization can be developed, and how sustainable will it be in the long term?

Commentators, scholars and policy makers, especially since the economic and global upheavals expressed since 2007–8, are now more openly and contestedly visioning the future and backcasting this to the present conditions of rurality; as indeed, as in the nineteenth century, many leading social theorists then questioned the emerging and quite rapid reorganization of capitalist industrialization, urbanization and the role of the peasantry. We are thus now in the realms of an emerging new set of prospectively defined agrarian and dialectical questions: How are we to manage the intensive cosmopolitan demands now being made on rural resources? And who will have the power to govern and direct these processes? Will this process lead to a more rural emancipation or devalorization? What will be the most effective balances between the rural and urban spheres? And, what role will the state play, given recent phases of neo-liberalization?

Here, in conclusion, there are several key components which can be identified from the preceding analysis. These are in themselves, far from unilinear or pre-determined, for as we have argued, the rural is now, more than ever, a place of contestation, not least about which visions and dialectics about sustainability take root.

From post-productionism to the bio-economy:
The role out of the new rural paradigm

We have seen, in the preceding analysis, how, and especially since the early 2000s, the British countryside becomes a basis for the uneven and volatile development of both the more integrated bio-economy/eco-economy on the one hand, and as a continued base for exclusive residential development on the other. These in many ways are new and reconstituted expressions of what my colleagues and I depicted in the 1980s as productionist and consumerist framings of the British countryside (see Marsden et al., 1993; Murdoch and Marsden, 1995; Murdoch et al., 1993). Now, however, the national and regional state governance frameworks are playing a far less positive role, than they were ten and, indeed, twenty years ago. In the 1980s and well into the 1990s, under successive governments, there was still a strong sense of national and regional governance leadership and, indeed, consensus expressed with regard to the national rural state. This was not only expressed by continued support for CAP productionist and post-productionist measures, but also in a raft of policy documents and white papers on the conditions of rural areas. This was institutionally backed up by proactive rural remits in the English Regional Development Agencies, the reorganized Countryside Agency, as well as active regional government offices of DEFRA.

Towards the end of the first decade of the twenty-first century, a new confluence, or we may see it as a coincidence, of neo-liberalizing tendencies was created which denuded this state-led framework. These included the food, fuel and fiscal crises ensuing from 2007 to 2008; the election of a more neo-liberal coalition national government in 2010 and a conservative government of 2015; and a related dismantling of previous institutional frameworks, whereby regional development agencies, government offices, the Countryside Agency, the rural development commission and a raft of semi-independent advisory bodies such as the Royal Commission for Environmental Pollution and the Sustainable Development Commission were disbanded. These shifts were clearly locally and regionally experienced in our case study regions analysed here (Devon and Shetland) over this period. The impending fiscal restraints placed upon local government structures and, indeed, their particular interpretation and reaction to these restraints in developing neo-liberal and city-region-based approaches to regional economic development policy (administered in part by the new Local Enterprise Partnerships in England), further served, as we soe clearly both in Devon and Shetland, to marginalize rural and agri-food concerns and initiatives, in favour, often, of more urban and centralized economic projects geared to attracting inward investments.

At least, then, from 2010, and partly as a result of this withdrawal of the national state as a national protector of the rural domain and its interests, rural areas have been further exposed to and faced with the growing and volatile pressures of globalization, demographic change and the rise of the bio-economy on their own, largely without a strong and coherent political voice. At the same time, the traditional and originally strong corporatist/productivist agricultural lobbies (especially the farmers unions) have also been increasingly marginalized in the corridors of power, especially as the crises of FMD abated, and the problems of bovine TB rose in public concern.

While we might have expected this most recent period to have reasserted a revised type of neo-productivism among agricultural production interests, this has not led to a coherent lobbying force in Westminster or in the Shire counties. Central government has been more concerned to promote agri-industry, retail power and biotech than it has to protect its dwindling farm population. In the twenty-first century then, and despite the growing concerns around food and energy security, we have witnessed the further demise of the corporatist politics of agricultural productivism. In its place, of course, has been the growth of retailer-led private-interest governance (see Marsden et al., 2010); a process which has prioritized more internationalized systems of food trade over any notions of national food (or energy) self-sufficiency. Much of this book has argued that this neo-liberal shift in governance will become all the more untenable as the recombinant natural resource and energy crisis unfolds (see Marsden and Morley, 2014). Under these conditions of debilitating declines in the resilience of rural and agri-food systems, new and more proactive governance frameworks are required.

What these neo-liberalizing tendencies suggest is the need for rural areas to more urgently adopt what the OECD in 2006 termed the 'new rural paradigm', by really embracing multifunctionality, new urban–rural linkages and decentralized post-carbon and renewable production systems. This, given these circumstances, becomes more critical and a necessity for the regeneration and sustainability of rural areas now than it did in the early 2000s when, indeed, it might have been seen as an optional benefit for rural development. During the last decade, my colleagues and I have thus been attempting to conceptually and empirically build this new paradigm as a major regenerative and potentially post-neo-liberalizing force for achieving rural sustainable development (see van der Ploeg et al., 2008; Horlings and Marsden, 2014). The actions of the UK governments since 2010 and 2015 have not necessarily assisted this endeavour, as we see in Devon and Shetland from the recent evidence outlined in this book. The UK rural space, indeed increasingly relies upon European funding mechanisms to support these 'new paradigm ventures'. And there are indeed significant counter forces of combined neo-liberalization and connected and centralized development models for the bio-economy, not only around agri-food, but also around renewable energy, waste recycling and fibre production.

Unlike our empirical experiences in Finland, Italy and parts of the Netherlands, the UK tendency is to absorb and promote the bio-economy into a more corporate and centralized grid system built upon economies of scale and vast transport costs which seem to be largely blind to the distributed needs and demands of many rural dwellers and businesses. In this sense the real threat to UK rural space, a threat that has been clearly expressed and experienced over the past decade by rural communities, has been the increased effects of centralized oligopoly of its main natural resource sectors. This includes not only food, but also energy, waste, water, minerals, housing, retailing, education and health services, telecommunications, library and care services, etc. This geographical draining of functions and services from rural areas has not only been detrimental in itself, leading to many rural areas being far less attractive for the young and skilled than need be. In addition, it has also led to the diminution of local and regional infrastructures – the disappearing middles – whereby there are fewer existing hubs in rural areas from which real multifunctionality and the eco-economy can now flourish. Thus, we have a rather paradoxical experience, at the time of writing, in many rural areas where there may well be growing local community support and a dense 'rural web' of assemblages from which to launch a new local and place-based rural development pathways; but there is no infrastructural capacity – either physical or virtual – upon which to channel this adaptive capacity. In short, many rural areas have experienced a regressive 'hollowing out' of their multiple and once dense infrastructures – that is, village farmsteads, shops, public houses, telephone kiosks, banks, library services, abattoirs, schools – just at the time when we are all realizing the necessity to rebuild sustainable rural communities through more effective and place-based means. This is now the profound eco-economic paradox of rural UK; just as we see the emergence of innovative community and local business eco-developments, much of the surrounding infrastructures upon which these could be built seem to be declining or disappearing.

A major challenge for much of UK rural space, outside, but not totally excluding parts of the more prosperous south-east region, is to consider and enact ways of *re-creating these social and physical infrastructures in ways which can then create positive and circular economy feedbacks between different types of urban and rural communities.* Of course, these 'hollowed out' conditions are not exclusive to many rural areas, as we see in many post-industrial regions (such as the South Wales Valleys, see Adamson and Lang, 2014) with similar sets of conditions. Nevertheless, given the potential opportunities that rural areas now face, from playing a far more proactive role in the multiplex development of the bio-economy, is bringing this particular type of rural hollowing out into sharp relief. It, of course, remains to be seen how and if the progressive dimensions of the digital revolution can resolve at least some of these structural problems of lack of rural infrastructure; but I wish to argue that 'the digital panacea' will not be able to surmount these problems alone. It will also need new local and distributed physical hubs and community-based businesses, new 'rural labs', food hubs community energy and alternative financial networks. Community-based and shared finance schemes are one important part of the eco-economic armoury, for redeveloping local rural capacities.

More conceptually, as I outline here in conclusion, it will require a more effective articulation of a distributed and place-based model of rural and regional development which may stand a chance of gaining more political traction at regional and national levels.

From a scholarly point of view, this will require academics and sustainability scientists to be more proactively engaged in enacting as well as critically describing and interpreting these new development pathways. Here, in conclusion to the book, I highlight four key conceptual dimensions, all of which I wish to argue need progressing in tandem: (i) developing 'post-normal' and coproduced sustainability science; (ii) critically understanding and combatting the inherent vulnerabilities which have emerged out of the current and dominant agri-food private, corporate governance and financial system; (iii) progressing and building translocal and reflexive governance processes; and (iv) conceptually and politically building a more heterodox and socially and spatially distributed agri-food and rural economy.

These four dimensions require uplifting and repositioning the rural and agri-food domain into the highly contested worlds of wider macroeconomic and policy debates, as we indicated in our introduction. In the recent past, the rural dimension has only risen up the political agenda when a periodic 'crisis' has hit – such as FMD, issues about badgers, fox hunters and a range of ever-present plant and animal diseases. This conveniently marginalizes its real sustainable development potential and assumes a need to maintain a 'business as usual approach'. This is now not so much a 'pipe dream' as a necessary key dimension of making the further transitions towards a post-carbon rural economic space that mainstream society and future generations will require.

The need for a new science paradigm as part of the new rural agri-food sustainability paradigm: Making science part of the solution

Food sustainability and security dilemmas are now typical sustainability problems often defined as 'wicked' problems in that they are life-threatening and urgent, have long-term impacts, are highly complex and cannot be solved by simple remedies (Funtowicz and Ravetz, 1993; Dovers, 1996; Wiek et al., 2012). A great deal of disciplinary and interdisciplinary research addresses these challenges. However, these efforts alone are not sufficient to capture the multidimensionality of sustainability which transcends the boundaries of disciplinary and interdisciplinary science, encompassing different magnitudes of scales, multiple balances and interests.

To begin to tackle this insufficiency, new research approaches and initiatives have prominently responded – for example, transdisciplinary research, interactive social research, participatory action research, sustainability science – initiating novel forms of collaboration between researchers and other communities of knowledge and values (Nowotny, Scott and Gibbons, 2001; Kasemir, Jaeger and Jäger, 2003; Clark and Dickson, 2003; Robinson, 2008). These require a reconsideration and reconceptualization of science which progressively advances 'certainty' in knowledge to a 'post-normal' view where the science enterprise is systemic, uncertain, normative and 'democratic' – allowing for a plurality of legitimate perspectives (Funtowicz and Ravetz, 2003a,b).

As Funtowicz and Ravetz (2003a,b) claim, in the case of science-related complex policy issues – such as those related to sustainability challenges – where risks cannot be quantified, when possible damage is irreversible, where values are in dispute, the stakes high and decisions urgent, that the application of routine techniques of normal applied science are not sufficient. In practice, most science-related complex policy problems have more than one plausible answer, and many have no well-defined scientific answer at all. The aim is thus not about arriving or deriving a single truth, but rather the exploration and enactment of new tasks and practices for science concerning the wider application of knowledge- production and decision-making processes. Here, the knowledge(s) and solution(s) produced have to represent the whole set and range of concerned perspectives which need to be taken into consideration in the problem framing as well as in the decision-making and implementation processes (Funtowicz and Ravetz, 2003a,b).

A second argument for this re-enactment is based on a wider consideration of knowledge production in science. Different types of knowledge – including normative, anticipatory, prospective and action-oriented knowledges (Grunwald, 2004; Wiek, 2007; Christen and Schmidt, 2012) – are needed so as to understand the complex and coupled human–nature interactions, the performing 'social–ecological systems', while being immediately of use for policy and management stakeholders for solving sustainability problems (van Kerkhoff and Lebel, 2006). These somewhat more 'uncommon' knowledge types complement rather than necessarily contradict 'more normal' descriptive–analytical knowledge. They support sustainability decisions, actions and transformations with direction-coherent visions and goals and – with operational structures – strategies and tactics for transformation (Wiek et al., 2012).

Third, non-academic sources of knowledge and values – local, experiential, practical and, as we shall argue here, 'place-based' knowledges – become central. Provided by a wide range of users, they are increasingly acknowledged as relevant, valid and legitimate for sustainability research (Kasemir, Jaeger and Jäger, 2003; Talwar, Wiek and Robinson, 2011). These arguments advocate a new type of science (what has been termed 'Mode 2', post-normal science) which is characterized by the continuous involvement of non-academic actors in the knowledge-production process, and by the adoption of a wider vector of research practices, such as transdisciplinary, community-based, interactive or participatory approaches (Kasemir, Jaeger and Jäger, 2003; Savan and Sider 2003; Robinson and Tansey, 2006; Hirsch et al., 2006; Jahn, 2008; Scholz et al., 2006). Such practices are strongly consistent with a new science–policy–society interface or a 'new social contract for science', which claims that science ought to address and 'solve' demanding 'real-world' problems; a claim that is renewed in the context of the global environmental change debate (Gibbons, 1999; Wiek et al., 2014).

As a solution-oriented, transformative endeavour, built on post-normal and Mode 2 paradigms, sustainability science has emerged as a new field of enquiry, aimed to provide a response to the crisis of normal sciences, enabling it to contribute more effectively to sustainable development through a holistic and transformative approach. It is characterized by the following main features (Spangenberg, 2011 and Wiek et al., 2012): (i) A focus on understanding the dynamic interactions between nature and society. This is usually lacking in 'normal' science, where a specific focus is given, for example, to separate biophysical aspects one at a time; (ii) The adoption of a transdisciplinary approach, based on a strong link with the specific social/local/place context and institutional setting from where sustainability problems originate. This is expressed in the inclusion of public and civic values and common goods perceptions in the characterization of the problem and identification and implementation of solutions. This iterative, circular coproduction process, linking scientific and experiential knowledge, enables mutual learning among researchers from different disciplines as well as from actors outside academia, promoting societal learning, transformation and reflexivity; (iii) The aim of practically contributing to societal learning and change, and attention posed to social acceptability of scientific and technology innovation (Jaeger, 2009); and (iv) The capability to provide direction through visions, designs and goals: it addresses the normative question of how coupled human – environment systems would function and look in compliance with a variety of explicitly value-laden goals and objectives.

We will explore here in the development of this chapter how this wider conceptualization of post-normal sustainability science is highly relevant in providing a revised scientific space for developing and shaping a more place-based, sustainable agri-food energy-land nexus. More specifically, we argue, this first entails an understanding of the current contested framings surrounding the bio-economy and the eco-economy.

Place-making as part of sustainability science

It is thus possible following the discussion above to position the rural eco-economy and its sustainable place-making practices at the centre of the current resource governance problematics we outlined earlier. This allows us to conceive of how it can begin to incrementally 'solve', or at least contribute to, the multiple agri-food and wider long-running environmental nexus concerns of sustainability, security, sovereignty and governance. In the latter case (governance), for example, it unlocks a potentiality for a post-neo-liberalizing set of governance processes (see Bevir, 2012; Collier, 2008) which create places and sites of experimentation and innovation for a post-carbon reorganization of nature-society (see also Hodson and Marvin, 2010a,b). As Collier (2009: 88), following Foucault (2007), argues:

> One technology of power may provide guiding norms and an orienting telos. But it does not saturate all power relations. Rather it suggests a configurational principle that determines how heterogeneous elements – techniques, institutional arrangements, material forms and other technologies of power – are taken up and recombined.' Such 'conditions of possibility' (95): 'are situated precisely amid upheaval, in sites of problematisation in which existing forms have lost their coherence and their purchase in addressing present problems, and in which new forms of understanding and acting have been invented.

In this sense then the very existence of sustainable place-making and the eco-economy becomes a way of articulating places of experimentation amidst contested 'conditions of possibility', and it provides a means of articulating its successes and failures into the wider policy and into the political-scientific realm associated with the more dominant framings of the bio-economy. So far, we are only at the beginning of this process of articulation, and it is here that a real contribution of a critical 'post-normal' sustainability science can make a major contribution. Thus, these arguments and conceptualizations have significant implications for the utility and societal importance of 'post-normal' sustainability science.

First and foremost, it is necessary for sustainability science to comprehend the differences in the paradigms of the bio-economy and the eco-economy, and to examine how both, from their different standpoints and socio-technical perspectives, can lead to more effective and societally engaging sustainable pathways and transitions. With regard to the eco-economy and its links to sustainable place-making we can begin to identify some of the key conceptual and methodological building blocks for inclusion in a transdisciplinary sustainability science approach.

These features have emerged from engagement over recent years in a range of international research projects mainly, but not exclusively, in the agri-food field. Clearly, they demand a move beyond 'normal' science to post-normal science (Sala, Farioli and Zamagni, 2013), whereby a strong emphasis is placed upon participatory action research techniques working with place-based communities (Mount and Andrée, 2013), and on the creation of 'live-labs' where coproduction of knowledges and practices can go hand in hand. This also entails, as we indicate here, what we can call 'deep locality studies', such as those conducted in Tredegar, South Wales, by Adamson and Lang (2014). They place emphasis upon many parts of the place-based eco-economy which go unseen in conventional economic analysis, including the local food system, informal and formal social caring arrangements, and the provision of local transport and energy infrastructures. They adapt the concept of the 'foundational economy' to study these deep localities, with an explicit and ongoing attempt to engage policy makers at various spatial scales.

Engaging these methodologies with place-based communities research can also allow understanding of what can and cannot work in the field, whether it is associated directly with collective farmer plant-breeding techniques, or with the wider setting up and orchestration of new short food supply chains between collections of small farmers and local schools and hospitals (as is occurring in parts of Brazil). Research which sifts and organizes local knowledges and feeds these into more reflexive governance arrangements is also a key function of sustainable place-making science. And, while this places a renewed and critical emphasis upon the relocalization of social, economic and ecological assets, it is by no means associated with a sort of defensive localism. Indeed, the conventional notions of globalization and externalization are upended, with viable attempts not only with the assistance of researchers to develop translocal participation and recognition of diversity but also reciprocity.

Here, aspects of social innovation become as important as technical innovation, where sites of experimentation (such as a small farm biogas plant) can become a basis for new social networks to take hold. Indeed, unlike the bio-economic model which prioritizes the technical over the social, the eco-economy takes the alternative point of departure in order to create, through trial and error, new forms of coproduction out of social innovations and networks. In this sense, the eco-economy cannot just rely upon or start with strict technical criteria or frameworks. Indeed, the field or the village, and their associated assemblages of knowledges and practices, cannot be controlled or managed by digital or bio-economic applications. Rather, the foundations of the eco-economy have to start and end with the social and with the constant re-embedding of social and technical innovations and networks.

Clearly, all of these features outlined here as variable assemblages of actions and practises are 'bundled' (Pearce, Barnett and Moon, 2012) in and through places, in often unordered and somewhat seemingly chaotic ways. This is why some expanded notion of social and ecological planning based upon multiple levels of reflexive resource governance become an essential institutional vehicle for creating more than the sum of parts in the eco-economy. Social design is, thus, a critical element here and needs to be built into more established governance processes. Such moves and shifts of emphasis have important implications for those practising sustainability science because they require demonstrations of 'what works', 'what works better' and, more particularly, how we can assist community leaders and actors to visualize new and adjusted social designs. Hence, a strong element of sustainable place-making science needs not just to move into the realms of the traditional linearities of 'survey, action, plan' but also to broaden this in line with the recent raft of post-structuralist theories in the social and cultural sciences which open the door to experimental, mixed and deeper topologies of social nature (see Collier, 2012).

What we are currently seeing and witnessing in the sustainable place-making field is the beginning of these scientific and practice shifts specifically in the agri-food realm, where the coproduction priorities necessary to solve problems of sustainability, security and sovereignty are most clearly expressed. As further progress is made, however, in nexus thinking – whether in the bio-economy or the eco-economy – whereby the solving of the resource crisis is recognized as an integrated and coupled set of socio-ecological concerns (including water, soils, wastes, energy, protein, germ plasm), we can expect calls for a more engaging and normative sustainability science to embrace the historically awkward realm of place and social design.

A key research question to address will be how rural areas and their land, fibre and water bases can potentially create multifunctional and more sustainable rural development from these new demands? Could the onset of the eco-economy be the basis for more sustainable rural development? Or, will it descend into 'business as usual' cost-price squeeze conditions, whereby the rural primary sector becomes devalorized again? Partly, this will depend upon how these rural spaces are to be governed and regulated, by whom and for whom. In conclusion here, we can begin to demonstrate how this creates a research agenda for sustainability science through both policy and practice engagement and with regard to place-based interdisciplinary and action-based sustainability research.

Box 6.1 SPM Process

- Networked value creation rather than GVA/GDP squeeze
- A recapturing of multiple flows of knowledge, goods and services
- Reflexive spatial governance
- A relocalization of social assets, capitals and market practices
- A commitment to social and technical design, social innovation as well as new product innovation
- A recognition of space as place
- Filling in the social and infrastructural 'missing middle' between individualized behaviours and aggregated abstractions
- Nexus (food, energy, water, landscape) thinking turning into practices
- Community-based action research and capacity-building

Box 6.2 Key features of SPM

- Foundational economy: deep locality studies (Williams, CREW, 2014)
- Endogenous–exogenous equations and networks
- Innovations scaling out, in and under the nexus
- Engagement with multilevel and reflexive governance and scales: village neighbourhood, catchment, city-region, bio-region, province
- Enrolment of community into the active reappraisal of assets, infrastructures, entrepreneurial networks, landscapes
- Evolutionary collaborative/collective informal planning and project development around place-based assets
- Reworking strategies with existing regulatory and institutional structures and creating new 'spaces for action'
- Reorganization of bio-sphere property rights
- Participation in translocalism agenda.

Creative connections and convergences between post-normal science (PNS) and the sustainable place-making approach (SPM)

Having reviewed both the bio-economy and eco-economy framings, it is necessary to begin to link SPM, and especially the development of the eco-economy, into the wider sets of arguments we introduced at the start of the chapter with regard to the progress of post-normal sustainability science. In order to progress the eco-economy and its associated place-making potentialities, it will be necessary to challenge the 'normal' science assumptions which tend to underpin the dominant bio-economy framings that we have also outlined here. There are several dimensions to this challenge which a post-normal sustainability science for the eco-economy could address and progress. These include the following.

Contested framings

Both PNS and SPM challenge the conventional and commodity-based consumption and production system ('sustainable intensification'), as well as the assumptions of control and predictive power of science and deployment of remedial techno-scientific systems to make sound policy decisions for a sustainable future. The SPM approach calls for new resource governance models, and the building of an alternative eco-economic paradigm to address the current contested policy/technology/production/consumption arena. At the same time, PNS calls for different forms of hybridizations to abandon modern divides and pitfalls and engage in new kinds of collective diagnosis and responsible action. PNS claims that modern frameworks, as the dominant discourse about sustainability, show contradictions and paradoxes (Benessia et al., 2012).

A first level of contradiction lies in the trust and privileged position assigned to (reductionist) techno-scientific systems and to its predictive abilities as the primary epistemic tool for shaping 'sustainable' policies and actions. This reliance on the control and predictive power of science tends to sidestep the evidence that future developments are more and more indeterminate and contingent particularly because of our public and collective power of transformation (see Collier quotation above).

A second level of contradiction concerns the firm conviction, seen indeed in British agri-food and rural policy debates, that narrow science and technologically based innovations lead the way to 'progress' in solving sustainability problems. This derives from the traditionalist-modernist assumptions that traditional scientific and technological practices are value(s)-free knowledge production, based upon reason, as opposed to deliberation, moral-ethical and relational-based constructs, subjected to human, economic, social and political values and interests (Benessia, et al., 2012).

Thirdly, there is a dominant and grounded conviction to the privileged position of Western science in providing diagnosis and solutions to 'real-world' problems, while the increasing complexity, indeterminacy and place and temporal context dependency require open-ended and reflexive dialogue between different kinds and coproduced knowledge arising from inherently diverse natural and cultural systems.

As Benessia (2012: 23) argues, one way out of this contradiction is 'a (responsible) reflection and action based on constant feedback between short- and long-term concerns, between natural and culturally specific needs and global issues, between the place-specific knowledge resource of local communities and the science-based innovation, this can be achieved by sharing experiences of scientists, artists, policy-makers, and civil society'. The active combination of the different expertise becomes a creative catalyst for SPM.

Coproduction of social nature and of its knowledges becomes a second key bridging point between the endeavour of PNS and SPM. This indeed brings back some key principles of classical agronomy from the nineteenth and early twentieth centuries (see van der Ploeg, 2013; Chayanov, 1927) and recasts them in terms of the contemporary and diversified eco-economy outlined in this book. It is the active engagement of the social and the natural in and through place. Takeuchi, for instance, discusses – using the *Satoyama* and *Satoumi* concepts of community-based management of forests and coastal eco-systems informed by traditional knowledge systems in rural Japan – how place-based communities reconstruct wetlands to create buffer zones, stimulate tourism and manage coastal eco-systems. Alternative plant-breeding practices mentioned in Chapter 2 as an eco-economic alternative to the dominant reductionist bio-economic plant breeding are also examples of eco-economic and place-based ways out of the dominant and science-led control of plant breeding. This potentially creates a hybridized and more sustainable model of agronomy (Waltener-Jones and Lang, 2000) in which the relations with food and food production are coproduced and embedded in a democratized constellation of social, cultural and ecological public values.

These emerging and bridging systems of PNS and SPM confront, however, aspects of a continued and crisis-prone corporate-controlled agri-food governance built around, as we shall see here, increasingly unstable and vulnerable financialized systems which continue to reduce the resilience of rural resilience more generally.

Corporate food governance, financialization and the reproduction of food security vulnerabilities: Changing food governance in the UK

The food, financial and resulting fiscal crisis emerging from 2007 to 2008 has led to a rejuvenation and reproduction of a series of interconnected food vulnerabilities. In this section we concentrate upon an analysis of these expressions with regard to the dominant, corporate, private-interest model of food governance. We have documented for some time in the 2000s the complex nature of this system of food governance both in the UK and in Europe more generally (see Marsden, et al., 2010), and more recently it has become linked more generally to the crisis tendencies associated with overall neo-liberal regulation (see Wolf and Bonanno, 2014; Busch, 2014).

In the UK since the crisis emerged we have witnessed both the rejuvenation of the private-interest model, and at the same time an intensification of its social impacts and vulnerabilities, such that a renewed discourse around 'food security' has emerged (see *Feeding Britain* report 2014). This is leading to a new set of conjunctures which are far more unstable in comparison with the late-twentieth-century private-interest model which delivered what seemed to be socially legitimate food provision at a relatively cheap price for the majority of the population (see Chapter 1). Now, as Bonanno (2014: 27) argues:

> The limits of neo-liberalism are theoretically clear and empirically evident. Arguably, the crisis of the regime can be seen more as a demonstrated fact rather than a hypothesis. Additionally, existing contradictions make it problematic to argue about the existence of an organised system. Neo-liberalism appears more like a project in crisis, rather than a regime. Yet, and despite claims of economic unsustainability and lack of substantive democracy, neo-liberalism remains the dominant ideology and, in many instances, the preferred political choice of the second decade of the twenty first century.

The food system is a central subset of these new set of contingencies, and it is one which now, as we shall delineate in this chapter, more openly displays these contradictions and vulnerabilities to such an extent that it reduces the overall legitimacy of the regulatory system as a whole. In this sense, we agree with Hall and Massey (2010: 57) when they argue for a post-neo-liberal state whereby 'history moves from one conjuncture to another rather than being an evolutionary flow. And what drives it forward is usually a crisis. ... Crises are moments of potential change, but the nature of their resolution is not given'.

It is important therefore to see the current neo-liberal-dominated conjuncture as a more highly contested and contingent process. Under these conditions we can expect new tendencies and countertendencies in food nutritional and provision systems (FNS) both operating in parallel times and spaces. For instance, we can see the continued intensification of production and supply of food at the same time as a growth in alternative assemblages is occurring as very much a reaction to these trends. What thus seems clear, and the UK governance seems particularly prone to this, is a lack of coherence and proactivity on the part of the state to act (and especially intervene) in and on behalf of the wider public interest, over and above its private-interest obligations to corporate private food interests. Figure 6.1 depicts these panarchical sets of relationships. These currently, and interestingly, tend to devalorize significant groups of consumers and producers, such that value is continually abstracted from both in the dominant private-interest model. (See Figure 6.1). This is more evident today than it was a decade ago when we were writing about the dominant private-interest food governance model. Then, before the multiple crises, that model could rely upon a fairly stable procurement of food materials from around the world at a relatively cheap and externalized cost. At the same time, general levels of economic growth and state welfare spending also tended to uphold the effective demand and consumption of food goods more for the majority of the low-income population.

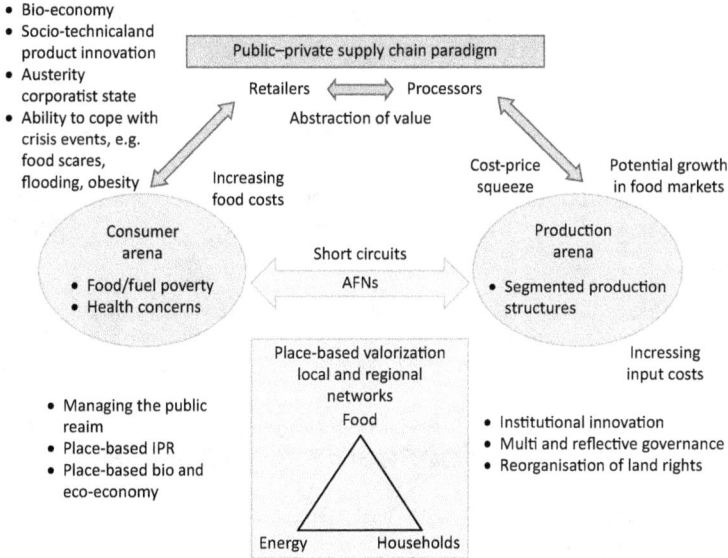

Figure 6.1 Coping with food disorder post-2008.

These conditions have now significantly changed as Moore (2010; 2015) and Marsden and Morley (2014) have recently pointed out, with the conjuncture of resource depletions on the one hand and the continued withdrawal of state welfare nets on the other. As we shall see below this combination of circumstances, together with the upholding of a neo-liberal corporate food system, has led to the reproduction of a new set of food security vulnerabilities. At the same time, it has also further stimulated the corporate-controlled financialization of key aspects of the food system as scarcities have led to speculative financial investments in land and key natural resources. The reaction to the crisis has thus been to continue to shift financial resources to resource-based 'safe havens', further reducing social and public good investments in reducing vulnerabilities and inequalities. So let's look at some of the evidence taken recently (Transmango Research, 2015).[1]

System Vulnerabilities

Ecological: soil fertility, bio-diversity, production losses and declines in self-sufficiency, water imports.

Social: declines in health and well-being, skill shortages on the farm and in the kitchen, rises in social inequality and low incomes, reductions in food sovereignty.

Corporate and financial: oligopoly and power concentration, concentrated rather than distributed food infrastructures, unsustainable 'food choice' editing, dependency upon imports and specific non-renewable inputs, corporate dominance of land markets constraining smallholdings and horticulture and public access to growing, weakness of public regulation and greater food safely risks.

Financialization: food as an increasingly financial asset to be traded over time (hedge) and space. Growth in financial packages by banks, agricultural commodity trading firms and investment funds. Serving to drive up, or at least create more volatility in food prices, land and bio-sphere markets.

Enacting resilience and managing vulnerability: Some concepts to progress

Rebuilding public legitimacy and reflexive governance

It is clear from recent research evidence (see Delphi study, Transmango, 2015[2]) that there is a general and growing lack of legitimacy facing current food governance systems in Europe. As Garnett and Godfray (2012: 49) have argued 'A system of food production that is socially or ethically unacceptable to a large fraction of the population will lack continuality, or resilience, however ecologically attuned it may be.' There is a need to ensure that more multilevel, reflexive, governance systems ensure more effective food security strategies which can recalibrate both food sustainability and security.

New PNS approaches need to connect with ecological, social and civic interests, and this needs to be organized and progressed by state bodies. As we have seen from our British case studies in Chapter 5, this is far from being the case, particularly since 2010 when fiscal austerity has been combined with more concentrated and exogenous models of economic development which has marginalized more state-based reflexive thinking.

As Feindt (2012: 5–6) portrays it, reflexive governance needs to embrace PNS by finding a lasting arena, and platforms for a range of actors from 'various levels of governance and/or various epistemic backgrounds in an effort to reflect on and possibly adapt their cognitive and normative beliefs, in ways which take account and acknowledge alternative understandings of the problems; in an attempt to integrate multiple approaches to problem solution'.

One example of how this can occur concerns food procurement (see Otsuki, 2014; Sonnino, Torres and Schneider, 2014). In their cases of Brazil where efforts to promote quality food procurement worked to shape reflexive governance in a decentralized political environment and created an institutional device based upon cooperative civic participation and state-engagement. However, the process highlighted socio-economic inequality due to uneven local capacities to connect good quality services to citizens' everyday practices and places. The work identifies the following paths to tackle this unevenness: improvements of place-based infrastructure, promotion of translocal cooperation and the building upon existing informal institutional arrangements.

Building translocal networks

A related and further key mechanism concerns the opportunities to create translocal (as opposed to conventionally globalized) networks between place-based agri-food initiatives. These are showing the capabilities to transgress existing and formalized systems of regulation which often tend to marginalize more distributed agro-ecological initiatives (such as in the area of community and participatory plant breeding and urban-based food community programmes). There is now a growing literature on the rise of translocal networks, not least around media and digital communication (see Appadurai, 1995; Brickell and Datta, 2011; Carpentier, 2007). However, it is clear that both in North America and in Europe, alternative food initiatives are finding distinct advantages in 'scaling-out' their activities and linking across, in some cases, vast territories. This is particularly interesting in Canada, with a range of community food initiatives creating more resilience and reducing vulnerability and isolation in what are vast terrains of landscape (e.g. the Northern Territories).

McFarlane (2009) deploys the analytic of 'translocal assemblage' as a means of conceptualizing space and power in social movements. Here, translocal assemblages are composites of place-based social movements which exchange ideas, knowledges, practices, materials and resources across sites. The assemblage is more than just the connections between sites, in that they are not just 'nodes' in a network; rather, they come with their own histories, the labour required to produce and sustain them, and their capacity to exceed the connections between other groups. They add innovative capital across places. Finally, therefore, they are not just another spatial category, output or resultant formation, but they also signify doing, performance and events (see also Oakes and Schein, 2006, on the case of translocal China).

The emergence of the distributed economy

The rise of the notion of the circular economy (see EU, 2015; McArthur Foundation, 2016) together with an emerging antidote to the competitive city-region debates around notions of the regenerative city (Girardet, 2015) are giving further weight to the ways in which the urban and rural economies can be reconnected via a more distributed set of economic linkages. Again, the onset of the bio-economy, and especially its more ecologically grounded conceptualization of the eco-economy (Marsden and Farioli, 2015), is providing a basis for re-conceptualizing more distributed ecological and economic systems (see Barbero et al., 2010; IIIEE, 2009). Building historically, for instance, on Cronin's analysis of the rise of Chicago and its hinterland in the nineteenth century, recent works have relinked these distributed connections. Johansson et al. (2005) see the distributed systems as a new engine of sustainable innovation and a fundamental part of the 'circular economy', whereby both material and economic flows of goods and services are recycled, minimizing wastes and generating more place-based value capture.

They call for the realization of the unsustainability of carbon-based centralized systems favouring neo-classical economic (and indeed aggregated and centralized) drivers. Rather than abandoning large-scale production, a selective share of production can be distributed to regions where a diverse range of activities are organized in the form of small-scale, flexible units which are connected with each other, with more self-organizing business environments (see also, Mirata, Nilsson and Kuisma, 2005; Ouma, Boeckler and Lindner, 2013). Staffas, Gustavsson and McCormick, (2013) compare current bio-economic approaches adopted in the EU and North America, and this indicates that national and regional policies will be critical as to whether the rise of the more integrated bio-economy takes either more concentrated or distributed pathways of development. These policies are particularly critical for rural areas, as in the case of Finland, where, for example, the ability to capture more local and distributed value networks from the bio-economy is being realized (Chapter 3).

Once one applies a more circular economy approach to the full cost-accounting of ecological resources flows in and between rural and urban spaces, the spectre of a more distributed spatial economy becomes far more realistic and necessary as part and parcel of the post-carbon transition. Here, then, we can see some important conceptual linkages emerging between the multifunctional 'new rural paradigm' (as empirically examined in Chapters 3 and 4) SPM and the recent emergence of a more distributed circular economy. So far, however, there are significant gaps in the communications between urban, regional and rural scholars and scientists on this agenda, although recent international debates around sustainable food and cities are making these connections. In this sense the case of agri-food becomes a major site for addressing these transitions and, indeed, in relinking the urban with the rural in rebuilding more regenerative cities on the one hand and more sustainable and distributed rural regions on the other.

Conclusions

Building resilience, reducing vulnerability: Re-enter the state

The twin processes of centralization and financialization have been central hallmarks of the neo-liberal agri-food and rural regime in the UK, especially since the FFFFc hit in 2007–8. This has tended – both in literally physical and infrastructural terms – to reinforce the 'hollowing-out' of much rural infrastructure just at the time, it becomes so essential to reinvest in it. At the time of writing, dairy farmers, having lost nearly half of their farms in the UK over the past decade, are again directly protesting about retailer buying power, the squeeze of farm-gate prices and the ratcheting up of their input costs. As we saw in our two case study regions, since 2010 in particular, both in Devon and in Shetland, the place-based rural web has been seriously diluted by the twin processes of centralization of services infrastructure (as indeed a particular response to local and regional government cuts and austerity) and the onset of a particular model of economic development which marginalizes agri-food and, indeed, rural development.

These are, then, hardly the bases upon which a more distributed and post-carbon rural paradigm would begin to prosper. What we see from this analysis is, however, a very uneven temporal as well as spatial dynamic about these very contested transitions which rural and urban areas are now facing. It is a process of, as we indicated in the introduction, 'contested sustainabilities', as both neo-liberalism and post-neo-liberal (eco-economic) experiments vie for places where they can enact their particular framings of sustainability – for instance, in the framings of the bio-economic and eco-economic models outlined in this book.

So, will we see a slow but painful death of the centralized and financialized neo-liberal model in the face of the growing realization of the need to progress the post-carbon transition? It will not be straightforward, and it depends, we can argue, on the further embedding of many of the conceptual parameters developed and introduced in this book. We need to promote more distributed models of landholding and land-using in rural areas as the optimum means of ensuring more eco-economic resilience in the future. Here the small family farm is a place which would not only grow food sustainably, but would also create a hub for bio-energy and waste recycling. We should remember that the vast majority of the 570 million farms in the world are small or very small. They occupy around 70 to 80 per cent of farmland and produce more than 80 per cent of the world's food in value terms. These tend to have higher agricultural crop yields per hectare and manage their natural resources and labour more intensively (see FAO, 2015; van der Ploeg, 2014). It is increasingly becoming recognized that small farms now offer a way out of the tensions in achieving both food security and sustainability around the world. But why not in countries like the UK? We need a debate about farm structures in countries like the UK as part of a wider concern relating to food and energy security. There has been a significant dwindling of productive capacity among the farm structures in the UK over the past 20 years, and this needs to be addressed. The question is where will this be addressed, by whom and for whom?

In Paris in December (2015), the global authorities will again focus upon the national and international reduction of carbon emissions. In the past, agri-food has been something of a bystander to these debates, as the focus is placed largely upon heavy industry. This needs to change. We need to see, as Mckibben recently reminds us (*New York Review of Books*, September 2015), and as recent EU research (Transmango) confirms, that agri-food is both a central part of the problem and part of the solution regarding the transition to the post-carbonized economy. Now, and with the onset of Paris and the new Sustainable Development goals, there is clear evidence, not least from the financial investment sector (see Caldecott, 2013), that carbonized investments are increasingly becoming 'stranded investments'. Even reliance upon the biogenetic GM technologies is now being seen as further asset 'stranding', as they are shown to exacerbate pests and diseases through the hybridization of related transgenic organisms, produce harm and risks to non-target species, such as soil organisms, non-pest insects, birds and other fauna, and disrupt biotic communities, including agro-ecological systems and genetic diversity. More generally, several leading financiers are warning investors to watch out for stranded assets with respect to further carbon exploitation, at the same time that on both sides of the Atlantic several major institutions, not least the Norwegian Sovereign Wealth fund, and several funds in Canada and the United States, are proceeding to divest from carbon-based investments.

As Mark Carney, head of Bank of England and chair of the Financial Stability Board, (Bank of England, 2015: 11) recently admitted:

> 19% of FTSE 100 companies are in natural resources and extraction sectors; and a further 11% by value are in power utilities, chemicals, construction and industrial good sectors. Globally, these two tiers of companies between them account for around one-third of equity and fixed income assets.

On the other hand, financing the de-carbonisation of our economy is a major opportunity for insurers and long-term investors. It implies a sweeping reallocation of resources and a technological revolution, with investment in long-term infrastructure assets at roughly quadruple the present rate. For this to happen, 'green' finance cannot conceivably remain a niche interest over the medium term.

There are a number of factors which could influence the speed of transition to a low carbon economy, including public policy, technology, investor preferences and physical events. ... An abrupt resolution of the tragedy of the horizons is in itself a financial stability risk. The more we invest with foresight; the less we will regret in hindsight.

Hence, looking into the not-too-distant future, we may be witnessing the deeper and more widespread reaction to the vulnerabilities we have created in the intensive agri-food and financialized model operating especially since 2007. Many of our expert respondents in the Transmango project, for example, are now calling for the state to again provide a consistent framework to resolve the recognized systems vulnerabilities witnessed in the European agri-food system (see Transmango, Delphi, full report; and Stakeholders report D2.3, 2015). Many respondents from the private, NGO and public sectors consider that the government should lead vulnerability assessments in order to create a comprehensive account of the challenges facing the UK FNS system as part of 'their duty to have proper understanding of food security' (p.18). This is in many ways a wider call for more reflexive food governance in the UK and EU; and a recognition that there is a lack of 'type 2–3' thinking and assessment about what the vulnerabilities are, how they are interlinked and how they could be addressed. Instead, the emphasis from national governments is to stimulate more trade as a solution – very much a 'type 1' market-led approach. At the time of concluding this work, the UK referendum to leave the EU has just been announced. This could lead to further (carbonized) deregulation and a further removal of protectionst, EU-environmental and -rural development policy. On the other hand, it could act as a significant stimulus for developing a real, globally responsible and sustainable agri-food and rural development policy embracing the bio-economy. In sum, the intensity of the contestations we have traced in this book is set to intensify as the debate over the British agri-food and rural policy takes a more post-EU track.

This is then partly a battleground between neo-liberalized (non-reflexive) governance and the growing need for more reflexive governance, which once again recognizes the decisive and fundamental role of the state and the public realm in resolving the contradictions between food security and food sustainability (Marsden, 2013). This is the new contested resource governance terrain that 'post-normal scientists' along with other sustainability stakeholders are engaged with. It is one which needs to integrate agri-food and rural development into these debates far more centrally than in the past, and to challenge these contested transitions in ways which reflexively position agri-food and sustainable rural development as part of the (resilient) solution rather than as part of the (vulnerability) problem. We will see ...

Beyond national state ruralities

It is becoming increasingly clear that in most advanced economies the necessary transitions towards a more sustainable food system will not be mobilized or realized by national governance systems. We can postulate that this is a clear departure in the fourth vector of Figure 6.2, whereby in all the three earlier vectors, the nation state was proactive in designing and implementing its policies for creating balances and compromises between food sustainability and food security concerns on behalf of the public policy need. While the 'alternative' food movement has for a long period argued for more local and regional forms of mobilization, it is becoming increasingly clear that these

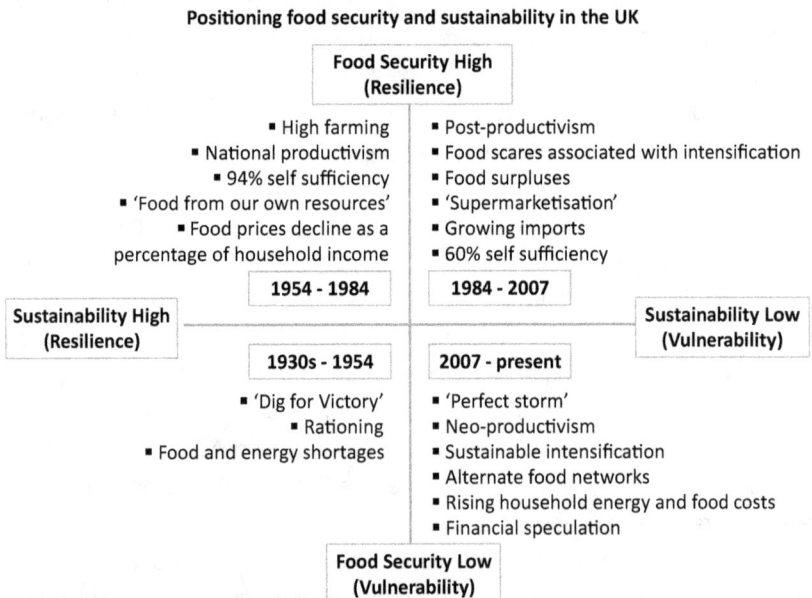

Positioning food security and sustainability in the UK

Food Security High (Resilience)

- High farming
- National productivism
- 94% self sufficiency
- 'Food from our own resources'
- Food prices decline as a percentage of household income

- Post-productivism
- Food scares associated with intensification
- Food surpluses
- 'Supermarketisation'
- Growing imports
- 60% self sufficiency

1954 - 1984   **1984 - 2007**

Sustainability High (Resilience)   **Sustainability Low (Vulnerability)**

1930s - 1954   **2007 - present**

- 'Dig for Victory'
- Rationing
- Food and energy shortages

- 'Perfect storm'
- Neo-productivism
- Sustainable intensification
- Alternate food networks
- Rising household energy and food costs
- Financial speculation

Food Security Low (Vulnerability)

Figure 6.2 Positioning food security and sustainability in the UK.

levels of agency are likely to be key drivers for the sustainable and security transformations that are needed.

This is not just happening because of the current and growing vitality of local and community food initiatives, as we now see in Canada; or because of the growing demands for food access from low-income groups faced with cuts in welfare and rises in household living costs. It is also occurring because in many countries the national policy and political systems of governance are intentionally or unintentionally abandoning their commitments to protecting and enhancing food sovereignty and security for significant parts of their populations. This is now becoming increasingly clear, seven or eight years after the food crisis merged with the neo-liberal financial and fiscal crisis. In most nation states in Europe and North America, there is, instead, a merging of political and governance priorities with the corporate food and financial sectors operating on a global and concentrated basis. Further financialization of the food sector is continuing to go hand in hand with national neo-liberal corporate-interest governance which protects and supports the regulation of market mechanisms which support agri-food oligopoly, especially in the food inputs, processing and retailing sectors.

Faced with this neo-liberal governance 'lock-in', and an absence of positive national policies to tackle rising food insecurities, it is being left to the civic and voluntary sectors to address the public consequences of this. Hence we see a significant rise in the mobilization of territorial-based civic and community-based organizations, not least at the city level and, indeed, with the assistance of some support from municipal and local forms of governance. We are facing, therefore, what we might typify as two parallel agri-food universes. First, a continuance of a commodity-based, highly financialized and bio-economic food provisioning system which relies upon further ecological damage and human vulnerability around a range of health and welfare conditions. Let us understand that this system is highly regulated through nationally supported and governed private-interest-organized supply chains which extract growing levels of value from both food producers and consumers. At both ends of the sophisticated and concentrated supply chains, therefore, and particularly since 2007–8, we have seen the further vulnerability of groups of producers and consumers in this system.

Second, faced with these sets of conditions, the local and community-based systems of provision based in particular places and regions have attempted to provide a more eco-economic alternative and sustainable system of food supply for a growing proportion of the population. This lies largely outside of the national systems of regulation and relies upon creating translocal rather than globalized relations and knowledge flows. These new systems are creating new and innovative connections between producers and sets of consumers, as well as linking social and welfare concerns with questions of ecological sustainability and healthy, affordable food.

A major, but so far limited, agent and driver for relocalized and translocalized food will indeed be, and need to be, the more mutlifunctional agricultural producer sector (as we typify in Chapters 4 and 5). So far, despite the growing development of agri-ecological niches, this system is still far too locked-in and dependent upon the national and International systems of supply chain management as well as the CAP. These are continuing to reduce the number of farms, and growing protests, not least in the dairy sectors this summer (2015), demonstrate the inadequacy and current weaknesses of the established farming unions in national policy. So how can the local community food sector unlock more of the potential of the farm producer sector? How can a wider group of producers be enrolled into territorially organized and more distributed systems of provision and consumption? How can new rural–urban linkages be created so as to scale-out the sustainable food transformation?

To sum up, this is where a deeper exploration and articulation of the key concepts of reflexive governance, translocalism and the evolution of the distributed economy need to be engaged, such that they begin to fill the spaces and places left from neo-liberal national state withdrawal. For instance, translocal assemblages and networks need to nourish social innovations as well as physical and ecological infrastructures and demonstrations of good practice across places and existing multilevel governance structures. This is a potentially rich field of innovation and social experimentation. This is now happening across cities and some regional territorial networks, but it also requires more reflexive food and broader bio-economic governance which facilitates new spatially distributed platforms across both urban and rural domains (see Northwest Ontario study and network, (Nourishing Communties 2017)).

In these ways we may energize the transitions away from the dysfunctional vector in Figure 6.2, whereby the current conditions of corporate and neo-liberalized governance are allowing further declines in both food sustainability and security. Territorial initiatives and translocal food networks are beginning to repopulate this vector in ways which make the vector more variable overall.

The need for a new place-based politics in agri-food and rural development

So far it can be argued that despite the 'wake-up' calls of 2007–8 regarding the onset of concerns over food security and wider aspects of resource depletion, there has been only marginal increases in a new food and rural politics which can engage and link to progressing a wider post-carbon transition in the UK at least. The long-running decline in agri-food corporatism from the 1980s, which we depicted in earlier volumes (Marsden et al., 1993; Murdoch et al, 2003), has so far not been replaced with an equivalent politics for progressing the new or neo-productivist concerns as they have particularly arisen since 2007–8. Rather, as we have argued earlier, it has led to a continued neo-liberalized and technologically driven modus which espouses a particular faith in a rather narrow conception of the bio-economy.

As much of this book and its thesis contends, this needs to be theoretically, conceptually and empirically challenged from deep and comparative insights into what really constitutes real sustainability in the agri-food and rural sphere. As we have argued this is essentially place-based, and depends upon a re-embedding of economic and social practices in and across local and regional spaces and places. This will also mean reintegrating multifunctional agriculture with far wider conceptions of sustainable rural development and place-making. This now carries huge potential, but as we have seen, can also become 'blown off course', as is partly happening, for instance, in Devon and Shetland, by the refreshed dominant combinations of neo-liberalist governance and the espousal of a highly technocratic framing of the bio-economy. In order to build upon this potential, and to concurrently reduce its vulnerabilities, we need new connections to be made between 'post-normal' sustainability science, SPM practices and their local and translocal communication and political translation. As Sheppard (2015) has more broadly argued in his recent critique of conventionalized notions of globalized capitalism (1126):

> Mainstream accounts of globalising capitalism conceptualise humans and the more-than-human world as fixed characteristics, exogenous to the economy. The non-human world is conceptualised as fixed bundles of 'natural resources' to be traded like any produced commodity. ... Missing here, however, is any conception of the role of non-human agency (bio-physical processes etc.): its co-constitutive, dialectical relationships with economic processes are simply assumed away.

But, as Sheppard asserts (1129):

> Thinking (or unthinking) geographically about globalising capitalism has uncovered a wide variety of forms of economic life that resist, exceed, or simply are tangential to commodity production and market exchange, not only in supposedly traditional or less developed societies but also close to the heartbeat of globalising capitalism. Given globalising capitalism's tendency

to reproduce socio-spatial inequality, failing to deliver on its promise, such alternatives should no longer be regarded as residual practices, withering away naturally in the shadow of capitalism's inexorable development trajectory. They are a valuable and diverse experimental eco-system of norms, practices, and trajectories – the seed banks, if you will, of alternatives to globalising capitalism.

Sheppard is writing here not only about the worlds of agri-food or rural development, but also about the arguments directly relevant in progressing their sustainability at a time of growing malfunctionality and, indeed, public illegitimacy in the particular globalized and competitive processes which are still dominant in these domains.

Notes

1. http://www.transmango.eu/
2. http://www.transmango.eu/

References

Acland Committee (1913). The rural economy: report of findings.

Adamson, D. and Lang, M. (2014). Towards a new settlement: a deep place approach to equitable and suitable and sustainable places, Centre for Regeneration Excellence in Wales, http://regenwales.org/upload/pdf/042814110151CREW%20Deep%20 Place%20Study%20April%202014.pdf [accessed 14 July 2016].

Advertising Standards Authority (2009). ASA Adjudication on Viking Energy Partnership. Available at: http://www.asa.org.uk/Complaints-and-ASA-action/Adjudications/2009/11/ Viking-Energy-Partnership/TF_ADJ_47582.aspx. [accessed 14 July 2016].

Agarwala, M., Atkinson, G., Baldock, C. and Gardiner, B. (2014). Natural capital accounting and climate change. *Nature Climate Change*, 4(7), 520–2.

Alberta Innovates (2013). RECOMMENDATIONS TO BUILD ALBERTA'S BIOECONOMY, Report, Available at: http://bio.albertainnovates.ca/media/57924/bioe_final_report_ web_may2013.pdf [accessed 12 July 2016].

Alkon, A. H. and Traugot, M. (2008). Place matters, but how? Rural identity, environmental decision making, and the social construction of place. *City & Community*, 7(2), 97–112.

Amin, A. (2004). Regions unbound: Towards a new politics of place. *Geografiska, Annaler*, 86B, 33–44.

Anderson, C. R., Brushett, L., Gray, T. W. and Renting, H. (2014). Working together to build cooperative food systems [Editorial]. *Journal of Agriculture, Food Systems, and Community Development*, 4(3), 3–9.

Anderson, M. S. and Massa, I. (2000). Ecological modernization – origins, dilemmas and future directions. *Journal of Environmental Policy and Planning*, 2, 337–45.

Anderson, K. et al. (2008). Beyond the Rural – Urban Divide: Cross-continental Perspectives on the Differentiated Countryside and its Regulation. *Research in Rural Sociology and Development series*, Vol 14, Emerald, UK.

Anderson, K. et al. (2015). Metropolitan Ruralities. *Research in Rural Sociology and Development*, Vol 23, Emerald, UK.

Andrée, P., et al. (2014). *Globalisation Food Sovereignty: Global and Local Change in the New Politics of Food*, Toronto: University of Toronto Press.

Anex, R. (2004). Something new under the sun? The industrial ecology of biobased products. *Journal of Industrial Ecology*, 7(3–4), 1–4.

Ansar, A., Caldecott, B. and Tilbury, J. (2013). Stranded assets and the fossil fuel divestment campaign: what does divestment mean for the valuation of fossil fuel assets. Stranded Assets Programme, SSEE, University of Oxford.

Appadurai, A. (1995). The production of locality. In R. Fardon (ed.), *Counterworks: Managing the Diversity of Knowledge*, 204–25, London: Routledge.

Árnason, A., Shucksmith, M. and Vergunst, J., eds (2009). Comparing rural development. *Continuity and Change in the Countryside of Western Europe*, Aldershot: Ashgate Publishing.

Arthur, W. B., Durlauf, S. N. and Lane, D. A. (1997). *The Economy as an Evolving Complex System II*, Reading, MA: Addison-Wesley.

Balakrischan, M. S. (2009). Strategic branding of destinations: A framework, commentary. *European Journal of Marketing*, 43(5/6), 611–29.

Balmer, J. M. T. (2001). Corporate identity, corporate branding and corporate marketing – seeing through the fog, *European Journal of Marketing*, 35(3/4), 248–91.

Bank of England (2015). Breaking the Tragedy of the Horizon – climate change and financial stability: a speech given by Mark Carney, Governor of the Bank of England. Available at: http://www.bankofengland.co.uk/publications/Documents/speeches/2015/speech844.pdf [accessed 14 July 2016].

Barbero, S., Johnson, A., Ravikumar, R., Newton, R. M., Wong, C. Y., Khong, C. W., and Burns, L. D. (2010). Local bio-energy promotes distributed economy for sustainable development: Systemic design approach and case-studies. *Design Principles & Practice: An International Journal*, 4(4): 21–8.

Benessia, A., Funtowicz, S., Bradshaw, G., Ferri, F., Ráez-Luna, E. F. and Medina, C. P. (2012), Hybridizing sustainability: Towards a new praxis for the present human predicament. *Sustainability Science*, 7(1), 75–89.

Berkes, F. and Folke, C. (1998). *Linking Social and Ecological Systems: Management Practices and Social Mechanisms for Building Resilience*. New York: Cambridge University Press.

Bevir, M. (2012). *Governance: A Very Short Introduction (Vol. 333)*. Oxford: Oxford University Press.

Bevir, M. (2013). Interpreting governance: Intentionality, historicity, and reflexivity. *Revue française de science politique (English Edition)*, 63(3–4), 115–32.

Birch, K., Levidow, L. and Papaioannou, T. (2014). Self-fulfilling prophecies of the European knowledge-based bio-economy: The discursive shaping of institutional and policy frameworks in the bio-pharmaceuticals sector. *Journal of the Knowledge Economy*, 5(1), 1–18.

Blay-Palmer, A. (2014). Editorial introduction sustainable local food spaces: Constructing community of food. *Local Environment Special Issue*, 18(5): 521–641.

Bonanno, A. (2014). The legitimation crisis of neoliberal globalization: Instances from agriculture and food. In S. A. Wolf and A. Bonanno (eds), *The Neoliberal Regime in the Agri-food Sector: Crisis, Resilience, and Restructuring*, 12–28. London: Routledge.

Bowen, A. and Hepburn, C. (2014). Green growth: An assessment. *Oxford Review of Economic Policy*, 30(3), 407–22.

Boyd, E. and Folke, C. (2012). *Adapting Institutions: Governance, Complexity and Social-ecological Resilience*. Cambridge: Cambridge University Press.

Brenner, N., Peck, J. and Theordore, N. (2010). After neo-liberalism? *Globalisations*, 7(3), 327–45.

Bressler, D. (2012). Transforming technologies: Game changers for the bio-economy in North America. 'Growing the Bio-economy conference', 2–5 October, Banff, Canada.

Brickell, K. and Datta, A., eds (2011). *Translocal Geographies: Spaces, Places, Connections*. Burlington: Ashgate Publishing, Ltd.

Bridge, G. and Smith, A. (2003). Intimate encounters: Culture – economy – commodity. *Environment and Planning D: Society and Space*, 21(3), 257–68

Bristow, G. (2009). Limits to regional competitiveness. In J. Tomaney (ed.), *The Future of Regional Policy, Smith Institute and Regional Studies Association*, 26–32. London: Smith Institute.

Bristow, G. (2010). Resilient regions: Re-'place'ing regional competitiveness. *Cambridge Journal of Regions, Economy and Society*, 3(1), 153–67.

British Columbia (2013). BC Bioeconomy, Available at: http://www.gov.bc.ca/jtst/down/ bio_economy_report_final.pdf [accessed 11 March 2015].

Bruckmeier, K. (2000). LEADER in Germany and the discourse of autonomous regional development. *Sociologia Ruralis*, 40(2), 219–27.

Buck, N. Gordon, I. and Harding, A., eds (2005). *Changing Cities: Rethinking Urban Competitiveness, Cohesion and Governance*. Basingstoke: Palgrave Macmillan.

Busch, L. (2014). Governance in the age of global markets: Challenges, limits, and consequences. *Agriculture and Human Values*, 31(3), 513–23.

Busch, L. and Bain, C. (2004). New! Improved? The transformation of the global agrifood system. *Rural Sociology*, 69(3), 321–46.

Business, Innovation and Skills (BIS) (2010). A strategy for Sustainable growth, July 2010, Crown Copyright.

Busta House Hotel (no date). Food. [Available Online] http://www.bustahouse.com/ features/62/food.

Buttel, F. H. (2000). Ecological modernization as social theory. *Geoforum*, 31(1), 57–65.

Caldecott, B. (2013). Are we facing a multi-trillion dollar agri-bubble?, Business Green. Available at: http://www.smithschool.ox.ac.uk/research-programmes/stranded-assets/Are%20we%20facing%20a%20multi-trillion%20dollar%20agri-bubble%20 %E2%80%93%2009%20Aug%202013%20%E2%80%93%20BusinessGreen%20 print%20view.pdf [accessed 12 July 2016].

Caldecott, B., Howarth, N. and McSharry, P. (2013). Stranded assets in agriculture: Protecting value from environment-related risks. Smith School of Enterprise and the Environment, University of Oxford, Oxford, United Kingdom. http://www.smithschool. ox.ac.uk/research-programmes/stranded-assets/Stranded%20Assets%20 Agriculture%20Report%20Final.pdf [accessed 12 July 2016].

Cantrill, J. G. and Senecah, S. L. (2001). Using the 'sense of self-in-place' construct in the context of environmental policy-making and landscape planning. *Environmental Science & Policy*, 4(4), 185–203.

Carpentier, N. (2007). Translocalism, Community Media and City. Working Papers 7. Centre for Studies on Media and Culture (CeMeso)-Free University Brussels, Belgium.

Castells, M. (2012). *Networks of Outrage and Hope: Social Movements in the Internet Age*. Cambridge, UK: Polity.

Ceccarelli, S. (2014). Diversity for specific adaptation and evolutionary processes: Improving food security by cultivating diversity. International Congress on Diversity Strategies for Organic and low input agricultures and their food systems, 7/9th July 2014, Nantes, France.

Chatham House (2009). Food futures: Re-thinking UK strategy. London. Royal Institute of International Affairs [accessed 12 March 2015] https://www.chathamhouse.org/sites/files/chathamhouse/public/Research/Global%20Trends/r0109foodfutures.pdf [accessed 12 July 2016].

Chayanov, A. (1927). *The Theory of Peasant Co-operatives*. Columbus: Ohio state University Press.

Christen, M. and Schmidt, S. (2012). A formal framework for conceptions of sustainability – a theoretical contribution to the discourse in sustainable development. *Sustainable Development*, 20(6), 400–10.

Christensen, C. M., Baumann, H., Ruggles, R. and Sadtler, T. M. (2006). Disruptive innovation for social change. *Harvard Business Review*, 84(12), 94.

Christoff, P. (1996). Ecological modernisation, ecological modernities. *Environmental Politics*, 5, 476–500.

Clark, R. (2013) Why we need to frack, slash, build, *The Sunday Times*, Available at: http://www.thesundaytimes.co.uk/sto/news/focus/article1280837.ece [accessed 10 March 2015].

Clark, W. C. (2007). Sustainability science: A room of its own. *Proceedings of the National Academy of Sciences*, 104(6), 1737.

Clark, W. C. and Dickson, N. M. (2003). Sustainability science: The emerging research program. *Proceedings of the National Academy of Sciences*, 100(14), 8059–61.

Clarke, J. (1996). Farm accommodation and the communication mix. *Tourism management*, 17, 611–16.

Clarke, J. (1999). Marketing structures for farm tourism: Beyond the individual provider of rural tourism. *Journal of Sustainable Tourism*, 7, 26–47.

Cloke, P. J. and Little, J. (1997). *Contested Countryside Cultures: Otherness, Marginalisation, and Rurality*. Routledge and London: Psychology Press.

Collier, S. J. (2008). Enacting catastrophe: Preparedness, insurance, budgetary rationalitzation, *Economy and Society*, 37(2), pp. 224–50

Collier, S. J. (2009). Topologies of power foucault's analysis of political government beyond 'Governmentality'. *Theory, Culture & Society*, 26(6), 78–108.

Collier, S. J. (2012). Neoliberalism as Big Leviathan, or…? A Response to Waquant and Hilgers. *Social Anthropology*, 20(2), 86–95.

Commission for Rural Communities (2010). State of the Countryside Report; available at: http://webarchive.nationalarchives.gov.uk/20110303145243/http://ruralcommunities.gov.uk/files/sotc/sotc2010.pdf [accessed 11 March 2015].

Community Council for Devon (2006/2007). Rural Trends 2006/07 Report 3: Agriculture and Community. Exeter.

Constance, D. H., Renard, M. C. and Rivera-Ferre, M. G., eds (2014). *Alternative Agrifood Movements: Patterns of Convergence and Divergence*. London: Emerald.

Cooke, P. (2008). Regional innovation systems, clean technology and jacobian-cluster platform policies. *Regional Science, Policy and Practice*, 1 (1), 23–45.

Cooke, P. (2010). Socio-technical transitions and varieties of capitalism: Green regional innovation and distinctive market niches. *Journal of the Knowledge Economy*, 1(4), 239–67.

Cooke, P. (2011). Transition regions: Regional–national eco-innovation systems and strategies. *Prog Plan*, 76, 105–46.

Corporate Edge (2003). Project Selkie: The Recommended Brand Strategy for Shetland Report.

Crew, M. A. and Kleindorfer, P. R. (1999). Stranded assets in network industries in transition. In M. A. Crew (ed.), *Regulation Under Increasing Competition*, Vol 30 of Series Topics in Regulatory Economics and Policy, 63–78. New York, US: Springer.

Cronon, W. (2009). *Nature's Metropolis: Chicago and the Great West*. New York: WW Norton & Company.

Dana, L., Korot, L. and Tovstiga, G. (2005). A cross-national comparison of knowledge management practices, *International Journal of Manpower*, 26(1), 10–22.

Darnhofer, I. (2005). Organic farming and rural development: Some evidence from Austria. *Sociologia Ruralis*, 45, 308–23.

DCC, Devon County Council (2004). *The Focus on Devon report*, Exeter.

DCC, Devon County Council (2007). Devon Rural Strategy 2007, Exeter.

DEFRA (2013). Rt Hon Owen Paterson MP speech to Rothamsted Research, available at: https://www.gov.uk/government/speeches/rt-hon-owen-paterson-mp-speech-to-rothamsted-research [accessed 12 July 2016].

DEFRA (2015). Great British Food and Farming Plan events held across the country, gov.uk. Available at: https://www.gov.uk/government/news/great-british-food-and-farming-plan-events-held-across-the-country [accessed 12 July 2016].

Deibel, E. (2013). Open Variety Rights: Rethinking the Commodification of Plants. *Journal of Agrarian Change*, 13(2): 282–309.

De Schutter, O. (2014). Report of the Special Rapporteur on the right to food, Olivier De Schutter. Final report: The transformative potential of the right to food. Human Rights Council of the United Nations. Retrieved from http://www. srfood. org/images/stories/pdf/officialreports/20140310_finalreport_en. pdf.

Dovers, S. R. (1996). Sustainability: Demands on policy. *Journal of Public Policy*, 16(3), 303–18.

Dryzek, J. S. (1997). *The Politics of the Earth: Environmental Discourses*. New York: Oxford University Press.

e-architect (2008). BDP's Shetland Museum Wins Top Prize At Wood Awards. [Available Online] http://www.e-architect.co.uk/scotland/shetland_museum.htm.

Edwards, G. and Roberts, J. T. (2014). A HIGH-CARBON PARTNERSHIP? CHINESE-LATIN AMERICAN RELATIONS IN A CARBON-CONSTRAINED WORLD, Report for Global Economy and Development at BROOKINGS, Available at: http://www10.iadb.org/intal/intalcdi/PE/2014/14080.pdf.

Ekman Ehn, K. and Kassab, Z. (2014). Asset Valuation in a Low Carbon World-Value Implications of Oil Price Scenarios for US Oil and Gas Assets.

Enticott, G. (2014). Biosecurity and the bioeconomy: The case of disease regulation in the UK and New Zealand. In T. K. Marsden and A. Morley (eds), *Sustainable Food Systems: Building a New Paradigm*, 122–42. London: Earthscan

EPIQ (no date). Dutch Auction. [Available Online] http://www.epiqtech.com/auction_software-Dutch-Auction.htm.

Eriksson, A., Allee, V., Cooke, P., Harmaakorpi, V., Sotarauta, M. and Wallin, J. (2010). *The Matrix-Post Cluster Innovation Policy*. Stockholm: Vinnova.

Errington, A. and Gasson, R. (1994). Labour use in the farm family business. *Sociologia Ruralis*, 34(4), 293–307.

European Commission (EC) (1988). The future of rural society, available at: http://ec.europa.eu/agriculture/cap-history/crisis-years-1980s/com88-501_en.pdf [accessed 20 July 2016]

European Commission (EC) (2005). Territorial state and perspectives of the European Union, towards stronger territorial cohesion in the light of Lisbon and Gothennburg ambitions Scoping document endorsed by Ministers of Spatial Development and the European Commission. *Ministerial Meeting on Regional Policy and Territorial Cohesion*.

European Commission (EC) (2010a). Investing in Europe's future: Fifth report on economic, social and territorial cohesion. *Report from the European Commission*. Luxembourg: Publications Office of the European Union.

European Commission (EC) (2010b). From challenges to opportunities: Towards a Common Strategic Framework for EU. *Green Paper, European Commission*, 9 February 2011. Brussels.

European Commission (EC) (2012). Directorate-General for Research and Innovation. Innovating for Sustainable Growth: A Bioeconomy for Europe. Publications Office of the European Union. Available at: http://ec.europa.eu/research/bioeconomy/pdf/bioeconomycommunicationstrategy_b5_brochure_web.pdf [accessed 10 March 2015].

European Commission (EC) (2015). Closing the loop: An EU action plan for the circular economy. Brussels. Available at: http://ec.europa.eu/environment/circular-economy/index_en.htm.

European Geoparks Network (no date). Appendix A1: Shetland's Economy [Available Online] europeangeoparks.org/repository/photos/135_Shetland_A1_Shetlands_Economy.pdf [accessed 30 June 2016].

EU (2007). Territorial agenda of the European Union. In *Towards a more competitive and sustainable Europe of diverse regions, agreed on the occasion of the informal ministerial meeting on urban development and territorial cohesion*, 24–25 May 2007. Leipzig.

Evans, N. J. and Ilbery, B. W. (1989). A conceptual framework for investigating farm-based accommodation and tourism in Britain. *Journal of Rural Studies*, 5, 257–66.

Evans, N. J. and Ilbery, B. W. (1992a). Advertising and farm-based accommodation: A British case study. *Tourism Management*, 13, 415–22.

Evans, N. J. and Ilbery, B. W. (1992b). Farm-based accommodation and the restructuring of agriculture: Evidence from three English counties. *Journal of Rural Studies*, 8, 85–96.

Evans, N., Morris, C. and Winter, N. (2002). Conceptualizing agriculture: A critique of post-productivism as the new orthodoxy. *Progress in Human Geography*, 26(3), 313–32.

FAO (2015). WFP. 2015. In The State of Food Insecurity in the World 2015. Meeting the 2015 international hunger targets: Taking stock of uneven progress.

Feindt, P. H. (2012). Reflexive Governance, public goods and sustainability-conceptual reflections and empirical evidence in agricultural policy. In E. Brousseau, T. Dedeurwaerdere and B. Siebenhüner (eds), *Reflexive Governance for Global Public Goods*, 22–45. Cambridge, MA: MIT Press.

Florida, R. (2002). *The Rise of the Creative Class: And How It's Transforming Work, Leisure, Community and Everyday Life*. New York: Basic Books.

Flynn, A. and Marsden, T. (1992). Food regulation in a period of agricultural retreat: The British experience. *Geoforum*, 23(1), 85–93.

Folke, C. (2006). Resilience: The emergence of a perspective for social – ecological systems analyses. *Global Environmental Change*, 16(3), 253–67.

Folke, C., Carpenter, S. and Walker, B. (2010). Resilience thinking: Integrating resilience adaptability and transformability. *Ecology and Society*, 15(4), 20.

Foresight (2011). The future of food and farming. Challenges and choices for global sustainability. The Government Office for Science, London.

Foresight (2012). Foresight annual review 2012, The Government Office for Science, London.

Forster, T., Egal, F., Getz Escudero, A., Renting, H. and Dubbeling, M. (2015). *Milan Urban Food Policy Pact. Selected Good Practices from Cities*. Milan, Italy: Fondazione Giangiacomo Feltrinelli.

Fort, M. (2008). Shetland on a Plate: The inaugural Shetland Food Festival took place this month. About time, says Matthew Fort – the islands' culinary heritage is well worth celebrating. *The Guardian*. 25 October 2008. [Available Online] http://www.guardian.co.uk/travel/2008/oct/25/shetland-food-festival?page=2.

Foucault, M. (2007). *Security, Territory, Population*. Berlin: Springer.

Frenkin, K., van Ort, F. and Verburg, T. (1995). Related variety, unrelated variety and regional economic growth, *Regional Studies*, 41, 685–97.

Friedmann, H. (2007). Scaling-up: Bringing public institutions and food service corporations into a project for a local sustainable food system in Ontario. *Agriculture and Human Values*, 24, 389–98.

Frouws, J. (1998). The contested redefinition of the countryside: An analysis of rural discourses in the Netherlands. *Sociologia Ruralis*, 38, 54–68.

Funtowicz, S. O. and Ravetz, J. R. (2003a). The emergence of post-normal science. In R. Von Schomberg (ed.), *Science, Politics and Morality*, 85–123. Dordrecht, The Netherlands: Springer.

Funtowicz, S. O. and Ravetz, J. R. (2003b). Post-normal science. International Society for Ecological Economics (ed.), Online Encyclopedia of Ecological Economics at http://www.ecoeco.org/publica/e

Garnett, T. and Godfray, C. (2012). Sustainable intensification in agriculture. Navigating a course through competing food system priorities. *Food Climate Research Network and the Oxford Martin Programme on the Future of Food*. Oxford, UK: University of Oxford, 51.

Garud, R. and Karnoe, P., eds (2001). *Path Dependence and Creation*. New York: Psychology Press.

Gasson, R. and Errington, A. J. (1993). *The Farm Family Business*. London: CAB International.

Geels, F. W. (2002). Technological transitions as evolutionary reconfiguration processes: A multi-level perspective and a case-study. *Research Policy*, 31(8), 1257–74.

Geels, F. W. (2004). From sectoral systems of innovation to socio-technical systems: Insights about dynamics and change from sociology and institutional theory. *Research Policy*, 33(6), 897–920.

Gibbons, M. (1999). Science's new social contract with society. *Nature*, 402, C81–C84.

Gibbs, D. (2000). Ecological modernisation, regional economic development and regional development agencies. *Geoforum*, 31, 9–19.

Gibson-Graham, J. K. (2006). *A Post Capitalist Politics*. Minneapolis: University of Minnesota Press.

Girardet, H. (2006). *Creating Regenerative Cities*. New York: Routledge.

Goodman, D. (2004). Rural Europe redux? Reflections on alternative agro food networks and paradigm change. *Sociologia Ruralis*, 44(1), 3–16.

Goodman, D. and Redclift, M. (1991). *Refashioning Nature: Food, Ecology and Culture*. London: Routledge.

Goodman, D., Sorj, B. and Wilkinson, J. (1987). *From Farming to Biotechnology: A Theory of Agroindustrial Development*. Oxford: Basil Blackwell.

Goodman, D., DuPuis, E. M. and Goodman, M. K. (2012). *Alternative Food Networks: Knowledge, Practice, and Politics*. London: Routledge.

Goven, J. and Pavone, V. (2014). The bioeconomy as political project a polanyian analysis. *Science, Technology & Human Values*. DOI:10.1177/0162243914552133.

Grant, W. (Ed.) (1987). *Business Interests, Organizational Development and Private Interest Government: An International Comparative Study of the Food Processing Industry (Vol. 8)*. Berlin and New York: Walter de Gruyter.

Green New Deal Group (2013). National Plan for the UK: from austerity to the age of the new deal. New Weather Institute, Available at: http://www.greennewdealgroup.org/wp-content/uploads/2013/09/Green-New-Deal-5th-Anniversary.pdf [accessed 10 March 2015].

Grin, J., Rotmans, J. and Schot, J. (2010). *Transitions to Sustainable Development: New Directions in the Study of Long Term Transformational Change*. New York: Routledge.

Grunwald, A. (2004). Strategic knowledge for sustainable development: The need for reflexivity and learning at the interface between science and society. *International Journal of Foresight and Innovation Policy*, 1(1), 150–67.

Guba, E. G. and Lincoln, Y. S. (1981). *Effective Evaluation: Improving the Usefulness of Evaluation Results through Responsive and Naturalistic Approaches*, San Francisco: Jossey-Bass Publications.

Gunderson, L. H. and Holling, C. S. (2002). *Panarchy: Understanding Transformations in Systems of Humans and Nature*. Washington: Island.

Haarmann, W. and Horlings, I. (2010). *Dorpen aan de rivier; Nieuwe markten voor recreatie en toerisme*, Telos: Tilburg.

Habermas, J. (1987b). *The Theory of Communicative Action, Vol. 2, Lifeworld and System: A Critique of Functionalist Reason*, Boston: Beacon Press.

Hajer, M. A. (1995). *The Politics of Environmental Discourse: Ecological Modernisation and the Policy Process*. Oxford: Oxford University Press.

Hall, A. D. (1941). *Agriculture after the War*. London: John Murray.

Hall, P., Thomas, R., Gracey, H. and Drewett, R. (1913). *The Containment of Rural England*. London: Allen and Unwin.

Hall, P., Thomas, R., Gracey, H. and Drewett, R. (1972). *The containment of Urban England*. London, Allen and Unwin.

Hall, S. and Massey, D. (2010). Interpreting the crisis. *Soundings*, 44(1), 57–71.

Hall, S., Massey, D. and Rustin, M. (2013). After neoliberalism: Analysing the present. *Soundings: A Journal of Politics and Culture*, 53(1), 8–22.

Havra (no date). The Hand-Made Fish Company. [Available Online] http://www.havra. co.uk/handmadefish.shtml.

Head, L. (2015). The Anthropoceneans. *Geographical Research*. http://onlinelibrary.wiley. com/doi/10.1111/1745-5871.12124/full

Hermans, F., Horlings, I., Beers, P. J. and Mommaas, H. (2010). The contested redefinition of the sustainable countryside; revisiting Frouws' rurality discourses. *Sociologia Ruralis*, 50(1), 46–63.

Hilgartner, S. (2007). Making the bioeconomy measurable: Politics of an emerging anticipatory machinery. *BioSocieties*, 2(3), 382–6.

Hirsch H., G., Bradley, D., Pohl, C., Rist, S. and Wiesmann, U. (2006). Implications of transdisciplinarity for sustainability research. *Ecological Economics*, 60(1), 119–28.

HM Government (2013) A UK Strategy for Agricultural Technologies, Available at: https:// www.gov.uk/government/uploads/system/uploads/attachment_data/file/227259/9643-BIS-UK_Agri_Tech_Strategy_Accessible.pdf [accessed 10 March 2015].

HM Government (2015) Building a high value bioeconomy, HM Government, Available at: https://www.gov.uk/government/uploads/system/uploads/attachment_data/ file/408940/BIS-15-146_Bioeconomy_report_-_opportunities_from_waste.pdf [accessed 17 July 2016].

Hoff, H. (2011). Understanding the Nexus. Background Paper for the Bonn2011 Conference: The Water, Energy and Food Security Nexus. Stockholm: Stockholm Environment Institute.

Horlings, I. (2010). *Vital Coalitions; Partnerships for Rural Regional Development.* Wageningen, The Netherlands: Wageningen Academic Publishers.

Horlings, I. and Padt, F. (2009). Leadership in rural-urban networks, paper for the ISSRM conference, July 2009, Vienna.

Horlings, I. and Hinssen, J. (2010). Sustainable innovation in intensive animal husbandry in the Netherlands: Putting your money where your mouth is, Scaling and governance conference, November 2010, Wageningen.

Horlings, I. and Marsden, T. (2010a). The new rural paradigm and redefining the rural web. In P. Milone and F. Ventura (eds), *Networking the Rural: The Future of Green Regions in Europe*, 213–44. Assen: Van Gorcum.

Horlings, I. and Marsden, T. (2010b). Pathways for Sustainable Development of European Rural Regions: Eco-Economical Strategies and New Rural-Urban Relations. Working paper, published on the BRASS website, http://www.brass.cf.ac.uk/

Horlings, I. and Marsden, T. (2010c). The role of social capital, leadership and policy arrangements in European rural regional development, BRASS working paper, Cardiff, published on the website.

Horlings, I. and Marsden, T. K. (2011a). Towards the real green revolution? Exploring the conceptual dimensions of a new ecological modernisation of agriculture that could feed the world. *Glob Environ Change*, 21, 441–52.

Horlings, I. and Marsden, T. (2011b). Rumo ao desenvolvimento espacial sustentável? Explorando as implicações da nova bioeconomia no setor de agroalimentos e na novação regional. In *Sociologias*, Porto Alegre, ano 13, no 27, mai./ago. 2011, Vol. 13, No. 27, Issue May/

Horlings, I. and Padt, F. (2013). Leadership for sustainable regional development in rural areas: Bridging personal and institutional aspects. *Sustainable Development*, 21, 413–24.

Horlings, I., Bijsterveld, A. J. and Janssen, J. (2006). Het Groene Woud is vele landschappen. In *Zoeken naar nieuwe wegen*, Telos: Tilburg.

Horlings, L. G. and Kanemasu, Y. (2010). Towards an Eco-Economy? Rural development and farm tourism in Devon (UK), FAO, Available at: http://agris.fao.org/agris-search/search.do?recordID=NL2012089790 [accessed 13 July 2016].

Horlings, L. G. and Marsden, T. K. (2014). Exploring the 'New Rural Paradigm' in Europe: Eco-economic strategies as a counterforce to the global competitiveness agenda. *European Urban and Regional Studies*, 21(1), 4–20.

Horlings, L. G. and Kanemasu, Y. (2015). Sustainable development and policies in rural regions; insights from the Shetland Islands. *Land Use Policy*, 49, 310–21.

House of Commons Environment, F. A. R. A. C (2014). Food security: Second Report of Session 2014–15. House of Commons.

Houses of Parliament (2011). Biofuels from Algae, Parliamentary Office of Science and Technology (POST), Note Number 384, July 2011, Available at: http://www.parliament.uk/documents/post/postpn_384-biofuels-from-algae.pdf [accessed 11 March 2015].

Hodson, M., Marvin, S. (2010a). *World Cities and Climate Change: Producing Urban Ecological Security*. New York: McGraw-Hill.

Hodson, M., Marvin, S. (2010b). Can cities shape socio-technical transitions and how would we know if they were? *Res Policy*, 39(4), 477–85.

Huber, J. (1982). Die verlorene Unschuld der ökologie. Frankfurt am Main: S. Fischer Verlag.

Huber, J. (1985). Die Regenbogengesellschaft; Ökologie und Socialpolitik. Frankfurt am Main: S. Fischer Verlag.

Huber, J. (2000). Towards industrial ecology: Sustainable development as a concept of ecological modernization. *Journal of Environmental Policy and Planning*, 2(4), 269–85.

Huttunen, S. (2013). Sustainability and Meanings of Farm-based Bioenergy Production in Rural Finland, PHD, Faculty of Social Sciences, University of Jyväskylä, Finland.

Ilbery, B. and Maye, D. (2007). Marketing sustainable food production in Europe: case study evidence from tow Dutch labelling schemes. *Tijdschrift voor economische en Sociale Geografie*, 98, 507–18.

Ingram, J., Ericksen, P. and Liverman, D., eds (2010). *Food Security and Global Environmental Change*. New York and London: Routledge.

International Institute for Industrial Environmental Economics (IIIEE) (2009). The Future is distributed: a vision of sustainable economies. Lund: IIIEE. Available at: http://lup.lub.lu.se/luur/download?func=downloadFile&recordOld=1545920&fileOld=1545922

Jackson, T. (2005). Motivating sustainable consumption: A review of evidence on consumer behaviour and behavioural change: A report to the Sustainable Development Research Network. *Centre for Environmental Strategy*, UK: University of Surrey.

Jaeger, J., (2009). Sustainability Science in Europe. *Background Paper for the European Commission DG Research*, May 2014.

Jaffee, D., Kloppenburg, J. R. and Monroy, M. B. (2004). Bringing the 'moral charge' home: Fair trade within the North and within the South. *Rural sociology*, 69(2), 169–96.

Jahn, T. (2008). Transdisciplinarity in the practice of research. In M. Bergmann and E. Schramm (eds), *Transdisziplinäre Forschung: Integrative Forschungsprozesse verstehen und bewerten*, 21–37. Frankfurt/Main, Germany: Campus Verlag.

Jänicke, M. (1984). *Umweltpolitische Prävention als ökologische Modernisierung industrieller Strukturpolitik*. Berlin: Wissenschaftszentrum Berlin, IIUG dp 84–1.

Jauhiainen, J. S. and Moilanen, H. (2011). Towards fluid territories in European spatial development: regional development zones in Finland. *Environment and Planning C: Government and Policy*, 29(4): 728–44.

Javalgi, R. G., Cutler, B. D. and Winas, W. A. (2001), At your service! Does country of origin research apply to services? *Journal of Services Marketing*, 15(7), 565–82.

Johansson, A., Kisch, P. and Mirata, M. (2005). Distributed economies – a new engine for innovation. *Journal of Cleaner Production*, 13(10), 971–9.

Journal of Agrarian Change (2010). Special issue on food security.

Journal of Rural Studies (2013). Special issue on food security.

Juma, C. and Konde, V. (2001). *The New Bio-economy: Industrial and Environmental Biotechnology in Developing European Urban and Regional Studies 21(1) Countries.* New York: United Nations Conference on Trade and Development.

Kanemasu, Y. and I. Horlings (2010). The answer is blowing in the wind? Rural development and wind energy in Shetland, report, follow-up of the Etude project, UK: Cardiff University.

Kanemasu, Y. R., Sonnino, R. and T. Marsden (2008). The Rural 'Web' in Devon: Emerging Contours, Deliverable D 4.4, Regional case study Devon (UK) , WP4 report Etude project, UK: Cardiff University.

Kasemir, B. (ed.) (2003). *Public Participation in Sustainability Science: A Handbook.* Cambridge, UK: Cambridge University Press.

Kasemir, B., Jaeger, C. C. and Jäger, J. (2003). Citizen participation in sustainability assessments. In B. Kasemir (ed.), *Public Participation in Sustainability Science: A Handbook*, 3–36. Cambridge: Cambridge University Press.

Kates, R. W. (2001). Sustainability science. *Science*, 292, 641–2.

Kauffman, S. (1995). *At Home in the Universe: The Search for the Laws of Self-organization and Complexity.* New York: Oxford University Press.

Kemp, R. (2000). Technology and Environmental Policy – Innovation effects of past policies and suggestions for improvement. In A. Jasmison and H. Robvacher (eds), *Innovation and the Environment*, 35–61. Paris: OECD.

Kenter, J. O., Reed, M. S., Irvine, K. N., O'Brien, E., Brady, E., Bryce, R., Christie, M., Church, A., Cooper, N., Davies, A., Hockley, N., Fazey, I., Jobstvogt, N., Molloy, C., Orchard-Webb, J., Ravenscroft, N., Ryan, M. and Watson, V. (2014). UK National Ecosystem Assessment Follow-on. Work Package Report 6: Shared, Plural and Cultural Values of Ecosystems. UNEP-WCMC, LWEC, UK. Available at: http://www.lwec.org.uk/sites/default/files/attachments_video/WP6_FinalReport.pdf [accessed 10 March 2015].

Kirwan, J. (2006). The interpersonal world of direct marketing: Examining conventions of quality at UK farmers' markets. *Journal of Rural Studies*, 22, 301–12.

Kitchen, L. and Marsden, T. (2009). Creating sustainable rural development through stimulating the eco-economy: beyond the eco-economic paradox? *Sociologia Ruralis*, 49, 273–93.

Kitchen, L. and Marsden, T. (2011). Constructing sustainable communities: A theoretical exploration of the bio-economy and eco-economy paradigms. *Local Environment*, 16(8), 753–69.

Kloppenburg, J. (2010). Impeding dispossession, enabling repossession: Biological open source and the recovery of seed sovereignty. *Journal of Agrarian Change*, 10(3), 367–88.

Kneafsey, M. (2000). Tourism, place identities and social relations in the European rural periphery. *European Urban and Regional Studies*, 7(1), 35–50.

Kneafsey, M., Venn, L., Schmutz, U., Balázs, B., Trenchard, L., Eyden-Wood, T., and Blackett, M. (2013). Short food supply chains and local food systems in the EU. A state of play of their socio-economic characteristics. JRC Scientific and Policy Reports. Joint Research Centre Institute for Prospective Technological Studies, European Commission.

Lamine, C., (2005). Settling shared uncertainties: Local partnerships between producers and consumers. *Sociologia Ruralis*, 45 (4), 324–45.

Lamine, C., Renting, H., Rossi, A., Wiskerke, J. H. and Brunori, G. (2012). Agri-food systems and territorial development: Innovations, new dynamics and changing governance mechanisms. In I. Dashofer, I. Gibbon and B. Dedieu (eds), *Farming Systems Research into the 21st Century: The New Dynamic*, 229–56. Berlin, The Netherlands: Springer.

Langeveld, J. W. A., Dixon, J. and Jaworski, J. F. (2010). Development perspectives of the biobased economy: A review. *Crop Science*, 50(Supplement_1), S-142.

Lather, P. A. (1991). *Getting Smart: Feminist Research and Pedagogy With/in the Postmodern*, New York: Routledge.

Lawrence, G., Lawrence, G., Lyons, K. and Wallington, T. (2013). *Food Security, Nutrition and Sustainability*. London: Earthscan.

Levidow, L., Birch, K. and Papaioannou, T. (2012). EU agri-innovation policy: Two contending visions of the bio-economy. *Critical Policy Studies*, 6(1), 40–65.

Lincoln, Y. S. and Guba, E. G. (1985). *Naturalistic Inquiry*, Beverly Hills, CA: Sage Publications.

Little, J. (2002). *Gender and Rural Geography: Identity, Sexuality and Power in the Countryside*. New York, NY: Prentice Hall.

Lloyd, G. D. (1933). *War Memoirs of David Lloyd George*. London: Odhams press limited.

Lobley, M. and Potter, C. (2004). Agricultural change and restructuring: Recent evidence from a survey of agricultural households in England. *Journal of Rural Studies*, 20, 499–510.

Lowe, P., Marsden, T., Murdoch, J. and Ward, N. (2005). *The Differentiated Countryside*, 200, London: Routledge.

Lowe, P., Marsden T. K. and Whatmore, S., eds (1990). Agriculture and the Rural Environment. *Critical Perspectives on Rural Change*, London: David Fulton.

Markusen, A. (1994). Studying regions by studying forms. *Professional Geographer* 46, 477–90.

Marsden, T. (1984). Capitalist farming and the farm family: A case study. *Sociology*, 18, 205–24.

Marsden, T. (2003). The Condition of Rural Sustainability. Assen, The Netherlands: Uitgeverij Van Gorcum.

Marsden, T. (2004). The quest for ecological modernisation: Re-spacing rural development and agri-food studies. *Sociologia Ruralis*, 44, 129–46.

Marsden, T. (2007). *Etude Methodological Guideline for the Quick Scan, 25-6-2007, Internal Document*. Cardiff: Cardiff University.

Marsden, T. (2010). Mobilising the regional eco-economy: Evolving webs of agri-food and rural development in the UK, Cambridge Journal of Regions. *Economy and Society*, 3, 225–44.

Marsden, T. (2012). Towards a real sustainable agri food security and food policy: Beyond the ecological fallacies? *The Political Quarterly*, 83(1), 139–45.

Marsden, T. (2013). Sustainable place-making for sustainability science: The contested case of agri-food and urban-rural relations. *Sustainability Science*, 8(2), 213–22.

Marsden, T. and Sonnino, R. (2007). *How to Select Case Studies or the Quick Scan; Guidelines for ETUDE Document*. Cardiff: Cardiff University.

Marsden, T. and Sonnino, R. (2008). Rural development and the regional state: Denying multifunctional agriculture in the UK. *Journal of Rural Studies*, 24, 422–31.

Marsden, T. and Sonnino, R. (2012). Human health and wellbeing and the sustainability of urban–regional food systems. *Current Opinion in Environmental Sustainability*, 4(4), 427–30.

Marsden, T. and Franklin, A. (2013). Replacing neoliberalism: Theoretical implications of the rise of local food movements. *Local Environment*, 18(5), 636–41.

Marsden, T. and Morley, A., eds (2014). *Sustainable Food Systems: Building a New Paradigm*. London: Routledge.

Marsden, T. and Farioli, F. (2015). Natural powers: From the bio-economy to the eco-economy and sustainable place-making. *Sustainability Science*, 10(2), 331–44.

Marsden, T., Murdoch, J., Lowe, J., Munton, R. and Flynn, A. (1993). *Constructing the Countryside*. London: UCL Press.

Marsden, T., Milbourne, P., Kitchen, L. and Bishop, K. (2003). Communities in nature: The construction and understanding of forest natures. *Sociologia Ruralis*, 43, 120–56.

Marsden, T., Murdoch, J., Lowe, P., Munton, R. C. and Flynn, A. (2005). *Constructuring the Countryside: An Approach to Rural Development*. London: Routledge.

Marsden, T., Lee, R., Flynn, A. and Thankappan, S. (2010). *The New Regulation and Governance of Food: Beyond the Food Crisis?* London: Routledge.

Martin, R. (2010). Regional economic resilience, hysteresis and recessionary shocks. *RGs Conference*, 2, 225–38.

Massey, D. (2004). Geographies of responsibility. *Geografiska Annaler*, 86 B-1, 5–18.

Massey, D. (2005). *For Space*. London: Sage.

McAfee, K. (2008a). Beyond techno-science: Transgenic maize in the fight over Mexico's future. *Geoforum*, 39(1), 148–60.

McAfee, K. (2008b). Exporting crop biotechnology: The myth of molecular miracles. In G. Otero (ed.), *Food for the Few: Neoliberal Globalism and Biotechnology in Latin America*, 61–90. Austin: University of Texas Press.

McCarthy, J., (2005) Rural geography: multifunctional rural geographies – reactionary or radical? *Progress in Human Geography*, 29(6), 773–82.

McCormick, K. and Kautto, N. (2013). The bioeconomy in Europe: An overview. *Sustainability*, 5(6), 2589–2608.

McFarlane, C. (2009). Translocal assemblages: Space, power and social movements. *Geoforum*, 40(4), 561–7.

McKibben, B. (2015). The Pope and the Planet, The New York Review of Books, Available at: http://www.nybooks.com/articles/archives/2015/aug/13/pope-and-planet/

McMichael, P. (2009). Banking on agriculture: A review of the world development report 2008. *Journal of Agrarian Change*, 9(2), 235–46.

McMichael, P. (2013). Land grabbing as security mercantilism in international relations. *Globalizations*, 10(1), 47–64.

Mills, C. W. (1959). *The Sociological Imagination*. New York, NY: Oxford University Press.

Milone, P. and Ventura, F., eds (2010). *Networking the Rural: The Future of Green Regions in Europe*, 213–44. Assen: Van Gorcum.

Ministry of Environment Finland, (2014). *Sustainable growth from the bio-economy: the Finnish bioeconomy Strategy*, 213–44. Helsinki, 2014.

Mirata, M., Nilsson, H. and Kuisma, J. (2005). Production systems aligned with distributed economies: Examples from energy and biomass sectors. *Journal of Cleaner Production*, 13(10), 981–91.

Mol, A. (2008a). Boundless biofuels? Between environmental sustainability and vulnerability. *Sociologia Ruralis* 47, 297–316.

Mol, A. (2008b). I eat an apple. On theorizing subjectivities. *Subjectivity*, 22(1), 28–37.

Mol, A. P. J. (2000). The environmental movement in an era of ecological modernization. *Geoforum*, 31, 45–56.

Mol, A. P. J. and Sonnenfeld, D. A. (2000). *Ecological Modernisation Around the World: Perspectives and Critical Debates*. London: Frank Cass Publishers.

Moore, J. W. (2010). The end of the road? Agricultural revolutions in the capitalist world ecology, 14-50-2010. *Journal of Agrarian Change*, 10, 389–413.

Moore, J. W. (2015). *Capitalism in the Web of Life: Ecology and the Accumulation of Capital*. London: Verso Books.

Moragues-Faus, A. and Morgan, K. (2015). Reframing the foodscape: The emergent world of urban food policy. *Environment and Planning A*, 47(7), 1558–73.

Morgan, K. and Sonnino, R. (2010). The urban foodscape: World cities and the new food equation. Cambridge Journal of Regions, *Economy and Society*, 3(2): 209–224.

Morgan, K., Marsden, T. K. and Murdoch, J. (2008). *Worlds of Food: Place, Power, and Provenance in the Food Chain*. Oxford: Oxford University Press on Demand.

Moulert, F., MacCallum, D. and Hillier, J. (2013). Social innovation: Intuition, precept, concept. In F. Moulaert and A. Mehmood (eds), *The International Handbook on Social Innovation: Collective Action, Social Learning and Transdisciplinary Research*, 13.

Mount, P. and Andrée, P. (2013). Visualising community-based food projects in Ontario. *Local Environment*, 18(5), 578–91.

MOVE.SHETLAND.org (2009). New Body Will Promote Shetland. [Available Online] http://move.shetland.org/april-2009-newsletter.

Murdoch, J. and Marsden, T. (1995). The spatialization of politics: Local and national actor-spaces in environmental conflict. *Transactions of the Institute of British Geographers*, 20, 368–80.

Murdoch, J., Lowe, P. Ward, N. and Marsden, T. (2003). *The Differentiated Countryside*. London: Routledge.

Murphy, J. (2000). Ecological modernization. *Geoforum*, 31, 1–8.

Murphy, J. and Gouldson, A. (2000). Environmental policy and industrial innovation: Integrating environment and economy through ecological modernisation. *Geoforum*, 31(1), 33–44.

Negri, A. and Hardt, M. (2004). *Multitude: War and Democracy in the Age of Empire*, New York: Penguin Press.

Ness, B., Anderburg, S. and Olsson, L. (2010). Structuring problems in sustainability science: The multi-level DPSIR framework. *Geoforum* 41, 479–88.

Newby, H. (1979). *The Deferential Worker: A Study of Farm Workers in East Anglia*. Madison: University of Wisconsin Press.

NOMIS Official Labour Market Statistics (2009). Available Online. https://www.nomisweb.co.uk/

Nourishing Communties (2015). *Sustainable Local Food Systems Research Group*. Wilfred Laurier University.

Nowotny, H., Scott, P. and Gibbons, M. (2001). *Re-thinking Science: Knowledge and the Public in an Age of Uncertainty*. Cambridge: Polity, 12.

Oakes, T. and Schein, L., eds (2006). *Translocal China: Linkages, Identities and the Reimagining of Space*. London: Routledge.

O'Connor, D., ed. (2006). *Driving Rural Development: Policy and Practice in Seven EU Countries*. Assen, The Netherlands: Uitgeverij Van Gorcum.

OECD (2005). *The Bioeconomy to 2030: Designing a Policy Agenda. International Futures Programme*. Paris: Organisation for Economic Co-operation and Development March 2015].

OECD (2006). *The New Rural Paradigm: Policies and Governance*. Paris: Organisation for Economic Cooperation and Development.

OECD (2009). *The Bioeconomy to 2030: Designing a policy agenda*. Paris: OECD. Available at: http://www.oecd.org/futures/long-termtechnologicalsocietalchallenges/thebioeconomyto2030designingapolicyagenda.htm

OECD (2011). *A Green Growth Strategy for Food and agriculture. Preliminary report May 2011*, Paris: Organisation for Economic Cooperation and Development.

OECD (2013). *Rural-urban Partnerships: An Integrated Approach to Economic Development*. Paris: Organisation for Economic Cooperation and Development.

Office for National Statistics (2014) Office for National Statistics. Regional Labour Market Statistics October 2012.

Oostindie, H., van der Ploeg, J. D., van Broekhuizen, R., Milone, P., Ventura, F. and Brunori, G. (2010). The central role of nested markets in rural development in Europe. *Rivista di Economia Agraria*, 65(2), 191–224.

Otsuki, K. (2014). Social economy of quality food. *International Journal of Social Economics*, 41(3), 233–43.

Ouma, S., Boeckler, M. and Lindner, P. (2013). Extending the margins of marketization: Frontier regions and the making of agro-export markets in northern Ghana. *Geoforum*, 48.

Paddock, J. and Marsden, T. (2015). Revisiting Evolving Webs of Agri-food and Rural Development in the UK: The Case of Devon and Shetland. In P. Milore, F. Ventura and Y. Jingzhong (eds), *Constructing a New Framework for Rural Development*, Research in Rural Sociology and Development Series, 22, 301–24. London: Emerald Group Publishing Limited.

Palumbo, F. and P. Herbig (2000), The multicultural context of brand loyalty, *European Journal of Marketing*, 3(3), 116–24.

Parliament UK (2014). Feeding Britain A strategy for zero hunger in England, Wales, Scotland and Northern Ireland The report of the All-Party Parliamentary Inquiry into Hunger in the United Kingdom. Available at: https://foodpovertyinquiry.files. wordpress.com/2014/12/food-poverty-feeding-britain-final.pdf

Parry, B. (2007). Cornering the futures market in 'bio-epistemology'. *Biosocieties*, 2(3), 386–9.

Passmore, J. (2012). From the fur trade to the Bio-economy: Does Canada have what it takes? Keynote presentation and conference paper. Growing the Bioeconomy Conference 2–5 October 2012, Banff, Canada.

Pearce, J., Barnett, R. and Moon, G. (2012). Sociospatial inequalities in health-related behaviours Pathways linking place and smoking. *Progress in Human Geography*, 36(1), 3–24.

Pearce, J. R., Richardson, E. A., Mitchell, R. J. and Shortt, N. K. (2011). Environmental justice and health: A study of multiple environmental deprivation and geographical inequalities in health in New Zealand. *Social Science & Medicine*, 73(3), 410–20.

Pechlaner, G. (2012). *Corporate Crops: Biotechnology, Agriculture, and the Struggle for Control*. Austin: University of Texas Press.

Peck, H. (2005). Drivers of supply chain vulnerability: An integrated framework. *International Journal of Physical Distribution & Logistics Management*, 35(4), 210–32.

Pederson, S. B. (2011). Place branding: Giving the region of Oresund a competitive edge. *Journal of Urban Technology*, 11, 77–95.

Perfecto, I., Vandermeer, J. and Wright, A. (2009). *Nature's Matrix: Linking Agriculture, Conservation and Food Sovereignty*, London: Earthscan.

Pike, S. (2005). Tourism destination branding complexity. *Journal of Product & Brand Management*, 14(4), 258–9.

Poppy, G. M., Jepson, P. C., Pickett, J. A. and Birkett, M. A. (2014). Achieving food and environmental security: New approaches to close the gap. *Philosophical Transactions of the Royal Society B*, 369, 1–7.

Rangan, V. K., Elberse, A. and Bell, M. (2006). *Marketing New York City, Harvard Business Case Studies, April 27*. Boston, MA: Harvard Business School of Publishing.

Renting, H., Marsden, T. and Banks, J. (2003). Understanding alternative food networks: Exploring the role of short food supply chains in rural development. *Environment and Planning A*, 35, 393–411.

Renting, H., Schermer, M. and Rossi, A. (2012). Building food democracy: Exploring civic food networks and newly emerging forms of food citizenship. *International Journal of Sociology of Agriculture & Food*, 19(3): 289–307.

Rhodes, R. A. (1997). *Understanding Governance: Policy Networks, Governance, Reflexivity and Accountability*. Buckingham: Open University Press.

Robbins, K., Butler, A., Turner, M. and Lobley, M. (2006). Agricultural Change and Farm Incomes in Devon: An Update. *CRR Research Report No. 17*. Exeter: University of Exeter.

Robinson, J. (2008). Being undisciplined: Transgressions and intersections in academia and beyond. *Futures*, 40(1), 70–86.

Robinson, J. and Tansey, J. (2006). Co-production, emergent properties and strong interactive social research: The Georgia Basin Futures Project. *Science and Public Policy*, 33: 151–60.

Rooney, J. A. (1995). Branding: A trend for today and tomorrow. *Journal of Product & Brand Management*, 4(4), 48–55.

Ross. C. (2013). Why we need to Frack, Slash and Build', *Sunday Times*, 30 June 2013, Available at: http://www.thesundaytimes.co.uk/sto/news/focus/article1280837.ece

Rozenberg, J., Vogt-Schilb, A. and Hallegatte, S. (2014). Transition to clean capital, irreversible investment and stranded assets. World Bank Policy Research Working Paper (6859).

Sala, S., Farioli, F. and Zamagni, A. (2013). Life cycle sustainability assessment in the context of sustainability science progress (part 2). *The International Journal of Life Cycle Assessment*, 18(9), 1686–97.

Savan, B. and Sider, D. (2003). Contrasting approaches to community-based research and a case study of community sustainability in Toronto, Canada. *Local Environment*, 8(3), 303–16.

Saxa Vord (2004). Shetland's Culture. [Available Online] http://www.saxavord.com/shetland-culture.php. [accessed 30 December 2008].

Schermer, M., Renting, H. and Oostindie, H. (2011). Collective farmers' marketing initiatives in Europe: Diversity, contextuality and dynamics. *International Journal of Sociology of Agriculture and Food*, 18(1), 1–11.

Scholz, R. W., Lang, D. J., Wiek, A., Walter, A. I. and Stauffacher, M. (2006). Transdisciplinary case studies as a means of sustainability learning: Historical framework and theory. *International Journal of Sustainability in Higher Education*, 7(3), 226–51.

Schot, J. and Geels, F. W. (2008). Strategic niche management and sustainable innovation journeys: Theory, findings, research agenda, and policy. *Technology Analysis & Strategic Management*, 20(5), 537–54.

Self, P. and Storing, H. J. (1962). *The State and the Farmer*. Berkeley: University of California Press.

Sheppard, E. (2015). Thinking geographically: Globalizing capitalism and beyond. *Annals of the Association of American Geographers*, 105(6), 1113–34.

Shetland Community Trust (2009). *Trustees' Report and Consolidated Financial Statements*, 31 March 2009.

Shetland Enterprise, Shetland Islands Council and Highlands and Islands Enterprise. (2005) Opportunities for the Future of the Shetland Economy.

Shetland Fishermen (no date). Shetland Fishermen. [Available Online] http://www.users.zetnet.co.uk/sfa/. [accessed 25 June 2010].

Shetland Islands Council (SIC) (2000). The Shetland Structure Plan 2001-2016. Infrastructure Services, Grantfield, Lerwick, Shetland.

Shetland Islands Council (2007a). Sustaining Shetland: Annual Monitoring of Social, Economic, Environmental and Cultural Trends.

Shetland Islands Council (2007b). Shetland in Statistics, Economic Development Unit, Shetland Islands Council, 34th Edition.

Shetland Islands Council (2008). Sustaining Shetland: Annual Monitoring of Social, Economic, Environmental and Cultural Trends.

Shetland Islands Council (2009). *Shetland in Statistics*. Lerwick, Shetland.

Shetland Islands Council (no date). News Bulletin: Promote Shetland. [Available Online] http://www.shetland.gov.uk/news-advice/prdev0528.asp

Shucksmith, M. (2000). Endogenous Development, Social Capital and Social Inclusion: Perspectives from LEADER in the UK. *Sociologia Ruralis* 40(29), 208–19.

Simeon, R. (2006). A conceptual model linking brand building strategies and Japanese popular culture. *Marketing Intelligence & Planning*, 24(5), 463–76.

Simpson, J. and Stalker, M. (2004). Shetland's Food & Drink Sector: Workforce Development Plan and PESTLE Analysis. Report to Shetland Local Economic Forum Skills and Learning Subgroup September 2004.

SITRA (2012). *Local Solutions Create a Global Bio-economy*. SITRA, Helsinki.

Sjoblom, S., Andersson, K., Marsden, T. K. and Skerratt, S. (2012). *Sustainability and Short-term Policies*. Farnham, UK: Ashgate.

SLMG (2014). *Initiatives*. Retrieved from http://www.slmg.co.uk/

Smil, V. (2013). *Harvesting the Biosphere: What we have Taken from Nature*. Cambridge, MA: MIT Press.

Smith, K. (2008). The challenge of environmental technology: Promoting radical innovation in conditions of lock-in. Hobart: Report to Garnaut Commission.

Smith, A. and Stirling, A. (2007). Moving outside or inside? Objectification and reflexivity in the governance of socio-technical systems. *Journal of Environmental Policy & Planning*, 9(3–4), 351–73.

Smith, A., Stirling, A. and Berkhout, F. (2005). The governance of sustainable socio-technical transitions. *Research policy*, 34(10), 1491–1510.

Smith, A., Voß, J. P. and Grin, J. (2010). Innovation studies and sustainability transitions: The allure of the multi-level perspective and its challenges. *Research policy*, 39(4), 435–48.

Sonnino, R., Torres, C. L. and Schneider, S. (2014). Reflexive governance for food security: The example of school feeding in Brazil. *Journal of Rural Studies*, 36, 1–12.

Sotarauta, M. (2002). Leadership, Power and Influence in Regional Development. A Tentative Typology of Leaders and their Ways of Influencing. In M. Sotarauta and H. Bruun Nordic (eds), *Perspectives on Process-Based Regional Development Policy*, 182–207. Stockholm: Nordregio.

Sotarauta, M. (2005). Shared leadership and dynamic capabilities in regional development. In I. Sagan and H. Halkier (eds), *Regionalism Contested: Institution, Society, Governance*, 53–72. Aldershot: Ashgate.

Spangenberg, J. H. (2011). Sustainability science: A review, an analysis and some empirical lessons. *Environmental Conservation*, 38(3), 275–87.

Spaargaren, G., Oosterveer, P. and Loeber, A. (2012). *Food Practices in Transition: Changing Food Consumption, Retail and Production in the Age of Reflexive Modernity*. New York: Routledge.

Spaargaren, G., Oosterveer, P. and Loeber, A. (2013). *Food Practices in Transition*. London: Routlege.

Staffas, L., Gustavsson, M. and McCormick, K. (2013). Strategies and policies for the bioeconomy and bio-based economy: An analysis of official national approaches. *Sustainability*, 5(6), 2751–69.

Stockholm Environment Institute (SEI) (2011). Understanding the Nexus. Background Paper for the Bonn 2011 Nexus conference.

Sullivan, R. (2014). Climate Change: Implications for Investors and Financial Institutions. Available at SSRN 2469894.

Sustainable Shetland (no date) Sustainable Shetland. [Available Online] http://www.sustainableshetland.org/index.htm.

Talwar, S., Wiek, A. and Robinson, J. (2011). User engagement in sustainability research. *Science and Public Policy*, 38(5), 379–90.

Taylor, N. (2000). Eco-villages: Dream and reality. In H. Barton (ed.), *Sustainable Communities: The Potential for Eco-Neighbourhoods*, 19–28. London: Earthscan.

The Guardian (2010). Oil Companies Welcome Tax Breaks for Development of Shetland Fields. 27 January 2010. [Available Online] http://www.guardian.co.uk/business/2010/jan/27/oil-firms-shetland-tax-breaks.

The List (no date). Hand-Made Fish Co. [Available Online] http://www.list.co.uk/place/25021-hand-made-fish-co/.

The Scotsman (2010a) 'Council Slammed over £300k Payoff for Controversial Chief.' 7 May 2010. [Available Online] http://thescotsman.scotsman.com/news/Council-slammed-over-300k-payoff.6279256.jp.

The Scotsman (2010b) 'Islanders Demand Council Stands Down in March on Offices.'
    23 February 2010. [Available Online] http://thescotsman.scotsman.com/scotland/
    Islanders-demand-council-stands-down.6094601.jp

The Shetland Food Directory (no date). The Hand-Made Fish Company. [Available
    Online] http://www.foodshetland.com/listing.php?cat=7&p=350. [accessed 1 July].

The Shetland News (2008). Go Ahead and Build Mareel! The Shetland News 26 June
    2008. [Available Online] http://www.shetland-news.co.uk/features/Go%20ahead%20
    and%20build%20Mareel.htm.

The Shetland Times (2010a). Windfarm Developer Given Permission to Keep Test Mast
    Despite Conflict of Interest Dispute. 25 June 2010. [Available Online] http://www.
    shetlandtimes.co.uk/2010/06/02/windfarm-developer-given-permission-to-keep-test-
    mast-despite-conflict-of-interest-dispute.

The Shetland Times (2010b). Shetland Islands Council and Total Seal Deal for £500
    Million Gas Terminal. 19 March 2010. [Available Online] http://www.shetlandtimes.
    co.uk/2010/03/19/shetland-islands-council-and-total-seal-deal-for-500-million-gas-terminal.

Thompson, J. and Schoones, I. (2009). Addressing the dynamics of agri-food systems:
    An emerging agenda for social science research. *Environmental Science and Policy*,
    12, 386–97.

Thomson, R. and Holland, J. (2003). Hindsight, foresight and insight: The challenges
    of longitudinal qualitative research. *International Journal of Social Research
    Methodology*, 6, 233–44.

Trueman, M., Klemm, M. and Giroud, A. (2004), Can a city communicate? Bradford as a
    corporate brand. *Corporate Communications: An International Journal*, 9(4), 317–30.

Turner, B. L. (2010). Vulnerability and resilience: Coalescing or paralleling approaches for
    sustainability science. *Glob Environ Change*, 20, 570–6.

Tyner, W. (2012). Economic and Policy Issues for Cellulosic Biofuels. Conference Paper.
    Growing the Bioeconomy Conference, Banff, Canada. 2–5 October 2012.

Vanclay, F., Higgins, M. and Blackshaw, A., eds (2008). Making Sense of Place,
    Canberra: National Museum of Australia Press, 5.

van der Ploeg, J. D. (2013). *Peasants and the Art of Framing: A Chayanovian Manifesto*.
    Agrarian change and peasant studies series: Fernwood Publishing, Canada.

van der Ploeg, J. D. (2014). Peasant-driven agricultural growth and food sovereignty.
    Journal of Peasant Studies, 41(6), 999–1030.

van der Ploeg, J. D. and Renting, H. (2004). Behind the 'redux': A rejoinder to David
    Goodman. *Sociologia Ruralis*, 44(2), 234–42.

van der Ploeg, J. D. and Marsden, T. K., eds (2008) *Unfolding Webs: The Dynamics of
    Regional Rural Development*. Assen: Royal Van Gorcum.

van der Ploeg, J. D., Renting, H., Brunori, Knickel, K., Mannion, J., Marsden, T. K.,
    Ventura, F. (2000). Rural Development: From Practices and Policies Towards Theory.
    Sociologia Ruralis, 40(4): 391–408.

van der Ploeg, J. D., Long, A. and Banks, J. (2002). Rural development: The state of
    the art. In J. D. van der Ploeg A. Long and J. Banks (eds), *Living Countrysides: Rural*

Development Processes in Europe: The State of the Art, 8–17. Doetinchem, The Netherlands: Elsevier.

van der Ploeg, J. D., Van Broekhuizen. R., Brunori, G., et al. (2008). Towards a framework for understanding regional rural development. In J-D. van der Ploeg and T. K. Marsden (eds), *Unfolding Webs: The Dynamics of Regional Rural Development*, 1–28. Assen: Royal van Gorcum.

van der Ploeg, J. D., Ye, J. and Schnieder, S. (2015). Introduction, Constructing a new Framework for Rural Development. In P. Milone et al. (eds), op cit.

van Kerkhoff, L. and Lebel, L. (2006). Linking knowledge and action for sustainable development. *Annual Review of Environment and Resources*, 31, 445–77.

van Ostaaijen, J., Horlings, I. and Van der Stoep, H. (2010). In Horlings, I. (ed.), *Vital Coalitions, Vital Regions; Partnerships in Sustainable Regional Development*, 157–74. Wageningen: Wageningen Academic Publishers.

Vihinen, H., Kull, M., (2010). Policy implications to support and develop rural webs. Chapter 10 in 191–213. In P. Milone and F. Ventura (eds) (2010) *Networking the Rural: The Future of Green Regions in Europe*. Van Gorcum: The Netherlands.

Viking Energy (no date). News [Available Online] http://www.vikingenergy.co.uk/news-detail.asp?item=20

Waltner-Toews, D. and Lang, T. (2000). A new conceptual base for food and agricultural policy: The emerging model of links between agriculture, food, health, environment and society. *Global Change and Human Health*, 1(2): 116–30.

Wang. M. Q. (2004). A product-nonspecific framework for evaluating the potential of biomass-based products to displace fossil fuels. *Journal of Industrial Ecology*, 7(3–4), 17–32.

Ward, N. (2008). Rethinking rural policy under new labour. Chapter 2 in Woods, M. (ed.), *New Labour's Countryside*, 29–45. Bristol: The Policy Press, University of Bristol.

Wardrope, A. and Braithwaite, I. (2015). Unhealthy investments. Fossil fuel investment and the UK health community, Report, Centre for Sustainable Healthcare; and Climate and Health Council. Available at: http://www.unhealthyinvestments.uk/uploads/1/3/1/5/13150249/unhealthy_investments_final.pdf

Welsh Government (2012). Sustaining a Living Wales A Green Paper on a new approach to natural resource management in Wales, Consultation paper, Available at: http://gov.wales/docs/desh/consultation/120210nefgreenpaperen.pdf [accessed 14 July 2016].

Whatmore, S., Munton, R., Little, J. O. and Marsden, T. (1987). Towards a typology of farm businesses in contemporary British agriculture. *Sociologia Ruralis*, 27, 21–37.

Wiek, A. (2007). Challenges of transdisciplinary research as interactive knowledge generation–experiences from transdisciplinary case study research. *GAIA-Ecological Perspectives for Science and Society*, 16(1), 52–57.

Wiek, A., Ness, B., Schweizer-Ries, P., Brand, F. S. and Farioli, F. (2012). From complex systems analysis to transformational change: A comparative appraisal of sustainability science projects. *Sustainability Science*, 7(1), 5–24.

Wiek, A., Talwar, S., O'Shea, M. and Robinson, J. (2014). Toward a methodological scheme for capturing societal effects of participatory sustainability research. *Research Evaluation*, 23(2), 117–32.

Wield, D., Chataway, J. and Bolo, M. (2010). Issues in the political economy of agricultural biotechnology. *Journal of Agrarian Change*, 10(3), 342–66.

Wilson, G. A., (2001). From productivism to post-productivism … and back again? Exploring the (un)changed natural and mental landscapes of European agriculture. *Transactions of the Institute of British Geographers NS*, 26, 77–102.

Winter, M. (2003). Geographies of food: Agro-food geographies – making reconnections. *Progress in Human Geography*, 27, 505–13.

Wiskerke, J. S. C. (2009). On places lost and places regained: Reflections on the alternative food geography and sustainable regional development. *International Planning Studies*, 14, 369–87.

Wolf, S. A. and Bonanno, A., eds (2013). The Plasticity and Contested Terrain of Neoliberalism. In *The Neoliberal Regime in the Agri-Food Sector: Crisis, Resilience, and Restructuring*, 284. London: Routledge.

Woods, M. (2008). *New Labour's Countryside: Rural Policy in Britain Since 1997*. Bristorl: Policy Press.

Woolcock, N. and Narayan, D. (2000). Social capital: Implications for development theory, research and policy. *World Bank Research Observer*, 15, 225–49.

Worldwatch Institute (2015). *State of the World 2015: Confronting Hidden Threats to Sustainability*, Washington, Covelo, London: Island Press.

Wormell, P. (1978). Anatomy of agriculture: A study of Britain's greatest industry. London: Harrap Books.

WRR (1998). *Staat zonder land. Een verkenning van bestuurlijke gevolgen van informatie- en communicatietechnologie*. The Netherlands: WRR, Den Haag.

Ye, J., Fu, J., (2015). Peasant innovation and grassroots action in China. Chapter 5, 89: 127. In P. Milone, F. Ventura and J. Ye (eds) (2015) Constructing a new framework for Rural development *Research in Rural Sociology and Development Series*. Emerald, UK.

Ziegler, R. and Ott, K. (2011). The quality of sustainability science: A philosophical perspective. *Sustainability: Science, Practice, & Policy*, 7(1), 31–44.

Index

www.ingramcontent.com/pod-product-compliance
Lightning Source LLC
Chambersburg PA
CBHW062028270326
41929CB00014B/2365